Social care in Europe

Social care in Europe

Edited by
Brian Munday and Peter Ely
European Institute of Social Services,
University of Kent at Canterbury

PRENTICE HALL
HARVESTER WHEATSHEAF

London New York Toronto Sydney Tokyo Singapore
Madrid Mexico City Munich

First published 1996 by
Prentice Hall Europe
Campus 400, Maylands Avenue
Hemel Hempstead
Hertfordshire, HP2 7EZ
A division of
Simon & Schuster International Group

Typeset in 10/12pt Times
by Dorwyn Ltd, Rowlands Castle, Hants

Printed and bound in Great Britain by
Biddles Ltd, Guildford and King's Lynn

Library of Congress Cataloging-in-Publication Data

Social care in Europe/edited by Brian Munday and Peter Ely.
    p. cm.
   Includes bibliographical references and index.
   ISBN 0–13–354193–2 (pbk.)
    1. Public welfare–European Union countries. 2. Social security–
European Union countries. I. Munday, Brian. II. Ely, Peter.
HV240.5.S626 1996
361.94–dc20   95–34018
                                               CIP

British Library Cataloguing in Publication Data

A catalogue record for this book is available from
the British Library

   ISBN 0–13–354193–2 (pbk)

---

1 2 3 4 5   00 99 98 97 96

To Jill and Joy,
two enthusiastic Europeans

Contents

Figures and tables

Figures

Tables

Contributors

Karen Attridge works in the Family Services Division of the London Borough of Croydon Social Services Department.

John Baldock is a reader in social policy at the University of Kent at Canterbury.

Peter Ely is a lecturer in social work at the University of Kent at Canterbury.

Dr Nicola Madge is Principal European Research Officer at the National Children's Bureau, London.

Brian Munday is director of the European Institute of Social Services, University of Kent at Canterbury.

Antonio Samà is consultant to the European Institute of Social Services, University of Kent at Canterbury.

Andrew Swithinbank is the European projects manager, Kent social services department; and assistant director, European Institute of Social Services, University of Kent at Canterbury.

Vanessa Wilson is an information officer at the European Institute of Social Services, University of Kent at Canterbury.

Preface

The 'rediscovery of Europe' in recent years has been quite remarkable and due not least to the influence and growth of the European Union. In Britain a nationalistic press will seize on rumours that Brussels is about to dictate the standard size for the Euro banana, while a vociferous section of the Conservative party campaigns to keep Europe at arm's length. Meanwhile the European Union has recently increased from twelve to fifteen member states and others wait to join.

Jacques Delors, until recently President of the European Commission, was a strong advocate for a 'social Europe' in which citizens' social needs and interests would be given much greater priority. The writers of this book share this ambition, believing that social care in particular must achieve greater prominence in the work of the European Union and individual member states, because these services crucially affect the quality of life of so many European citizens. Too little is known of these services, their similarities and differences across the member states of the European Union. This book aims to help fill this gap in our knowledge of 'social Europe'.

The great upsurge of interest in things European is particularly noticeable in the academic world, with a steady stream of comparative texts on a wide range of subjects and many European research projects completed, under way and planned. The academic of Malcolm Bradbury's novels is now more likely to be on the Eurostar train to Paris or Brussels than in a 747 jumbo jet crossing to North America.

Courses for students in all types of academic institutions increasingly include comparative studies, concentrating particularly on European work. This may range from one or two lectures, to a comparative course within an undergraduate degree, or a new Master's course in a subject such as European social welfare. The growth in the European content of student courses is evident in the broad field of social policy in general and social care in particular.

This book is designed to help fill a significant gap in the literature needed in comparative social policy and social care teaching: namely, up-to-date material on *social care* in the European Union. It provides an overview of these services in the member states together with a discussion of policies, dominant issues and themes. It is designed for students and teachers, as well as the many state and independent agency staff who are taking an increasingly keen interest in policies, services and practice in other European countries.

With one exception the writers of this book are British and so inevitably have an outsider's understanding of social care outside the United Kingdom. However, all have considerable experience of collaborative work across Europe and several have written other major publications on European and international social care. While the book is aimed primarily at UK readers its content will be welcomed by students, teachers and practitioners in comparative social policy and social care throughout Europe and further afield.

The editors acknowledge with thanks the patient support of Clare Grist through the difficult last stages of this work. Maggie Bowers played a valuable part in the final preparation of the manuscript.

CHAPTER 1

Introduction

Definitions and comparisons in European social care

Brian Munday

A group of social workers board the Dover ferry *en route* for one of a series of meetings with their counterparts in northern France. Discussions will concentrate on their respective approaches to child protection work, learning from one another's policies and practices and deciding how to deal with cross-border situations that will increasingly arise in a frontier-free Europe. Meanwhile, residents of a Parisian old people's home are settling down with some curiosity – even misgivings – to lunch in a similar establishment in Kent as part of an imaginative exchange scheme funded by a European Commission programme. These and many other activities across Europe are all part of an exciting and accelerating Europeanisation of social care.

This book examines the many facets of this process, contributing to the modest volume of literature on European social care. Historically, the subject has suffered considerable neglect both academically and practically so that only relatively recently have we begun to understand similarities and differences in social care policies, traditions and practices across Europe. Happily, the situation is now changing quite quickly, both in relation to European countries within the boundaries of the European Union and most recently including eastern and central European countries.

Elsewhere (Munday 1989) this writer has discussed the long-standing problem of the marginalisation of social care and social work within Europe and internationally. Compared with more powerful and professionalised services such as health and education, social care has a relatively low status within individual countries and also in the policies and programmes of the European Union as a whole. This is considered more fully in chapter 3 of this book. Academically, comparative studies in social welfare typically concentrate on macro-studies of welfare states, referring to social protection for empirical material rather than the less certain world of social care.

This text focuses quite specifically on social care within the European Union, with detailed discussions of social care services for major user groups, drawing selectively on material from several but not all EU countries. Other chapters place this material in context with an overview of the main characteristics of social care systems in all member states of the European Union, and a review of a major trend in European social care, namely the development of 'mixed economies' of care. Ideally, the discussion should be set within clear conceptual models for comparing European social care systems but such an ambition remains frustratingly elusive for reasons considered later in this introductory chapter.

For mainly pragmatic reasons the book is concerned exclusively with countries of the European Union – Belgium, Denmark, France, Germany, Greece, Ireland, Italy, Luxembourg, the Netherlands, Portugal, Spain and the United Kingdom. The recent entry of Austria, Finland and Sweden to membership of the European Union came too late for those countries to be included in the coverage of this book. The writers completely accept the importance of understanding social care in all European countries – including eastern and central Europe – but there is an obvious danger of excessive superficiality in too wide a coverage in one text; and the European Union does provide a particular political, economic and social structure within which to consider patterns and trends in social care in the constituent states.

This book is written by staff from two leading UK-based European social care organisations – the European Institute of Social Services at the University of Kent, and the European Children's Centre at the National Children's Bureau in London. Given Britain's increasing and unenviable reputation as the 'anti-social' member of the European Union, it may seem strange to begin by arguing that these are exciting and positive times for social care in Europe. There is a widening gap between the negative position taken by a vociferous section of the Conservative party on Britain's membership of the Union and increasing co-operation between social services personnel in the United Kingdom and other member states.

The writers' position on European social care is certainly not one of naive, uncritical optimism. The problems faced by service users and staff are formidable, as illustrated at many points in this book. In its recent White Paper on European Social Policy (1994) the European Commission acknowledges the potentially long-term disadvantages experienced by groups of citizens across Europe who suffer as a result of economic restructuring. The Commission's response has been to give high priority in European social policy to measures to combat 'social exclusion', that is, the barriers and processes that operate to deny disadvantaged groups of citizens access to key social rights such as an adequate income and participation in the major social and occupational institutions of society (see Room 1993). As chapter 3 of this book illustrates, there are various specific social programmes initiated by the Commission designed to combat particular forms of social exclusion.

Until relatively recent years social care personnel in any one European country knew little of services and trends elsewhere in the continent. Social work in Britain particularly had been more influenced by American rather than European writings and practice models, with language differences being a powerful factor in this tradition. This situation is changing quite dramatically as illustrated in the following developments.

Agency partnerships

Encouraged by programmes and funding from Brussels, social care agencies are linking with counterparts elsewhere in Europe to make joint applications for European finance but also to understand and learn from one another's policies and practice. As illustrated above, staff and service users' exchanges develop within these agency partnerships. This is an ever-increasing movement with wide-ranging effects.

Publications

The literature on European social care is slowly increasing from a very modest base. There are now several books describing and analysing different aspects of social care in some or all EU countries, such as Cannan *et al.* (1992), Hill (1991), Lorenz (1994) and Munday (1993). In addition, the relevant networks and observatories of the European Commission regularly publish invaluable reports on subjects central to European social care concerns.

Research

As part of the growing interest to learn from other countries' experience and approaches to social care, comparative research projects are commissioned on a variety of topics. This has been particularly evident in relation to needs and services for elderly people, with an emphasis on seeking alternatives to residential care (see chapter 4). Some years ago the Dutch government was concerned to find that the Netherlands had the highest proportion of people over sixty-five in some form of institutional care. They commissioned a four-country study of innovations in domiciliary care of the elderly (see Kraan *et al.* 1991) to identify best practice in other countries in order to assist the Dutch authorities in maintaining a higher proportion of elderly people in their own homes.

Specialist organisations

Several organisations have been established to advance the cause of social care throughout Europe as part of this new social movement. Some, such as Eurolink Age and the European Children's Centre, concentrate on a particular age group and have a broader remit than just social care. Others, such as the European Institute of Social Services, work specifically in social care, in this case acting as a research, information, consultancy and training organisation covering the whole field of social care. The independent not-for-profit sector has become particularly well represented in Europe through a variety of co-ordinating umbrella organisations, many of them based strategically in Brussels – see Baine *et al.* (1992).

The Erasmus programme

This is a long-standing Brussels-funded scheme to enable large numbers of students in further and higher education to spend part of their study time in another member state. Social work students from all EU countries can participate in the scheme and so gain first-hand experience of social care work in at least one other European country. This has been more difficult for social work students from the United Kingdom than those from other countries because of factors such as the relative shortness of their courses and the constraints imposed by the national social work qualification. Nevertheless, Erasmus – shortly to become Socrates – makes an important contribution to the Europeanisation of social care.

Definitions

Any comparative study in the diverse field of social welfare faces a bewildering array of 'social' terms, often with quite different meanings in different countries. The potential for confusion, misunderstandings and even conflict is considerable. Therefore, we now state our understanding of certain key terms which are used extensively in this text. They are not neat, allegedly definitive definitions but a discussion of *meanings* – which is arguably more useful to the reader. Our view is that it is unwise to become bogged down in a pedantic over-concern with terminological exactitude in this uncertain field. Predictably, different terms will be used by European countries to refer to more-or-less similar activities in the social sphere and this should be accepted. The European Institute of Social Services has recently produced an elaborated dictionary of key social services terms in four European languages. This is urgently needed by agency personnel engaged in collaborative work with colleagues in other countries.

Social care

This book is concerned with social care in the European Union. A related text is entitled *European Social Services* (Munday 1993). Do the two terms have quite different meanings? In

Britain readers are familiar with the term 'the personal social services' referring to the wide range of social services provided by local authority social services departments and many independent not-for-profit and for-profit agencies. These services are mainly for specified user groups such as elderly people and children and families, and are provided in different locations such as the home, day centres and residential establishments. The services are staffed by personnel such as social workers, home helps and occupational therapists.

The term 'the personal social services' is peculiar to the United Kingdom and therefore is not useful in a comparative study of this kind. The shorter term 'social services' is used in some European countries as referring more or less to the territory covered by personal social services in the United Kingdom. Elsewhere the term 'social care' is employed to refer to the same field. Knapp (1984) uses this term in his text on *The Economics of Social Care* and we prefer it as a term that is widely used with a more-or-less common understanding across Europe. It also has the advantage of encompassing a broader range of activities and care resources than those confined to formal social services agencies. Social care often includes the informal support provided by families, friends and neighbours, as well as that provided by social services agencies and their paid staff. Chapter 4 discusses current social policy moves across Europe to place more emphasis on informal and non-state care, thus reducing the cost to the state.

To complicate matters further, social care does have a slightly different meaning in Britain, where it is used to define the responsibilities, tasks and competencies of certain groups of non-social work personnel working in statutory and independent agencies. They normally work in day centres and residential homes and – unlike their counterparts in most other EU countries – they may not have a full professional qualification. The Social Care Association in the United Kingdom exists to further their work and interests.

Social protection

It is important but sometimes difficult to distinguish between the mainly non-cash social care services above and a country's cash benefits system. The latter provides for financial payments to individuals and families when their income falls below a basic level, for a variety of reasons. This book is concerned predominantly with non-cash services, but the distinction is harder to maintain in the many European countries where the two services are combined and made the responsibility of one local government agency. In the United Kingdom social workers have traditionally been strongly opposed to having responsibility for cash benefits but staff argue otherwise in countries like Belgium.

The question of whether to integrate or separate cash and care services is a live issue in several European countries. Reference is made in chapter 2 to the separation of the services in Portugal, resulting in social care – known as 'social action' in that country – achieving a higher status than under integration. The integrated services in Finland and Poland have come under such strain from applications for cash benefits from the escalating number of unemployed people that they have been considering separation of the services to preserve a viable social work service.

Cash benefits are either insurance-based and paid to the individual as a right, for example in times of sickness, unemployment or old age (i.e. pensions), or they are paid according to exceptional need and means-tested. In the European Union a country's total system is referred to as 'social protection', while the special needs-based payments are usually referred to as 'social assistance'. Sometimes 'social security' is used instead of social protection and the two terms are used in places in this book. European Union policy is to work towards convergence of member states' social protection systems, fearing that wide disparities in systems will lead to serious distortions in the distribution of industry and labour across the Union. Industry may wish to move to countries with the cheapest social protection systems while labour will move in the opposite direction. This is a complex subject which cannot be discussed further here.

Social work

This is a notoriously difficult term to define, with significant variations across Europe in what constitutes a 'social worker'. In most EU countries social work is a protected title, to be used only by practitioners holding a recognised professional qualification and with their names on the professional register. This is not the case in the United Kingdom where the government remains opposed to its introduction. Lorenz (1994) provides an excellent up-to-date historical review of the development of social work in Europe. Sometimes the terms 'social services' and 'social work' have been used as if they were synonymous, but this is not so. Social work is an activity which social care agencies of all kinds need to undertake to meet their responsibilities; but it is only one of a range of activities they engage in. Social workers are probably the largest and most important occupational group in statutory and independent social care services in European countries. The difficulty of neatly delineating their professional territory is nicely conveyed by Jones (1985, p. 173):

> For all the seemingly general use of the terms 'social work' and 'social worker' (e.g. *Sozialarbeiter, assistante sociale*), this represents an outstanding example of semantic confusion. Even within countries, as any glance at the literature will confirm, social work can mean many different things to different people (Rodgers and Stevenson 1973). How much more so, therefore, might one expect to encounter variations, contrasts, and above all ambiguities of usage once there is a switch from national to cross-national review.

In most EU countries there is a second social profession alongside social work that has no counterpart in the United Kingdom. This is a profession which undertakes many of the tasks normally carried out by social workers here. The personnel are referred to as 'social pedagogues' in German-speaking countries and northern Europe, and *éducateurs specialisés* in French-speaking areas and the south. They have their own professional training courses, either separate from or alongside social workers.

Voluntary, private or independent social care agencies

In Britain a distinction is made between statutory and voluntary social care agencies. The former are organisations of central or local government and financed mainly by the state, but with a trend towards income from charges to users on a means-tested basis. Voluntary organisations may well receive state funding through grants or increasingly through contract payments, but they are separate from and not controlled by governmental organisations. Many UK voluntary organisations are registered as charities, which provides them with certain advantages, such as reductions in property tax and no liability for income tax.

In other European countries the word 'independent' or 'private' rather than voluntary is normally used to refer to non-state organisations. Independent is the preferred term in this book but the two terms are used interchangeably. Independent social care agencies may be either not-for-profit or for-profit. The former may be very large organisations employing many professional paid staff and with substantial annual budgets. However, unlike for-profit agencies, at the end of the financial year they are not allowed to distribute a cash surplus amongst people with a financial interest in the organisation. Surpluses are to be used for the development of the service, although this can include salary increases for staff. For-profit social care agencies are commercial enterprises and not found in Europe to the same extent as in North America, but they are becoming increasingly evident, for example, in residential care for elderly people.

Finally in this discussion of the meaning of key terms, reference must be made to the different groups of *users* of social care services. UK readers are very aware of the greater sensitivity in recent years to the terms used to identify groups such as elderly people, people with learning difficulties or disabilities, and people with mental health problems. Previous terms such as 'the elderly', 'mentally handicapped' and 'mentally ill' are regarded as demeaning and stigmatising and no longer acceptable. This is not an example of political correctness in the social care field but a genuine concern to accord proper status to fellow citizens whose needs place them in the potentially vulnerable position of being periodically dependent upon official social care services.

Some of the older terms still seem to be in partial use in some European countries, even allowing for the uncertainties of translation. The increasing meeting of social care staff and users across national boundaries within Europe should hasten this process of using agreed, non-stigmatising terminology. Meanwhile, this text uses terms which are well established in the United Kingdom. The older term 'client' is mostly avoided, with its connotation of inherent dependency, passivity and inequality. It is difficult to find the perfect alternative, but the term 'user' is adopted as acceptable to most interested parties. Any attempts to introduce the politically correct market term 'customer' to refer to often unwilling users of social care services should be firmly resisted. It is rumoured that even the police are now referring to their customers!

Comparing European social care services

Any discussion of European social care systems and services inevitably involves making comparisons between countries, not least to examine what may be learned from policies and practices elsewhere. This is not to say that services are evaluated or judged to assess whether a country's services for, say, children and families are up to some kind of agreed European standard. In many respects we are not in a position to do this, given the continuing uncertainties over what constitutes good or best practice in many fields. There is also the complicating factor of cultural relativity in assessing services in different countries. For example, in Britain it has long been considered against the interests of young infants in care to place them in residential nurseries – their interests are much better served through being fostered. Yet modern residential nurseries for infants are found in France and are not considered unusual. British social care staff may judge this provision as bad practice, or are they simply not taking cultural factors into account that render the provision understandable and acceptable in the French context? Alternatively, the answer may be that it is much more difficult to recruit the necessary number of foster parents in France.

Comparative studies in the broad field of social welfare – and social care in particular – are difficult to conduct satisfactorily. Years ago Rodgers (1979, pp. 11–12) wrote of the particular problems involved in making international comparisons of social services and social work:

> There is the initial problem of finding working definitions which will enable us to identify similar policies and institutions in different countries. Lack of agreed definitions has largely discouraged any systematic comparison of social work and the personal social services so far. There can be no meaningful analysis of parts or the whole of this area of social service provision unless it is firmly set within the context of a country's overall collective action for social welfare, and its current perception of the value and efficacy of government intervention in promoting individual welfare.

The tendency has been to produce largely descriptive case studies of aspects of social services in several countries and leave the readers to make comparisons, as no conceptual frameworks or models have been devised to aid more organised and useful comparisons. Lorenz's (1994) work is an exception in that his study of European social work is strongly analytical and historical, with greater attention to context. But all too often the social, economic and political context that Rodgers refers to is missing. Comparative studies of welfare states in Europe and internationally are more advanced, with several attempts (e.g. Esping-Anderson 1990) to develop concepts and theories to further analysis and explanation.

Studies such as those of Esping-Anderson invariably draw heavily on social protection systems for their data and illustrative material, with a conspicuous absence of substantial references to social care services. There are two main reasons for this which largely explain the underdeveloped state of comparative studies in the social care field. First, the differing definitions and boundaries of social care within Europe. It is a question of degree but the problems are not so pronounced with health, social protection and education. Secondly, there is very little comparable data on social care services at the European level. This is a serious impediment and is difficult to rectify. Munday's (1993) earlier work with writers on social services from each member state graphically illustrated the lack of reliable data within individual countries, rendering impossible valid data-based comparisons. The European Commission is making some inroads into the deficiency through the work of its observatories and networks in the social field, whose annual reports include comparative data on such subjects as child care and care of elderly people. Sipila's as yet unpublished research shows the advantages of concentrating comparative work in specific services such as children's services.

In the remainder of this section the writer will examine the possible application of some welfare state models to social care comparisons, together with the main findings from the most substantial study attempted of international social services. Abrahamson's (1992) work on models of welfare within Europe has particular relevance to attempts to construct models for comparing European social care. He identifies four different models of welfare evident across Europe as a whole:

1. The *latin welfare model* as seen particularly in Greece but also to varying degrees in Spain, Portugal and Italy. In this model the emphasis is on welfare provision by traditional sources such as the family, church and long-established charities like the Red Cross. Public welfare provision has been limited and secondary to that afforded by non-statutory sources, but with tendencies to reverse that tradition, for instance in the early years of post-Franco Spain.
2. The *institutional* or *corporatist* model associated with Germany, Austria and central European countries. Here the emphasis is on labour market solutions, with negotiated agreements between employers and employees covering social protection measures. People left outside the labour market are disadvantaged, often needing to rely upon charitable provision.
3. The *residual* or *liberal* welfare state associated with Thatcherite post-1979 Britain and, further afield, with the United States. Here the state progressively withdraws from being the primary provider of welfare and encourages maximum contributions from family, independent not-for-profit and commercial sectors.
4. The *social democratic* welfare model is associated with Scandinavian countries. The emphasis is on universal services with the statutory sector as the primary provider. In these countries the family has less responsibility for care and the independent sector has played a very limited role. Commercial care has been virtually non-existent. More recently countries such as Denmark, Finland and Sweden have taken measures to shift towards a more mixed economy of welfare approach.

Abrahamson (pp. 10–11) concludes that:

> The different European welfare states are converging towards the corporate model which implies a strengthening of the trend towards dualisation of the welfare state. Dualisation in this sense means a bifurcated welfare system where the (labour) market takes care of the 'well-to-do' workers through various corporate arrangements and leaves the less privileged groups in society to predominantly local institutions, either in the form of municipalities or private charity.

Other writers, such as Esping-Anderson (1990) and Lorenz (1994), refer to similar models in their writings, with variations in where they place certain countries. Esping-Anderson removes Italy from the latin/Catholic model, elevating it to inclusion in the corporatist welfare state. Lorenz includes Ireland in what he refers to as the *rudimentary* approach, which equates with Abrahamson's latin model.

Unlike the other main writers on European models of social welfare, Lorenz is concerned essentially with social work, and so draws out some of the implications for social care and social work of the models. In the latin/rudimentary model citizens have limited legal rights to social services, the development of which has been patchy and often poorly co-ordinated. There are proportionally fewer social workers and other professional staff to serve local populations.

Social work in the liberal/rudimentary approach tends to concentrate on the poor and deviant, with a limited mandate for proactive, inclusive and universal initiatives. An increasing element in the social worker's role is that of rationer of scarce resources and organiser and 'fixer' of the contributions of non-state care resources. Additionally, the role may also emphasise responsibility for the social control of deviant and difficult citizens whose behaviour is seen as unacceptable to the rest of society.

Corporatism in social care emphasises *subsidiarity*, seen particularly in Germany, where social care provision is dominated by the six huge independent not-for-profit welfare organisations and a myriad of smaller agencies and projects. Public social welfare organisations deal more with social control tasks and are generally seen as unattractive. In Scandinavian countries social services function to promote democracy and solidarity, with a high level of provision in terms of quantity and quality. Social workers are employed almost entirely by state agencies and enjoy relatively high status.

An interesting aspect of Abrahamson's writings on European social welfare models is his construction of *welfare triangles* and the way in which they have been adapted by other writers to make comparisons of specific aspects of European welfare systems. His basic triangle from his 1992 paper is *the welfare triangle of modern society*, figure 1.1 (p. 238). This is a simple model based on the understanding that in modern society resources can be obtained from the three spheres of market, state and civil society, with the welfare of the individual 'being dependent upon the extent and combination of his/her relation to these three spheres' (p. 6). The spheres operate through the different media of money, power and solidarity. In terms of social policies in post-war Europe, market

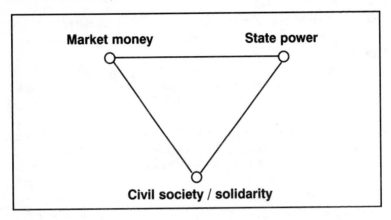

Figure 1.1 Welfare triangle of modern society, with money being the medium of the market, power being the medium of the state and solidarity being the medium of civil society. (Source: Abrahamson 1992.)

and state have been increasingly emphasised to the detriment of the solidarity of civil society. The triangle in Figure 1.1 shows the situation in Europe at the beginning of the 1990s.

Geographically, the division of welfare within Europe until recently could be represented in Abrahamson's second triangle, the *institutional organisation of welfare in post-Second World War Europe*, Figure 1.2 (p. 239). Abrahamson's rationale (pp. 6–7) for this model is that:

> Although all three spheres were active in organising welfare everywhere, the market dominated in Western Europe because of the emphasis on social insurance systems. The public sector dominated in Eastern Europe in accordance with the idea of 'real socialism'. The further one moves to the south of Europe, both in the east and west, institutions of civil society like the family, the church and other social networks become more dominant.

Of course, many other writers in recent years have written about European social policy and social welfare in similar terms – especially in referring to the widespread adoption of policies of mixed economies of welfare. But Abrahamson's graphic presentation is useful and creative because it allows for development to plot the direction of changes under way in European social welfare and social care.

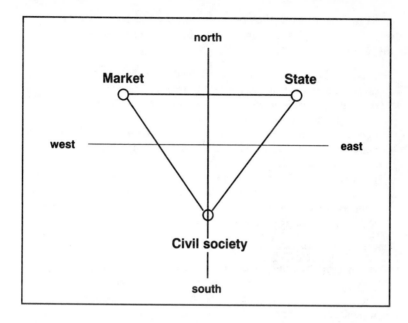

Figure 1.2 Institutional organisation of welfare in post-Second World War Europe. (Source: Abrahamson 1992.)

Kahn and Kamerman's (1976) comparative study of social services in eight countries (Canada, the United States, the United Kingdom, France, West Germany, Poland, Yugoslavia and Israel) remains one of the most substantial and satisfying studies in this difficult area for research. Their contextual discussion of the nature, purposes and uncertain boundaries of what they referred to as 'the sixth social service' has not been fully updated by subsequent writers, although others have addressed aspects of the subject (e.g. Munday 1989).

Kahn and Kamerman's work differs from that of writers such as Abrahamson and Esping-Anderson in that they did not articulate conceptual models within which to compare social services in the eight countries. Rather they consider some macro-level explanations for differences and similarities between countries, followed by a micro-level discussion of several key dimensions along which social services in different countries may be compared.

At the macro level they pose the question as to whether it is the wealthier countries that invest most in social services and conclude this is so (p. 2):

> Personal social services are needed in all social classes and under diverse economic systems. And they are not a transitional thing. For the reality which is apparent in a systematic overview in eight countries and a more general exploration in many others is that the most developed of industrial urban societies, those with the highest per capita personal consumption, invest heavily in general social services and do so in good times and bad. The services are permanent parts of the social infrastructure of modern states . . . one could with some basis even argue the hypothesis that economic development and industrialisation are more important determinants of social welfare focus and solutions than is political or economic ideology.

Later, they elaborate this view (p. 362):

> the investment in the personal social services and their growth comes only with national capacity, no matter how long standing the need. The more prosperous countries are further along. The more urbanised, whose populations have greater access to service centres, offer more services. The most developed states, or provinces, or regions, respond most adequately to needs and to 'wants'.

These are bold statements which remain difficult to test, given the chronic shortage of data on countries' social services inputs and outputs. Many observers of the international social services scene will find it hard to believe that the political and economic ideologies of 'Reaganism' in America and 'Thatcherism' in Britain have not had a profound and damaging effect on social welfare policies and programmes in those countries. Nevertheless, there is relevant data on economic indicators such as the standard of living of European countries, enabling some evaluation of the Kahn and Kamerman hypothesis in the conclusion to chapter 2.

Kahn and Kamerman reach a conclusion from their study which will also be examined in the review of member states' social services. They expected to find sharply delineated differences in the social services systems of the eight countries, based on well-defined concepts and structured options. Instead, they concluded that (p. 363):

> there are no pure and fully delineated general social service systems and that the various countries are more alike than different in

essentials. While there are important distinctions, not to be ignored, there are in fact more basic convergences. Response to task and shared objectives lead to commonalities which cross national boundaries.

Their view of the convergence of social services internationally is central to current discussions of social welfare and social care in Europe. Abrahamson's observation about the convergence of European social welfare systems towards the corporatist model has been reported earlier. In chapter 3 of this book there is a discussion of the EU policy of convergence rather than harmonisation in social affairs. Elsewhere in this book (e.g. chapter 4) there is discussion of how member states face very similar problems in the social care field and are formulating mostly common policy and service responses.

Dimensions along which social care services may be compared

At a more practical level of analysis and discussion Kahn and Kamerman suggest several dimensions along which social care services in different countries may be compared. These are not set within specific models or conceptual frameworks but provide a means of organising comparisons, compared with simply setting descriptive case studies alongside one another. Again, these are useful when comparing systems of the member states of the European Union:

1. Social services may be *free standing or adjunctive*. The United Kingdom is a good example of free-standing services, having broken away from an adjunctive position with health services in the early 1970s. The opposite is the case in Ireland where health and social services are organised within the one authority. In other EU countries social services and social protection – or more precisely means-tested social assistance – are the responsibility of the one department. It may be argued that as social services achieve better recognition and status within a society they are more likely to become free standing.
2. Services may be relatively *comprehensive and integrated* or subdivided along age-categorical lines. An alternative way to

express the difference is to define services as either 'generic' or 'specialist'. One approach may even seem fashionable for a time, to be followed by its alternative as disadvantages of the former become evident. There is no consensus that one way of organising services is inherently better than another.

3. Countries differ considerably in relation to who has *responsibilities* for which services, and which organisations *deliver* services. Chapter 4 explores these differences as there are strong moves now in some countries for local government to retain responsibility for services – including much of the funding – but to move service provision into the independent sectors. This has long been the position in countries such as Germany and the Netherlands.

4. Countries will differ in relation to social services *outputs* but as yet we lack reliable information on which to make valid comparisons. Even more basically, only rough and ready calculations of service inputs can be made. For example, it should be possible to compare the numbers of social workers employed in each country in relation to population size, but such an endeavour is fraught with difficulty, such as agreeing on what actually constitutes a 'social worker'.

5. Social services *legislation* in European countries is a major but rather neglected subject for comparative study. In the United Kingdom social service provision is based firmly on legislative mandate but less obviously so in some other European countries where there is more emphasis on first-stage prevention unrelated to specific client groups. The writer knows of only one comparative study of social services legislation (Rubiol 1986). In preparing new child care legislation for Ireland the Irish ministry of health looked closely at the 1989 Children's Act in Britain, demonstrating the potential for learning from one another's laws in social care. Further comparative work and dissemination in this field are required.

Conclusion

Other dimensions for comparing social care could be added but the above are sufficient at this stage. It has been shown that comparative work in both international and European social care remains relatively underdeveloped, although progress is being made. The lack of reliable data on social services in individual countries is a major constraint, as is the difficulty of formulating conceptual frameworks and models. In their absence higher-level formulations from studies of welfare states can be adapted to some extent for use in the specific field covered by this book, and lower-level dimensions used for practical comparisons of systems and services.

As has been emphasised, social services in any one country should be understood within their societal context, including historical development. Kahn and Kamerman suggest that there are discernible differences between countries' social services that depend on their stage of historical development. Their observation (p. 6) is the final point to be made here on the means for making comparisons:

> In general the personal social services seem to have focused more on developmental and socialisation tasks (i.e. 'prevention') as societies have become more affluent and the social sector or social welfare systems more elaborate. At the beginning, services tended to focus on substitute care, direct help and social control, often tied to providing material aid.

This conclusion, together with other observations by Kahn and Kamerman on similarities and differences between countries' social care systems, will be returned to following the discussion in chapter 2.

References

Abrahamson, P. (1992) 'Welfare pluralism: towards a new consensus for a European social policy?', in L. Hantrais, M. O'Brien and S. Mangen (eds), *Cross National Research Papers 6: The mixed economy of welfare*, Leicester: European Research Centre, Loughborough University.

Baine, S., J. Benington and J. Russell (1992) *Changing Europe: Challenges facing the voluntary and community sectors in the 1990s*, London: National Council for Voluntary Organisations Publications, and the Community Development Foundation.

Cannan, C., L. Berry and K. Lyons (1992) *Social Work and Europe*, London: Macmillan.

Esping-Anderson, G. (1990) *The Three Worlds of Welfare Capitalism*, Cambridge: Polity Press.

European Commission: Directorate-General for Employment, Industrial Relations and Social Affairs (1994) *European Social Policy: A way forward for the Union*, Luxembourg: Office for Official Publications of the European Communities.

Hill, M. (ed.) (1991) *Social Work and the European Community*, London: Jessica Kingsley.

Jones, C. (1985) *Patterns of Social Policy*, London: Tavistock.

Kahn, A. and S. Kamerman (1976) *Social Services in International Perspective*, Washington: US Department of Health, Welfare and Education.

Knapp, M. (1984) *The Economics of Social Care*, London: Macmillan.

Kraan, R., R. Baldock, J. Davies, B. Evers, A. Johansson, L. Knapen, M. Thurslund and C. Tunissen (1991) *Care of the Elderly: Significant innovations in three European countries*, Frankfurt: Campus; Boulder, CO: Westview Press.

Lorenz, W. (1994) *Social Work in a Changing Europe*, London: Routledge.

Munday, B. (ed.) (1989) *The Crisis in Welfare: An international perspective on social services and social work*, Hemel Hempstead: Harvester Wheatsheaf.

Munday, B. (ed.) (1993) *European Social Services*, Canterbury: European Institute of Social Services, University of Kent at Canterbury.

Rodgers, B. (1979) *The Study of Social Policy: A comparative approach*, London: Allen and Unwin.

Rodgers, B. and J. Stevenson (1973) *A New Portrait of Social Work: A study of the social services in a northern town from Younghusband to Seebohm*, London: Heinemann.

Room, G. (1993) *Social Services and Social Exclusion: Report of the European Community Observatory on National Policies to Combat Social Exclusion*, Lille: European Economic Interest Group 'Animation and Research'.

Rubiol, G. (1986) *Los servicios sociales*, vol. II: *Leyes de servicios sociales en Europa*, Madrid: Siglo XXI de Espana Editores, SA.

CHAPTER 2

Social care in the member states of the European Union

Contexts and overview

Brian Munday

Introduction

Any survey of a sample of texts on the European Union shows that most books are written to a thematic or topic structure, including books on social services or social care in Europe. The thematic approach is arguably inherently more interesting and intellectually satisfying, allowing for concentration on key, topical subjects without any pretence that the subject(s) can be covered exhaustively in relation to each of the twelve countries.

The disadvantage of this approach is that the reader rarely gets to know enough about each individual country as a necessary context for making best use of thematic study. It is surprisingly difficult to find a book that in one or two volumes contains summary accounts of each member state of the European Union, covering social, political, economic and cultural characteristics.

To understand social care for elderly or disabled people in Europe, for example, it is necessary to know something of the political and economic situation of the countries concerned and the social care systems that operate in those countries. Other writers have criticised the lack of context in accounts of social policy and social welfare in comparative studies. The main purpose of this chapter is to convey some of this contextual information about the twelve countries and their social care systems, prior to the more thematic or topic-based chapters in the rest of the book.

This is a daunting task, given the complexities of the countries and the impossibility of doing them sufficient justice within the constraints of one chapter. Of necessity, the emphasis will be on information and discussion of the different social services systems.

Some demographic and economic comparisons

Reference was made in chapter 1 to the problem of finding reliable up-to-date data on social care in member states of the European Union as a solid basis for comparative study. For example, international studies of health and welfare often include a statistic on the number of doctors per thousand population in each country. It ought to be possible to produce such a statistic for the number of social workers, occupational therapists and home helps in relation to population size of EU countries, but differences in terminology and other complications render this impossible – to say nothing of the often rudimentary state of basic data collection in some countries.

Selective data on demography and economic conditions in the member states will now be reviewed briefly as part of the context for a fuller understanding of social care in the twelve countries (Table 2.1).

Population size varies enormously across the European Union, ranging from Luxembourg, with a population no greater than that of a large London borough, to over 80 million people in the unified Germany. Eurostat estimated that at the beginning of 1992 the population of the European Union as a whole was well over 346 million – 6.4 per cent of the world's population, compared with 8.9 per cent in 1960.

Of particular relevance to future demand for social care services in the member states is the clear trend towards a decline in fertility, smaller families and ageing populations. The figure for natural population increases shows at the one extreme that the population is declining in Germany – the only EU country to experience this phenomenon in 1991. However, the net migration figure changes the picture substantially. Only Italy has a lower fertility rate than Germany, the rates for all the Mediterranean countries being lower than average for the European Union.

In 1991 the number of births dropped below 4 million for the first time since 1960 – a fall of 37.5 per cent compared with 1960.

Table 2.1 Main demographic indicators for the European Community, 1991

	Population at 1.1.1992 (1,000)	Natural increase (1,000)	Net migration (1,000)	Total increase (1,000)	Gross marriage rate (per 1,000 inhabitants)	Total fertility rate	Infant mortality rate (per 1,000 live births)	Life expectancy at birth Males	Females
Belguim	10,022.0	21.8[1]	14.1	35.0	6.1	1.62[2]	7.0[1]	72.8	79.5
Denmark	5,162.1	4.8	10.9	15.7	6.0	1.68	7.3	72.5	78.0
FR of Germany	80,274.6[1]	–81.2	600.7	521.3	5.7	1.33	6.9	72.1	78.7
Greece	10,279.9	7.1	152.9	159.9	6.4	1.40	9.0	74.6	79.8
Spain	39,055.9	48.3[1]	13.8	62.1	5.6[1]	1.33[2]	7.8[1]	73.3[2]	80.3[2]
France	57,217.5	234.3[1]	90.0	324.3	4.9	1.78[2]	7.3	72.9	81.1
Ireland	3,542.0	21.1[1]	1.7	23.0	4.8[1]	2.10	8.2[1]	72.2	77.7
Italy	57,788.2[1]	9.0[1]	33.3	42.0	5.3[1]	1.26[2]	8.2	74.0[2]	80.4[2]
Luxembourg	389.8	1.2	4.2	5.4	6.7	1.60	9.2	72.0	79.1
Netherlands	15,129.2	68.7	62.9	118.7	6.3	1.61	6.5	74.0	80.1
Portugal	9,846.0	12.1	–25.0	–12.5	7.3	1.50	10.8	69.8	77.3
United Kingdom	57,686.1[1]	146.3	27.6	156.1	6.2	1.82	7.4	73.2	78.6
EUR 12	346,393.3	493.6	987.2	1,451.1	5.7	1.51	7.5	72.8[2]	79.4[2]

Notes: [1] Provisional data.
    [2] 1990.

Source: Eurostat (1993).

Fertility rates overall have fallen from 2.61 births per woman in 1960 to 1.51 in 1991.

One factor explaining declining fertility rates is the significant rise in the number of women now active in the labour market in all EU countries. Denmark has the highest proportion of women in paid employment, the lowest proportions being in Catholic Ireland and the Mediterranean countries. As more and more women work outside the home they become less available for what has long been seen as their traditional role as informal carers within the home. This factor, allied to the trend towards smaller families, has long-term implications for the pattern of demand for formal caring services, whether provided by state, not-for-profit or for-profit services.

Chapter 7 discusses the changes in the proportion of elderly people in the European Union and the implications for demands on and funding of social care. The challenge posed to welfare states of a combination of declining fertility rates, smaller families, increased proportions of women entering the labour market and ageing populations was highlighted in the European Commission's Green Paper (1993a, p. 22) on the future for European social policy:

> The greatest challenge to the welfare state in the short run seems to be the serious financial difficulties it has to face as a result of the recession which is currently hitting most European economies. It can safely be assumed that under normal economic circumstances the financing of the European welfare states would not pose, at present, any major problems. However, it is well known that over the coming decades there will be a considerable shift in the demographic structure of our populations and an increasing number of older people will have to rely on the support of a shrinking number of people of working age.

Economic indicators

Social policy and social welfare provision must always be considered in relation to the economic position of the country or countries concerned. This has been a preoccupation for the European Union as a whole, with the Commission's Green Paper on future social policy followed by the 1994 White Paper (1994) emphasising that the future development of European welfare states must depend heavily on economic priorities, the future for jobs and the need for international competitiveness. All member states are seeking welfare and social care systems that are affordable in the context of their economic situation, predicted future trends and political preferences.

Table 2.2 contains some principal economic indicators for the member states in 1989.

Standard of living

Chapter 1 referred to Kahn and Kamerman's (1976) prediction that the most economically advanced and wealthier countries will be those with the most developed and extensive social services. Data on the standard of living in the member states is not strictly an indicator of the countries' wealth, but it is a useful yardstick for considering the Kahn and Kamerman view.

There are marked differences in the levels of economic activity of the twelve countries, as shown in the distribution of the European Union's total gross domestic product (GDP). More than 80 per cent is provided by four countries – France, Germany, Italy and the United Kingdom. Greece, Ireland, Luxembourg and Portugal account for only 2.8 per cent of EU GDP. These global figures take no account of major differences between countries such as population size and relative prices.

The figure in table 2.2 'GDP per capita in PPS' is much more useful as a guide to relative standards of living as it is a 'real-terms' figure, taking into account relative purchasing power. The diminutive Luxembourg is clearly in the lead using this measure, followed by Germany – although their position must have adjusted downwards following reunification. Belgium, Denmark, France, Italy, the Netherlands and the United Kingdom are all in a second group enjoying a relatively high standard of living within the European Union. Ireland and Spain are well below average, leaving Greece and Portugal as the two poorest countries. In 1991 Greece and Portugal had the highest inflation rates, Greece's rate of over 18 per cent being well over the norm of 3–5 per cent for the European Union as a whole.

Employment and unemployment

The Commission's White Paper on the future of European social policy emphasises the priority to be given to tackling persistent

Table 2.2 Principal indicators for the member states of the European Community, 1989

	EUR 12	B	DK	D	GR	E	F	IRL	I	L	NL	P	UK
Total population (1,000) [1]	343,470.3	9,947.8	5,135.4	79,346.5	10,046.0	38,924.5	56,304.0	3,506.5	57,576.4	378.4	14,892.6	10,336.9	57,409.0
Rate of activity (%)	54.2	47.7	66.8	55.5	49.7	47.1	55.2	51.3	49.0	50.4	55.3	57.9	62.0
Unemployment rate (%) [1]	8.4	8.1	7.4	5.1	7.5	16.1	9.0	15.6	9.8	1.6	8.1	4.6	6.4
Total taxes and social security contributions (% GDP)	39.5[2]	45.1[2]	52.1	37.4	35.9[2]	32.8	44.4	41.5	37.1	42.8[2]	48.2	34.6	37.3
GDP er capita in PS [1]	17,857	19,091	19,814	21,131	9,850	14,556	20,207	12,819	19,187	24,303	19,147	10,369	19,726

Notes: [1] 1990.
[2] 1988.

Source: Eurostat (1992).

high levels of unemployment, including long-term unemployment. Levels of spending on social protection and social services will be affected by countries' costs of addressing the unemployment problem.

The unemployment figures for 1990 show an average of 8.4 per cent overall, the rates for Spain and Ireland being nearly twice the average. Rates of over 20 per cent were found in the south and south-west of Spain – the regions of Andalusia and Estremadura – and the southernmost areas of Italy, including Sicily. Across the European Union more women than men were unemployed in 1990 – 11.1 per cent compared with 6.5 per cent, while the rate (16.1 per cent) for young people under 25 is particularly worrying. This latter problem is especially severe in Spain, where the rate for unemployed young people was 31.9 per cent in 1990, a problem compounded for the young unemployed by the absence of state benefits for those who have not worked. The expectation is that they will live with their families and be supported by them.

Long-term unemployment (i.e. over one year) remains very high in the Union, at around 45 per cent of the total unemployed in 1991. The rates declined for most countries between 1985 and 1991 with the exception of Italy and Greece. The Commission's Green Paper (p. 35) underlines the seriousness of continuing high levels of unemployment, not least to large numbers of disadvantaged European citizens who make heavy demands on both social protection and the social care resources of their countries:

> Increased unemployment to a forecast Community average of around 12% in 1994, following on already high structural unemployment, has reached the point where it is socially dangerous as well as politically and economically unacceptable. The 'ratcheting up' of unemployment with each recession has to be reversed because it now means that more than half the unemployed have been out of work for 12 months or more. Such a process partly explains escalating poverty and social exclusion.

Conclusion

This brief review of some comparative demographic and economic data provides part of the context for a fuller understanding of the social care systems of the different member states. Some prominent demographic trends have been highlighted that have major

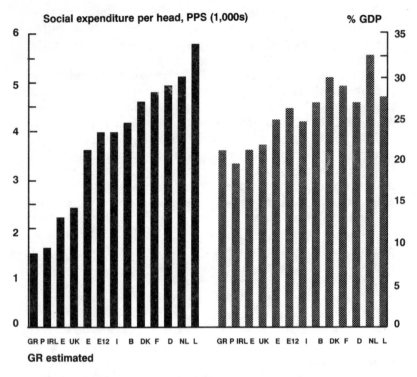

Figure 2.1 Social protection expenditure per head and in relation to GDP, 1991. (Source: Commission of the European Communities 1993b, p. 41.)

implications for likely future demand for formal social care services in all countries. Chapter 4 of this book discusses the policy and service response that is emerging strongly in most or all member states.

The economic data shows the considerable variations in the standard of living of the countries, leaving unanswered the question of whether there is a clear correlation with the level of social care development. Interestingly, there is evidence that *social protection* expenditure is higher per capita in EU countries that are economically most developed – see Figure 2.1. The Commission report (1993b) concludes from this data that: 'expenditure relative to GDP is higher in general in those countries where income per head is also relatively high, indicating that as economic development takes place proportionately more resources are devoted to social protection.' The two exceptions to this appear to be Italy and the United Kingdom, who, in relation to income per head, spend slightly less than the average for the European Union. Expenditure per capita on social care would be an important measure of the level of development of those services, but such data is extremely difficult to obtain. Figures for member states' expenditure on health care are available – see page 99 of the Commission's report on social protection – with some countries including some social care expenditure in their figures.

Social care systems in the member states

The rest of this chapter contains a concise country-by-country picture of social care systems in the twelve member states, relating this material to selected aspects of political and social structures. The writer draws on his earlier work on *European Social Services* (Munday 1993) and acknowledges the considerable contribution of the writers from the different countries in that volume.

Belgium

Belgium is one of the smaller EU countries, with a population of just over 10 million people in 1992. Economically, it is in the big league within the European Union, being eighteenth in the league table of world economies in the early 1990s, in terms of gross national product (GNP), and with a per capita export level twice that of Germany. The image of Belgium – fairly or not – amongst other Europeans is one of wealthy and rather dull respectability, attracting less interest as a country than do many of the other member states. It is, however, one of the strongest supporters of the European Union, which may well be related to Belgium being one state but not one nation.

The Belgian state was created in 1830 following the uprising against the Dutch, the new creation being a unitary state with a central government, provinces and municipalities. Belgium is now one of several European countries struggling to maintain its unity in the face of strong separatist movements, based on long-standing language and cultural differences. It is divided into three semi-autonomous language-based regions, the two main ones being the Flemish- (or Dutch-) speaking Flanders community and the French-speaking area of Wallonia. In the third, much smaller, Brussels region Flanders is responsible for the Flemish-speaking and bilingual population, leaving the French community for Wallonia.

Linguistic identification is so strong amongst sections of the population as to threaten the continuation of one nation state. From 1970 to 1988 the constitution was modified to create a federal state with sovereignty devolved to three horizontal authorities – central state, the communities and the regions. The three power levels have exclusive responsibilities with no one authority over another. The central state is responsible for social security, the communities for public health, welfare and education. Policy-making in the economy, transport and the environment has also been passed to the regions, with strong pressure to devolve social security, agriculture and some aspects of foreign policy. The Flemish community is most interested in the devolution of social security as it annually pays a large additional sum to support the larger numbers of elderly, sick and unemployed people in Wallonia. In the early 1990s the unemployment rate in Wallonia was double that for Flanders. This is a reversal of historic roles. Industrialisation came earlier to Wallonia, which used to subsidise the more rural areas. As Wallonia's basic industries declined into a 'rustbelt' Flanders attracted more modern manufacturing activity.

The process of devolving power to the local level has probably gone as far as possible, with uneasy agreement that there should be the maximum autonomy for the regions but not regional independence with the consequent break-up of the Belgian state.

Social care in Flanders

The communities have responsibility for welfare policy, the financing of social assistance and for social services. The social services systems in the two main communities will be reviewed here. The Flemish community publishes excellent information in English about their social services. The communities have well-defined legal responsibilities for the following so-called 'aid to persons':

- social welfare policy.
- family policy and all forms of assistance to children and families.

- reception and integration of immigrants.
- provision for disabled people, including vocational training and retraining.
- services for elderly people.
- special youth assistance.
- social assistance for ex-prisoners for the purpose of re-integration.

Although both communities are bound by the same legal responsibilities in social welfare, policies and services have evolved differently, partly because of the different levels of community financing. The Public Services for Social Welfare Act gives every citizen entitlement to social services, offering aid that is both curative and preventative. Services can be of a material, social, medical, social–medical or psychological nature. The Act requires that they respect the ideological, philosophical or religious convictions of the persons concerned.

General tasks for public social welfare include establishing hospitals, rest homes and homes for elderly people, retreats, service centres and housing for elderly people, day care centres for children and disabled people. Public social welfare centres are also responsible for urgent medical assistance, access to nursing institutions and the employment and protection of minors. The public service authorities may provide the services directly themselves, collaborate with other public services or contract with the independent sector. Services are financed by a mixture of grants from a special social welfare fund, payments from the municipalities, subsidies from higher authorities and payments by clients.

Mostinckx (1993) argues that a feature of the Flemish social care system is the emphasis on first-stage, open-for-all, preventative services. The government recognises and subsidises an extensive network of private centres for general social welfare which organise social and psycho-social aid designed to avoid, restrict or eliminate problems that threaten the welfare of the citizen. Their preventative services include reception of people in a state of crisis, provision of information, knowledge and skills for using social facilities and enabling independent living, assistance for individuals with problems such as personality development, their functioning in society or ability to form relationships.

These services are multidisciplinary and staffed by both professionals and volunteers, operating at the level of the individual, family and group. Other first-stage preventative work includes victim support, support for women and telephone reception centres. In each Flemish province a telephone reception centre offers a 24-hour telephone service, staffed by volunteers supervised by professionals. The service is carefully regulated and provides help with a very wide range of personal problems and needs. It does not have the mainly potential suicide focus of the British Samaritans service.

Extensive services are provided for children and families, elderly people and people with disabilities. With the former there is a close inter-relationship of health and social care, a major impetus having been given to this field by legislative reform in the early 1980s. In the field of child abuse the approach is primarily non-judicial and non-punitive, with a network of special assistance centres for abused children providing a 24-hour service staffed mainly by social workers.

A feature of social care for elderly people is the locality-based service centres providing material, health and social help. The centres are an accessible neighbourhood facility for senior citizens living in their own homes, each centre having a council with user involvement. At the other end of the age range there is a strong emphasis on services for young people, designed to enable them to integrate into society – see Munday (1993, pp. 50–5) for further details.

Overall, there is an impressive system of social care service in Flanders, as judged by the array of publicly financed services for the main client groups and the resources allocated to first-stage, preventative intervention. Other countries may have much to learn from Flemish experience in this aspect of social care.

Social care in Wallonia
Unfortunately, much less written information is available concerning the French community – see Wanlin (1993). In Wallonia each local authority district has to have a public centre for social welfare but the social action provision by the provinces – the governmental level between the Community and the districts – is optional and, in practice, diverse. As in Flanders, there is a mix of public and independent (mostly not-for-profit) social care provision.

The centres for social welfare are similar or even identical to the centres in Flanders. In addition to social care provision the centres assess applications and make payments of the *minimet*, with the state paying 50 per cent of the cost of these payments. Belgians have a right to payment of the *minimet* when they are not able to provide for themselves an income at a defined minimum level. As in most other EU countries, social care services and cash payments under means-tested social assistance are the responsibility of one local government agency – unlike the position in the United Kingdom.

Denmark

Denmark is of special interest as the only Scandinavian country in the European Union up to the end of 1994. Scandinavian countries have a reputation for relatively generous welfare state systems, paid for by high levels of personal taxation. This tradition is reflected quantitatively and qualitatively in their publicly financed and provided social care services. This has been the case with Denmark, although change has been under way in the 1990s.

Denmark, with a population of a little over 5 million, is the third-smallest member state, with its inhabitants enjoying one of the highest standards of living in the European Union – the fourth-highest in 1990. In the same year the unemployment rate was 7.4 per cent and below the average for the European Union. Personal taxation is high, with a basic income tax rate of 50 per cent in the late 1980s, people on high incomes paying a total of around 70 per cent in tax and other deductions. In 1989 total taxes and social security contributions as a percentage of gross domestic product were 52.1 per cent – easily the highest in the European Union.

The most comprehensive and up-to-date account in English of social care in Denmark known to the writer is the report for the European Commission's Observatory on Social Exclusion by Hansen *et al.* (1992). They refer to three outstanding characteristics of the Danish system:

1. There is an extensive range of services covering the main areas of social need.
2. The great majority of services are provided by public or publicly financed institutions.

3. Social services are financed almost exclusively by personal and commodity taxes.

They argue that the high level of social care provision is partly explained by the rapidly rising female participation rate in the labour market in the last thirty years. Denmark has the highest proportion of working women in the European Union – over 50 per cent in 1989 compared with an average of 34.9 per cent – with similar rates for both married and unmarried women. The writers refer also to significant changes in attitudes towards marriage and the family since 1960, with the number of divorces doubling between 1966 and 1971, and the number of marriages falling by more than a third between 1965 and 1981 during a period of a major increase in the number of couples living together without marrying. They conclude (p. 11):

> To sum up: the institution of the family, as the traditional bearer of a number of social and practical functions, has been greatly weakened in this period. A large part of the care functions for children, the elderly and the disabled which were formerly attended to by women have therefore been taken over by the public sector.

State-provided child care is generous by EU standards. From birth to two years around 44 per cent of children are in nurseries and full-time centres, while from three to six years 87 per cent are in kindergartens, preschool centres and other services. In addition, maternity leave is 14 weeks postnatal with 90 per cent of earnings up to a maximum level *and* two weeks statutory paternal leave on 90 per cent of earnings. Denmark is the only EU country to have this latter provision.

But in recent years Denmark – along with other Scandinavian countries – has been seeking a revised system of social care that it can afford and which is politically supportable. From 1982 Conservative–Liberal minority governments aimed to reduce the high level of public sector involvement in social affairs, with more emphasis in social care on increasing the contribution of the independent not-for-profit sector. One example was the setting up of a national Volunteer Centre similar to the one in the United Kingdom. The 1980s saw a clear government strategy to support community development and self-help projects as part of this shift away from the heavy dependence on public sector provision.

Responsibility for social care services

Local government reform in 1970 created 275 municipalities and fourteen counties, the population size of the former ranging from 6,000 to 55,000. A high degree of decentralisation was introduced, with local government taking on far more tasks and financial responsibility than before. Alongside these major changes a complex and expanded system of citizen participation at the local level became part of the new local government system.

Social care services are the responsibility of the Social and Health Administration (SHA) in each municipality. This body also administers some health services and is also responsible for the assessment and payment of social assistance to claimants. Smaller municipalities co-operate to provide certain social care resources, while counties can provide more specialist facilities. There is a very strong emphasis on responsibilities towards and services for children and young people, people with disabilities, and elderly people. This resulted a few years ago in the creation of a Danish social care export/consultation agency known as 'DANSOC'. The agency existed to make Danish expertise and excellence in child care, and services for disabled and elderly people available to interested organisations in other countries. Later, DANSOC became more broadly based, as the title SCANSOC indicates.

As Philpot (1989) points out, social care provision in Denmark has been based on the principle that the rights and obligations of people who are the main users of services are the same as those of all other citizens. This has resulted, for example, in a policy of integration of young and older people with learning disabilities into mainstream education, health and welfare services. The implementation of the principle of normalisation features strongly in the approach to provision for elderly people. There has been a strong reaction away from the relatively high level of institutional care, with no new residential homes for elderly people having been built since 1988. In sheltered home care there are formal requirements as to the minimum number and types of rooms. There has also been a long-standing provision for user participation in services, with 65 per cent of homes for elderly people having residents' councils as long ago as 1965.

Writing about community care in Denmark, Philpot (1989) emphasised the formal arrangements between health and social services that helped to ensure a coherent service. For example, a municipality had three days to create a home care package for a patient with an agreed date for discharge from hospital – a county service. Failing that, the municipality would pay the county £107 a month while the patient remained in hospital. If residential care was needed the municipality would have three weeks to find it, or suffer a significant financial penalty. The incentives to provide a community care service were very clear!

The extent and quality of Denmark's public social care services remain impressive and the envy of many other European countries. But as Hansen *et al.* (1992) conclude, the 'politics of modernisation' are now to the fore, with an emphasis on involving networks of citizens in social care, the development of the independent sector and new social experiments.

Eire

The Republic of Ireland covers around 80 per cent of the land area of the island and contains twenty-six of the island's thirty-two counties. As is well known, there has been a long-term and sometimes violent dispute over the division of the island into north and south, the north being part of the United Kingdom. The present cease-fire has led to real optimism that 'the troubles' may now be settled by negotiation rather than by force.

With a population of 3.5 million people, Ireland is the second-smallest member state. It also features at the extreme ends of other EU league tables in terms of demography and economic statistics. It has a relatively young population by EU standards, with the lowest proportion of elderly people over the age of seventy-five. In 1991 Ireland had the highest fertility rate – 2.10 against an EU average of 1.51 – but the trend as elsewhere is towards smaller families. There is increasing labour market participation by married women – from 5.4 per cent in 1961 to 23.6 per cent in 1990. Ireland has been characterised by persistent outward migration, with increased internal migration from rural to urban and suburban areas.

Economically, Ireland remains one of the poorest member states, with the third-lowest standard of living in 1990, the second-highest unemployment rate and the highest level of long-term unemployment. It has therefore qualified for a range of EU special funding, including those for social services developments as out-lined in chapter 3.

The amount of available written information on social care in Ireland is relatively modest. As Kavanagh (1993) comments, his-torically policy in health and social services has been shaped by Catholic social teaching and the principle of subsidiarity – the state should not undertake functions which could be fulfilled by individ-uals on their own or by the local community. This tradition is built into current policies in social care where the state plays a limited role as provider, while the religious and voluntary organisations figure more prominently – see below.

Organisation of social care services
These services do not enjoy a high priority, from central govern-ment downwards. There is no central department, minister nor budget heading. Social services have developed under the depart-ment of health and are administered by eight regional health boards. These vary in size from the Eastern, with over 1 million people, down to the smallest, with 200,000.

Health boards divide into three programmes: general hospitals, special hospitals and community care. Social services are located within 'community welfare', one of the three sub-programmes of community care. Community welfare also includes cash benefits payments and grants to voluntary organisations. The health boards have a limited legal obligation to provide social services which leads to uneven provision across the country, and considerable variations in the eligibility criteria used for similar services, for instance circumstances and levels of charges to service users.

Cinneide and Corrigan (1992) report that in 1989 the health boards employed 366 social workers, 255 working in community care services. The emphasis in their work has been on child protec-tion, child care and family work. Work with elderly people and people with disabilities has not been seen as mainline social work, these services being provided mainly by voluntary organisations, volunteers and nurses. Services for people with learning dis-abilities have been described as 'fragmented and patchy' (King 1989) – an example of the unevenness referred to earlier.

Religious orders play an important part in social care, such as residential services for people with learning disabilities; so do diocesan social services centres, which co-ordinate the work of religious and lay volunteers in a specific locality. By the early 1990s the role and activities of voluntary organisations had not been defined in law, policy or strategy.

Conclusion
The picture of Irish social services presented in the available literature is of relatively underdeveloped services, unevenly distributed across the country. More recently new child care legislation has been introduced, modelled on the United Kingdom law. Developments in adult services will benefit as Irish social care agencies form partnerships with their counterparts in other parts of Europe; and additional finance for social care is obtained from European programmes that target poorer countries, such as Ireland.

France

France is firmly in the big league of the member states of the European Union, being one of the founder members of the original Community and consistently one of its strongest supporters. It is big in terms of its population – the third-largest in the Union – and in the standard of living of its inhabitants, third in 1990 after Luxembourg and Germany. Its sometimes fierce determination to stick to its own language is probably a major reason why rather less is known about its complicated system of social protection and social care. Much of the following material is summarised from Ely and Saunders (1993).

France was a highly centralised state until the last two decades. Traditionally, there has been a high degree of consensus on the role of the state in social affairs, supporting intervention to improve the position of its people. The 1980s saw the introduction of a major programme of decentralisation affecting social services. Some of the powers of the central government *préfet* are transferred to locally elected representatives with responsibility for major services. Social services became the responsibility of the elected president of the *département* but decentralisation did not lead to a clear-cut division of responsibilities. Unlike the position in many other countries, one individual can hold office in up to three levels of government and an employee of the state can stand for political office.

As elsewhere in the European Union, current policies in social care services are heavily concerned with cost containment, as seen in the drive for efficiency savings in service delivery, better co-ordination and measures to make it easier for families to look after elderly relatives. Another feature is the strong growth of not-for-profit associations in most areas of national life, including social care.

Organisation of social care services

There are four levels of government in France: national, regional, departmental and commune. There are 22 regions, 96 departments and 36,000 communes, nearly a third with fewer than 200 people. At the national level there is the Ministry of Solidarity, Health and Social Protection, with twelve directorates. They relate to the regional and departmental directorates of health and social affairs.

The regions were established in the late 1960s mainly as units for social planning. The regional and departmental *préfets* directly manage the health service, with the regional council providing technical advice, financial assistance and co-ordination for social services at the next tier down. At the level of the *département* responsibility for management and provision of social services was transferred in the early 1980s to the elected president of the General Council, together with powers for contracting out services to not-for-profit associations.

Départements may not allow their level of provision of social services and social assistance (financial help for people not covered by insurance) to fall below the level set nationally. The responsibility of the General Council of the *département* should not interfere with those of judges who deal with children at risk; COTOREP, which assesses degrees of disability; the *préfet*, who is guardian of wards of state; and the commissions which hear applications for financial aid.

In the commune the local mayor is both the representative of the state and the elected representative of local government. His social services role is exercised through the *centres communaux d'action sociale*.

There is a separation of responsibilities for welfare services at the level of the *département*. The state, through the *préfet*, co-ordinates and oversees health-related services whose charges to service users will be reimbursed – at least in part – by the national sickness insurance funds. The *préfet* is responsible for implementing the regional plans for these services, for authorising the provision of local services or their contracting out, and for inspection and enforcement of national standards. Included in these services are reception and residential centres for people with severe disabilities, psychiatric services and school health services.

The president of the General Council in the *département* has responsibility for financial aid under *l'aide sociale* (financial allowances for people not covered by social security insurance schemes), and for certain social services which may be directly provided or contracted out. These include home help and other forms of domiciliary care, residential care for elderly and less severely disabled adults, field, day and residential care services for children, and the creation of *revenue minimum d'insertion* projects – see below.

Salient features of French social care services

The widely available computerised general information system known as *Minitel* includes information on social services topics for the general public and professionals. This is an excellent resource, given the long-standing difficulties for the general public in most countries in acquiring basic information about social services. In the United Kingdom, for example, such information could be incorporated in the 'Teletext' system.

In France the local point of access for social care assistance is the centre of social action in the commune. These centres provide an information and advice service, working proactively to help alleviate need on a collective basis. The centres are mostly financed by the *département* and their social workers employed by the social action section of the *département*. They work in generic and multi-disciplinary teams, covering a defined geographical area.

Given the European wide concern over how the cost of care for increasing numbers of very elderly and dependent people is to be financed, the French system is of particular interest. As Ely and Saunders explain, close relatives may have to contribute to the costs of residential care (1993, p. 133):

> If the old person lacks the means to pay the charges for residential
> care, then their children, childrens' spouses and grandchildren are
> obliged to contribute up to a certain ceiling, under the general legal
> principle of the *obligation alimentaire*, the duty to support one's close

family. And where their family's means are insufficient, the individual can apply to *aide sociale* who will loan the money and make arrangements to recover it from the individual's estate after his or her death.

Finally, the French measure to help combat some forms of social exclusion known as the *revenue minimum d'insertion* (RMI), established in 1988, has attracted considerable European attention. It was designed to address the growing level of poverty and disadvantage related to long-term unemployment and was available initially to people over twenty-five and younger people with dependent children. A feature of RMI has been that it can combine the payment of assistance to bring a person's income up to a guaranteed minimum level, together with a range of social actions in which the recipients must participate for their re-insertion into ordinary life. Ely and Saunders comment that (p. 145):

> RMI takes a holistic approach to considering an individual's or a family's needs, taking into account their financial circumstances, psychological state, social relationships, and life goals. It focuses on achievements in the programme as small steps towards these goals. A 'key worker' assesses needs and mobilises the necessary resources.

Social action programmes are provided by the department through its social services and not-for-profit associations. RMI has subsequently been reviewed nationally and its current position is not clear. Certainly, it has been seen as an innovatory, imaginative and relatively well-resourced approach to tackling a major form of social exclusion – a problem now high on the European Union's social policy agenda.

Germany

The reunification of Germany in 1990 made it substantially the largest EU country, with a population of over 80 million people, the great majority being inhabitants of the old west Germany. Its overall size contrasts with continuing concern over the falling birthrate – the second-lowest in the European Union – resulting in a negative natural increase in the population in 1991. But in the same year net inward migration of over 600,000 was nearly four times higher than for any other member state.

To date there is limited information available on social care in the former German Democratic Republic (GDR), so that much of this section's material refers to the situation of the Federal Republic of Germany (FRG). Social care in Germany is part of a comprehensive system of social insurance and social security, rooted in the Bismarckian system of the late nineteenth century, developed between the two world wars and modernised in post-Nazi Germany. Strong and continuing economic growth made possible the expansion of social services and social security at a relatively generous rate. More recently a declining birthrate, the growth in the proportion of elderly people and the heavy costs of reunification have led to a strong debate about the future for welfare in Germany.

The principle of subsidiarity is prominent in the German constitution and tradition, with Catholic social teaching placing emphasis on citizens' mutual responsibility for one another and for the family. Children and parents are mutually responsible for supporting one another and only when family and voluntary support is no longer sufficient does the state step in. The formal responsibility of the family is shown, for example, in the legal requirement that when social assistance is paid out to a recipient it can be reclaimed from the person's parents, if the recipient's position subsequently improves.

There has been excessive bureaucratisation and high administrative costs in the German welfare system, leading in the 1970s to a critique and reaction against bureaucratic, administrative social work and social services. That period saw the growth of countless grass-roots self-help initiatives that have been a particularly interesting feature of the total system.

The public social services sector

There are three sub-areas within the total system of social insurance: social insurance, public assistance and compensation, and welfare. 'Welfare' includes social services and social assistance regulated by law. Social assistance in turn is divided into social assistance, health assistance and child and youth assistance. It is provided on the basis of need and is not dependent on prior contributions. It is mostly financed out of local taxation.

The levels of government in Germany are the national or federal government, the *Länder* or states and local government – counties and cities. Public welfare is governed by laws at the federal level, with variations between the *Länder* in the levels and methods of financing benefits and social services. The role of federal government is mainly in planning, co-ordination, funding and legislation. A few social services are provided by the *Länder* (e.g. social services in prisons) and far more by local government. Here social services are administered through offices of social assistance, youth welfare departments and health offices. Two or more local authorities may combine to provide services which are especially complex and costly, such as institutions for mentally ill people.

Public welfare is responsible for two forms of help: 'subsistence help', which is means-tested financial help for people without other means, and 'help in particular conditions of life', such as help to integrate people with disabilities, help for homeless people and ex-prisoners, and various services to help integrate elderly people into the community. 'Help in particular conditions of life' accounts for about two-thirds of total expenditure.

There is a strong emphasis on work with children and young people in German social services. Unlike the division of local government responsibilities in the United Kingdom, youth and social services are integrated in the same agency in the public sector. The main areas of activity are youth work, youth social work and child and youth protection. In areas where legal norms have been set or where state obligations have to be met, the providers are public agencies – the youth welfare offices. All local authorities beyond a certain size have to establish youth welfare departments. Independent not-for-profit agencies (mostly the churches) are very involved in youth work, largely financed by the state. In the FRG there were also about 1,000 independent child welfare institutions.

The independent sector in social welfare
The centrality of the principle of subsidiarity in the German constitution ensures a substantial independent sector in social welfare. The many not-for-profit organisations are structured at all government levels from local to federal, working not on the basis of statutory responsibilities but according to religious or ideological criteria. Organisations range from the myriad of grass-roots, often politically radical groups referred to above, to the well-known six very large central associations, with co-ordinating functions.

These central associations have substantial budgets, employing many staff and unpaid volunteers. One of the big six – the Service Agency of the Protestant Church in Germany – employs about 86,000 social services staff, in addition to its health and education work. The associations in their many agencies provide social care services for the main user groups, and share common characteristics such as covering the entire FRG and providing a broad spectrum of services rather than being narrowly specialised. Their work is brought together in a national umbrella organisation, the Federal Association of Voluntary Welfare Agencies.

The division of labour between public and independent social care agencies is described by Landwehr and Wolff (1993, p. 174):

> The public providers are obliged not to establish their own agencies in so far as agencies of voluntary work already exist. . . . However, the municipalities and other public providers bear the final and overall responsibility for compliance with legal norms. At the same time, they are required to promote and support the associations of voluntary welfare work and the voluntary providers of child welfare.

The state by law has to provide direct and indirect grants from public finance to independent organisations. This includes payment for services provided by independent agencies where users have a legal claim to those services *and* prefer to use the services of an independent organisation. Other sources of finance for the non-state sector include – for church-based services – income from the national 'church tax', and lotteries.

At the national level public-private sector co-operation is mediated by the German Association for Public and Private Welfare, established in 1881. The relationship between the private and public sectors is said to be based on co-operation, with plurality and diversity characterising the system, offering real choice to the citizen. However, such lofty claims may not always be justified!

Social services in the former GDR

Writing of the situation shortly after reunification, Landwehr and Wolff (1993) referred to around 50 per cent of the population of the new *Länder* living on the edge of poverty. The *Länder* and local authorities were faced with problems *officially* unknown to them, problems which had been latent or ignored for ideological reasons – a familiar feature of former communist countries. Problems included juvenile delinquency and child abuse, homelessness, unemployment and the growth in potential poverty groups such as single parents and disabled people.

All energies initially were directed into setting up structures corresponding to those in the FRG – particularly departments of social assistance and youth welfare offices in the municipalities and counties. The problems have been great, both in terms of finance and personnel. There was an initial deficit of about 30,000 professional social welfare staff in the new *Länder*, east Berlin alone needing some 3,800 staff. Many of the new staff had to be trained in institutions of the former FRG.

Organised private social welfare work had to be started from virtually nothing, including youth, community and cultural social work. The need for social workers will be at least as great as in the FRG. In the old GDR there was a heavy dependency on unpaid and part-time social welfare personnel who are unlikely to be available in the future. However, given significant levels of unemployment among social workers in the FRG the personnel deficit may be partly met from that source.

The development of an adequate social protection and social care system in the former GDR presents a formidable challenge to the reunified Germany. It will be instructive to map progress alongside social welfare developments in other former communist central and eastern European states.

Greece

Greece – particularly its many islands – is well known as a popular holiday destination for vast numbers of Europeans, but it is one of the least well-known countries in the European Union in other respects. Greece is a republic established by referendum in 1974, with a constitution adopted in 1975. Prior to that the constitutional monarchy had been re-established after the Second World War, to be overthrown in turn by a military coup in 1967. The military dictatorship acted as a highly traditionalist force in Greek society, holding up the process of modernisation until its collapse after the Turkish invasion of Cyprus.

Economically, Greece developed rapidly, with a steep rise in the standard of living in the 1970s. Unfortunately, this was from such a low position in relation to other EU countries that by 1991 the standard of living for the population was still the lowest in the

European Union. Greece's poor economic position has undoubtedly been a major, but not the only, factor explaining the underdevelopment of social care services.

Social care services

There is relatively little written information about social care in
Greece to draw on. Two principal sources are the detailed report
for the European Commission by Karantinos *et al.* (1992); and the
chapter by Sokoly (1993). There has been no systematic study of
this sector and the general picture is of services developing in a
piecemeal fashion rather than on the basis of a rational planning
system. The result is that there are geographical inequalities in
provision, with a serious shortage of services in some areas and
wasteful duplication in others. The national organisation of services is highly centralised and hierarchical.

At central government level the Ministry of Health, Welfare and
Social Security is responsible for social protection, including social
services. Within the ministry the general secretariat of welfare is
responsible for social services. At the local level there are fifty-two
prefectures, each with a direction of health and welfare carrying
out policies and programmes elaborated by the ministry. Central
government assesses needs for social programmes and fixes a budget. Regional authorities are then responsible for implementation.
The centralised nature of the Greek system is illustrated by the
very low proportion of local authority expenditure as a proportion
of public expenditure – 6.2 per cent in 1984, the lowest of sixteen
European countries (see Blair 1991, p. 43).

The distinct impression is that the family and the private sector
still carry the main responsibilities for social care in Greece. Family ties remain close, with the family being protected by the constitution and government programmes aimed at strengthening the
family. Karantinos *et al.* (1992) comment that Greek women bear a
disproportionate burden in caring for family members.

Local government services have traditionally focused on three
groups: the young and their families, elderly people and people
with disabilities. More recently services have been developed for
Greeks returning from central and eastern Europe. Greek social
workers are trained on non-university courses of three to five
years' duration. In the early 1990s there were only three training schools and currently the shortage of finance, together with

political constraints, restricts employment opportunities for social workers. King's (1989) account of social work training refers to many social work students being poorly motivated, as they wanted to enter more prestigious professional training but failed to obtain high enough secondary school grades to do so. Training cannot change quickly enough to relate to changing social care needs, and social workers have strictly limited power and discretion.

The Greek Orthodox Church and the Red Cross have traditionally been important suppliers of social care services, their work being particularly evident in services for children, elderly people and people with financial problems. The church has probably been the main provider of residential care for elderly people, with the private for-profit sector moving into this service in recent years.

As in the rest of Europe, there is a policy to promote volunteering together with deinstitutionalisation and support for particularistic networks in their caring capacity. There is limited evidence to show that volunteering has spread significantly beyond that carried out through the church.

Private for-profit social care has increased greatly in the last decade, for example in child care services and homes for elderly people. Parents who can afford it prefer to pay for private child care services because of their quality. More generally, people often have little choice but to pay for commercial services because they are not available from the not-for-profit and state sectors.

Conclusion

This short account cannot do justice to social care in Greece but their services are arguably the least well developed of all member states in the European Union. Given the country's stage of economic development, there is evidence for the argument earlier in this book that the most advanced social care systems are found in the most highly industrialised and wealthier countries – and vice versa.

As a high-priority country for EU funding Greece's social care agencies have excellent opportunities to form partnerships with agencies in other EU countries and to obtain substantial EU finance for social care services and projects. Closer involvement with mainstream social care in Europe will assist the much-needed process of modernisation of the social care system in Greece.

Italy

Italy is another republic within the European Union, its written constitution dating from 1948. The constitution places social welfare responsibilities on the state, in broad terms. The country is divided into regions, provinces and communes, with the 1977 decree on decentralisation of administrative functions to local authorities handing over responsibility for planning, financing and implementation of all welfare activities. Two key principles following the 1977 decree are *pluralism* and participation.

In 1992 Italy had the second-highest population in the European Union but the lowest birthrate. There are strong regional differences, with deaths outnumbering births in the more prosperous north and the reverse in the much poorer south. Overall, average family size dropped from four in 1951 to three in 1981. As with most member states, Italy is faced with a marked ageing of the population, with all that entails for social and health care provision.

In 1990 Italy enjoyed the fifth-highest standard of living in the European Union but with the sharp north–south divide mentioned above. From the 1950s onwards there has been a shift from a rural society with high unemployment towards a more industrialised society. Fassolo (1993) refers to significant social changes in Italian society:

> from a rigid class society to a heterogeneous society with a
> remarkable degree of social mobility; from a society poor in material
> goods and traditional in its consumptions to a wealthy society with a
> high diffusion of income . . . ; from a society with static and rigid
> hierarchies of values to a society with changeable references and
> behaviours, geared towards recreating personal, family and group
> identity.

Alongside these changes there is the impression of widespread dissatisfaction with poor performance in public services, their uneven geographical distribution and excessive bureaucracy. As is the case elsewhere, the Italian welfare state is under attack, but its expansion is also advocated. The arguments over the virtues of 'welfare society' versus the 'welfare state' are evident in this context. Voluntary work is assuming a new significance in Italy, partly as a response to the perceived inadequacies of bureaucratic state services.

Organisation and characteristics of social care services
Health and social care in Italy attracted much European and international attention in the 1980s through the campaigning work of the 'psychiatrica democratica' movement, and the passing of the law earlier in 1978 leading to the widely publicised and controversial closure of large psychiatric institutions in Italy. Professionals from many other countries have visited Italy to observe this process at first hand, sometimes gaining inspiration to adopt the Italian approach in their own countries. Italy has certainly made an important if uneven contribution to the deinstitutionalisation movement and the growth of community care services.

Along with France and Germany in particular, the Italian approach to social care is based on Catholic social teaching, which emphasises mutual responsibility for one another and the family. Most care for children, elderly and disabled people is provided by the family and not-for-profit organisations. Public solutions tend to be seen as a last resort when an individual or the family cannot deal with their own problems. As mentioned above, attitudes are often ambivalent, with strong arguments for the extension of state services together with fierce criticisms of their perceived inadequacies.

Central government enacts laws and regulations concerning social services, and can direct and co-ordinate regional activities. The Ministry of Internal Affairs is responsible for social welfare, more specifically the Direction General of Civil Services within the ministry. The regions can in addition enact legislation, within the basic regulations established by state laws. They also have a planning and co-ordinating responsibility, promoting joint management of some services to overcome problems of the small size of some communes. A third of the population live in communes with fewer than 10,000 inhabitants, while 15 per cent live in communes with more than 500,000 people. The regions allocate funds to the communes for social welfare activities.

The communes are responsible for organising the delivery of social welfare services and all cash benefits, except for those that are insurance-based. Financial assistance to people in need is uniform throughout the country but there are considerable variations among the regions concerning the availability, quality and effectiveness of social care services. Health care is now a national service, having replaced the insurance-based system in 1978. The service is managed by local health units dependent on the communes. Some social services are provided within the health service but as a separate service. For example, local health units are responsible for the non-residential care of discharged psychiatric patients, with the communes providing such services as day centres, protected homes and the organisation of co-operatives, the latter being a particularly interesting feature of Italian social and health care.

The remit of local authority social care in Italy is sufficiently wide to include recreational and cultural activities as integral to provision. Services with these ingredients provide opportunities for encounter, communication, friendship, helping to prevent social isolation and passivity. Young animators and social workers accompany and guide groups involved in these activities. Loneliness and isolation are problems that social care is keen to help address in Italian society.

The independent sector

As in all other European countries, the contribution of the independent sector to social care in Italy is seen as particularly important. There is a relatively high level of volunteering, most volunteers belonging to associations, with their work being seen as essentially supplementary to the responsibility of welfare institutions. Parliament passed a law in 1991 to define 'voluntary activities' and form regulations concerning such matters as finance and registration.

Most regions and communes carry out their welfare functions through contracts with social co-operatives. These are staffed by a range of social service professionals, are not-for-profit but very businesslike in their approach. For-profit agencies in social care are now appearing in homes for elderly people and for psychiatric patients. They are used by public agencies for clients where good alternative provision does not exist.

Luxembourg

Luxembourg is a very untypical member state in the European Union. It has an extremely small population – 378,400 in 1990, of whom 27.5 per cent were foreigners who are excluded from all welfare provision, though their taxes do much to support it.

Together with the 'frontier workers' they comprise nearly 50 per cent of the population. The population enjoy the highest standard of living in the European Union (1990 figures) and in the same year an unemployment rate of 1.6 per cent against an EU average of 8.4 per cent. The country's wealth is based on the success of the iron ore industry from the beginning of this century, and more recently the growth of the large financial sector.

Luxembourg is a constitutional monarchy, its full title being the Grand Duchy of Luxembourg. The grand duke is the head of state who forms, along with the government, the constitutional organ of executive power. Legislative power is shared by the grand duke acting with the Chamber of Deputies, who represent the country. The population is predominantly Roman Catholic, with the Catholic principle of subsidiarity operating powerfully in policies on social care.

The country is divided into 118 communes, three districts and twelve regions. At central government level the Ministry of the Family has major social care responsibilities, such as financing services, paying the costs of placements of young people dealt with by the youth courts and a wide range of preventative and remedial services for children, families and elderly people.

The Ministry of the Interior oversees the work of the communes which by the law of 1987 have to provide welfare services for residents through the social communal offices. They should be the contact point for all services but only function as autonomous organisations in four of the 118 communes. Probation and youth protection are the responsibility of the Ministry of Justice, through its central service of social assistance. The Ministry of Health deals with drug and alcohol abuse, mental health, home care and residential homes.

The independent sector in social care
The private not-for-profit sector is very important in the history of social care in Luxembourg. Industrial patronage facilitated the growth of social work in the early twentieth century. During the same period the newly formed trade unions took on a social service role and there was a proliferation of associations, together with other types of private social services and institutions.

Caritas and the Red Cross became the two big socio-medical independent organisations, with the Roman Catholic Church

remaining very active through its local congregations and its associations grouped in the Caritas federation. Hartmann-Hirsch *et al.*
(1993) suggest that the total system of social care in Luxembourg is
a leading example in the European Union of the operation of the
mixed economy of welfare in social care, with a balancing mecha-
nism operating so that as the impact of one major provider grows
or diminishes, another withdraws or increases its intervention. No
doubt the system does not always work quite as beautifully as this
suggests.

Future developments

Hartmann-Hirsch *et al.* refer to recent discussions on the future
role of the state in Luxembourg. The aim is to avoid the two
extremes of non-involvement and nationalisation. Government
proposals of 1991 advocated a legal framework to regulate the
relationship between the state and other organisations in social
care, with the primary role of independent organisations to be fully
recognised.

There are to be formal agreements between the state and independent associations, the former to provide finance for staffing and
running costs, the latter to concentrate on experimentation and
new initiatives in social care. The state is to have a controlling role
in the co-ordination of services to avoid duplication and waste; and
to stimulate the creation of services seen as necessary. The issues
about the appropriate role of the state are similar to those debated
in other European countries. In the Luxembourg context they are
expressed by Hartmann-Hirsch:

> To what degree does a regulated association remain independent if it
> is funded 100 per cent by the state and this with a range of conditions,
> the necessity for an agreement as well as the fixing of working
> methods? If the working methods are fixed at the outset by the state,
> what remains a 'free field' for the association?

The degree of state support for independent social care developments has been uncertain. Both types of independent organisations provide services but Hartmann-Hirsch argues that the
commercial agencies provide less for the same price because they
have a worse staff-to-user ratio than that of the regulated
institutions.

Netherlands

Along with other European countries the Netherlands enjoyed a period of prosperity during the 1960s and 1970s. Bekke (1991) comments on how the government aimed at rebuilding Dutch society after 1945 by increasing public services, a process that continued during the later prosperous decades. Money was plentiful and social welfare developed rapidly.

The situation now is rather different. Bekke refers to the declining belief that government alone can solve modern societal problems; it is only one of a number of players in the social field. This realisation, together with budgetary problems for central and local government, has led to a re-appraisal of the position of government in Dutch society. To quote Bekke (p. 125):

> The image has emerged of a super-caring and super-regulating government which has gone beyond its capability to manage itself as well as its ability to manage society. The solution for government in the 1980s is on the one hand to step back, and on the other hand to carry out its remaining tasks in a more businesslike fashion. . . . Especially for the local authorities, development is in the direction of a network of agencies and of competition with other (independent) organisations for the delivery of services.

This change in the position of central and local government partly explains the Netherlands' reputation as the European leader in developing the mixed economy in social care. When the mixed economy was 'discovered' by the Thatcher government in the United Kingdom the Netherlands was high on a list of countries to visit to examine its operation in social welfare. It has long been the tradition in the Netherlands for social care services to be provided by independent not-for-profit organisations, many belonging to churches of the different Christian denominations in Holland. Although independent in origin, the services are now heavily subsidised by the national or local government.

In line with the general change in the role of government, the state in recent years has reduced its involvement in social affairs – what Pijl (1993) refers to as 'the sector of well being'. It has changed its approach to financing independent social care organisations, from subsidising agencies with fixed tasks to financing projects.

Organisation and responsibilities
Pijl (1993) comments that the continuing process of restructuring
and decentralisation in the Dutch political and administrative system makes it difficult to know who is responsible for what in social
services. The twelve provinces in the Netherlands have increased
their responsibilities under decentralisation, to include planning
and budgeting for youth and elderly care, and co-ordination of
smaller towns to enable them to provide certain services. There
are differences in the degree of decentralisation concerning youth
care and care of elderly people, and in the level of provision between the regions.

At the next level down from provinces the municipalities are
responsible for many social services, but not residential care. The
four big cities have some of the powers of the provinces in addition
to their municipal powers. The general picture, according to Pijl, is
that over the past decade social services have declined in importance and coherence, with some services integrated into health or
social security, while others have been decentralised and left to the
municipalities. Services are still mostly paid for with state funding
but the European trend for service users to contribute to the cost
of services is increasingly evident in the Netherlands.

Examples of services
As stated earlier, most social care services are provided by independent not-for-profit agencies, many with a religious foundation. There
is an emphasis in the Dutch system on providing open-for-all preventative services at a primary level. Citizen's Advice Bureaux concentrate particularly on young people, offering general social information
and a service specialising in legal rights and social security.

Generic social work bureaux are open to all citizens without the
need to fit into a defined client category. The bureaux assist people
with problems of social functioning, the services including information and advice, material help, mediation and advocacy, group
work and counselling. There may be discrete projects to concentrate on particular needs and problems such as AIDS/HIV, and to
transmit 'know-how' to other workers dealing with these problems. In 1989 there were 178 agencies for generic social work,
employing 2,934 professional social workers.

As might be expected, there are many volunteer organisations at
the local level in social services, with a tendency to use volunteers

to fill gaps left by the professionals. The Netherlands National Centre for Voluntary Work was established in 1991 to support and develop volunteering and their organisations.

An interesting innovation in the 1970s was the setting up of a network of crisis centres and shelters, designed for people needing shelter at short notice because of an acute crisis, such as family breakdown or a mental health crisis. These facilities provide short-term stay and active support to users to enable them to work out longer-term solutions. In the early 1990s there were thirty-six centres run by Protestant church agencies, with about 750 places. These centres are in addition to the forty or more special centres for battered women.

Portugal

In 1990 Portugal had the second-lowest standard of living in the European Union. Demographic data underlines the relatively underdeveloped state of the country compared with other member states. In 1991 infant mortality at 10.8 per 1,000 live births was the highest in the European Union, while life expectancy for men and women was the lowest. In the same year Portugal was the only country to experience a net reduction in population size, because of continuing emigration.

Perhaps surprisingly, the 1990 unemployment figure was only 4.6 per cent, the second-lowest after Luxembourg. The housing problem has been particularly serious in Portugal, due to substantial internal migration into the cities of people from rural areas looking for work and suitable housing.

The year 1974 saw the end of a period of dictatorship in Portugal and transition to representative parliamentary democracy. The constitution of 1975 guarantees basic social protection and social care rights to all citizens, such as in case of illness, unemployment, disability, together with a more general right of protection for the family, children and elderly people.

Political structure

Apart from mainland Portugal there are the two autonomous regions of Azores and Madeira. At the head of the political system are the president and parliament, the president occupying a powerful political position akin to the US president. The mainland is divided into eighteen administrative regions or districts, with the 275 municipalities at a lower level of local government. Historically, the municipalities have played an important part in public administrative life (Pereira 1991) but it is only since the end of the dictatorship that they have become established as democratic local governments. Previously they acted essentially as units of administration of the state.

Responsibility for social care services

The Ministry for Employment and Social Security is responsible nationally for these services, and for social policy generally. Within the Ministry the General Direction for Social Action carries the more specific responsibility. In 1977 a unified social security system was created to include *social action*, that is, the field of social care and social work. A law of 1984 maintained the unified system but further legislation in 1991 separated social action from social security, giving an enhanced status to the former beyond the role of complementing social security payments. This change is interesting in the context of continuing international debate over the advantages and disadvantages of combining or splitting responsibility for the two related services – cash and care – as referred to in chapter 1.

At the regional level social security centres were set up in 1977 with responsibility for social services. Their main responsibilities include social action in protection for children, young people, disabled and elderly people and families in poverty, promoting social integration, supporting independent not-for-profit initiatives and licensing and supervising profit-making providers of social care. There are local social security services dependent on the regional centres. They are responsible for direct work with service users and for 'dynamising the community'.

The independent sector

This sector is extremely important in social care in Portugal. For example, the large Catholic not-for-profit organisation Santa Casa da Misericordia is the main provider of social services in Lisbon. Marques and Bras Gomes (1993) estimate that there were some 2,334 independent non-profit social solidarity institutions in 1992. The first institution was created in the fifteenth century; most are local organisations and some are linked to the church. Independent services that are registered by the central directorate for social action are considered to be public utility institutions and entitled to certain tax exemptions. Pereirinha *et al.* (1992) report a 42 per cent increase in government funding for non-profit organisations between 1989 and 1990 – one indication of the importance of this sector in the total Portuguese social care system.

As with Greece, there is limited published material available on social care in Portugal. Pereirinha *et al.* (1992) observe that there is no tradition of studying what the Portuguese refer to as 'social action', so that information is scarce and diffuse. The impression is that, compared with other EU countries, social care is relatively underdeveloped in Portugal, with a strong dependency on provision by the independent sector. This situation is understandable given the poor economic position and the legacy for public services of Portugal's period of political dictatorship.

Spain

This writer observed first hand the excitement, pride and enthusiasm that characterised the early days of the growth of public services in the immediate post-Franco period in Spain – a country that had been denied more than minimal public welfare services during the long period of dictatorship. The mood in Spain was refreshingly different from that evident in social services in some other European countries, where social services were well developed but feeling the chill wind of serious financial restraint and increasingly hostile political environments.

In the 1980s Spanish politicians and welfare professionals were keen to study social services models and systems in other European countries so that they might construct the right kind of welfare state for their new democracy. That willingness to learn from others is still evident, even if the Spaniards have joined the European preoccupation with the mixed economy of social care as they too face a mounting problem in funding their social security and public social care services.

Like its neighbour Portugal, Spain suffered under a long period of dictatorship, which ended with the death of Franco in 1975, to be followed by the establishment of a new constitution and a democratic parliamentary system in 1978. But unlike Portugal, Spain rapidly improved its economic position from the 1960s to achieve a much higher standard of living than Portugal by 1990. It has the fifth-largest population but, along with Germany, the second-lowest birthrate in the European Union.

In recent years the economy has shown distinct signs of strain, with the third-highest inflation rate in 1994 and a serious unemployment problem that is concentrated heavily in the younger age group. In seeking reductions in state expenditure the socialist government has proposed highly unpopular cuts in social protection payments, leading to national public service strikes.

Implications of the political change for social care

Under the Franco regime Spain had been a unitary state with strong centralisation. Public services were mainly the police and armed forces, although the public administration did provide traditional public relief services and a form of social work in the regions. Most formal social care was provided by approved traditional charities such as Caritas and the work of the Catholic Church. The rapid economic advance of Spain in the 1960s did lead to expansion and modernisation of social services, particularly in independent agencies like Caritas, and in social security.

The establishment of democracy had important implications for social care. Under Franco there were strict controls over citizens associating together in voluntary associations, so voluntary action was liberalised by the new socialist government. Secondly, there was a growing demand for commercial social care services such as for elderly people and drug abusers. Thirdly, and more fundamentally, there was an acceptance in the early 1980s of an ideology supporting widespread public intervention and the decentralisation of government responsibilities for social services. This was formalised in the responsibilities the constitution places upon the public authorities.

Organisation of services

It can be difficult to understand which level of government has responsibility for which services in the Spanish system. The country is divided into a number of autonomous communities on the mainland, plus the Balearic and Canary Islands. Spain also has two territories in north Africa, Ceuta and Melilla. The central government in Madrid has legal and financial responsibility for the nationwide social security system, which is administered by the autonomous communities. Central government controls services for migrants and other categories of foreigners and social services in the two north African territories.

The autonomous communities can pass their own laws relating to social services, with considerable differences being found in the type and level of social service provision between the communities. Some commentators argue, for example, that social care provision in Cataluña and the Basque territory is superior to that in other parts of Spain. Below the level of the autonomous communities are the provinces and municipalities. The basic law allows for considerable flexibility as to what they provide in social services. In practice, first-stage/preventative services are normally the responsibility of municipalities, under the direction and economic support of the communities. Other social services are shared differently between the communities and lower-level authorities.

Social services are financed essentially through taxation, with each territorial level supporting its own services, with some exceptions. Casado (1993) reports that charges are rarely levied on users, the main exception being contributions by elderly people towards the cost of residential care. Independent organisations are financed from their own resources, some charges to users, and grants or contracts with public authorities. Voluntary action has received strong governmental support in recent years, with a particular emphasis on the development of volunteering. This is in contrast to policy in the early years of the new democracy, when the emphasis was on building up professional services in the public welfare sector. There are still relatively few independent for-profit services in social care in Spain, this sector comprising mostly kindergartens, homes for elderly people and addiction treatment centres.

Spain has a network of offices providing basic or first-aid social services. They cover populations of 5,000–25,000, their main functions being to provide information on resources, home aid management, meeting needs for residential care and community development. The national Instituto Nacional de Servicios Sociales also has a network of first-stage services, mainly for elderly and disabled people, and refugees. Similar services are provided by the Red Cross and Caritas.

An interesting feature of Spanish social care is the strong functional connection between social and cultural activities, programmes and services. This is very evident in provisions for elderly people, as described by Casado (pp. 342–3):

> An extensive network of social day centres for the elderly has been
> developed. These are usually known as 'hogares', homes or clubs.
> Both urban and village communities have services of this kind. In
> their simplest version they consist of a social centre for meetings,
> conversation and table games. The most sophisticated version includes
> such services as counselling, pedology, rehabilitation, occupational
> therapy, gymnastics, cultural activities etc. Apart from these services,
> they manage demands for residential care and home aid.

Conclusion

Spain has had a relatively short time in which to develop a modern social care system in a country where the autonomous communities have considerable freedom to decide what they wish to provide. The early commitment to establish a western European style of welfare state has been tempered more recently by economic realities and a switch in social care to the familiar policy emphasis on building up the independent sector.

Fortunately, there is now more information available on social care in Spain than is the case with countries such as Greece, Portugal and Ireland. Casado's work has been referred to and he is probably the leading writer on Spanish social services. For readers of Spanish his basic text (1994) is essential reading. Other writings in English include Rossell and Rimbau's work (1989).

United Kingdom

It is assumed that most readers will be more familiar with social care in the United Kingdom than in other member states. This section therefore concentrates mainly on any significant differences in arrangements in the countries that comprise the United Kingdom.

The UK government's ambivalent attitude towards its membership of the European Union has already been referred to. Certainly, any move to extend Brussels' authority in the social care field would be strongly resisted, as the Commission is only too well aware. Traditionally, other European countries have looked to the United Kingdom as a leader in social welfare and social services, based on its reputation for a comprehensive welfare state system and well-developed statutory and independent social services. The extent of our independent not-for-profit sector is still the envy of most other countries, but less so in the case of the statutory sector. But even there it could be argued that local government social services compare favourably with their counterparts elsewhere in Europe, having been modernised through the introduction of general management and economic criteria.

Current UK preoccupations in health and social care with contracting out and purchaser–provider splits cause puzzlement among colleagues in other parts of Europe. Discussions with a large group of Belgian social work students revealed that they had never heard of case or care management and elsewhere in Europe the emphasis is still on direct service provision by social care practitioners.

Warner *et al.* (1993) point out that in the three parts of the United Kingdom (England and Wales, Scotland, and Northern Ireland) policies and social services delivery forms are similar, but there are separate legislative and organisational patterns. At central government level the Department of Health and the Secretary of State are responsible for social services, aided by a corps of civil servants known as the Social Services Inspectorate. Three types of local authorities hold responsibility for providing social care services: county councils, metropolitan districts and London boroughs. Major local government reform is under discussion, with the possibility that at least some of the larger county councils will be broken into smaller district units who will have responsibility for social services.

The 1990 National Health Service and Community Care Act has sharply accelerated a move to change the traditional role of local authority social services departments from being predominantly direct providers of services, to becoming 'enabling authorities' as part of the implementation of government policy towards a mixed economy of social care. The trend is to separate the organisational management of social service provision from the planning and purchasing of services, and for the statutory agencies to act as regulators of the quality of care provided by the other sectors in the mixed economy.

Finance for social services comes from a mix of central government tax-based funding, local government finance and, increasingly, charges to service users. Health care in Britain remains free at the point of delivery, whereas community-based social care is means tested – an extremely controversial subject in late 1994. First-stage open-for-all preventative services are less a priority for statutory social services in the United Kingdom compared with other member states. As Warner argues, the emphasis for these agencies is now more on targeting finite resources on those in greatest need. Preventative services are more likely to be provided by the independent sector.

In *Scotland* the 1968 Social Work (Scotland) Act was followed by the reorganisation of social work services under the regional authorities in 1975. Note that local authorities in Scotland have *social work* departments rather than the *social services* departments in England and Wales. The distinction probably reflects a greater emphasis on the contribution of the social work profession north of the border. There are two tiers of local government: nine regional councils, fifty-three districts and three island area councils. The regional councils have responsibility for social work services. A major difference between England and Wales and Scotland is that in the former there is a separate probation service, whereas in Scotland probation work is included in the responsibilities of the social work departments.

The long-awaited cessation of hostilities by the paramilitary organisations in *Northern Ireland* should lead to significant political and economic benefits that will be to the advantage of social service users and the agencies themselves. The continuing conflict has acted to keep investment in the province at a depressed level, resulting in one of the highest levels of long-term unemployment and deprivation in the whole of the European Union. As Bamford (in Warner *et al.* 1993) underlines, the long-standing conflict has been an important context for understanding social services in the north, for example the allocation of funds to independent organisations had to be done on an equitable basis between Catholic and Protestant groups.

Since 1973 health and social services have been linked in a single administrative structure, with four Health and Social Services Boards responsible for all services in their areas. Bamford argues that this system allows for the better co-ordination of health and social services, with care programmes being managed on a multi-disciplinary basis.

The social care legislation is different from that in the rest of the United Kingdom: for instance, the 1989 Children's Act does not apply to Northern Ireland. The usual position is for welfare laws passed in England and Wales to be implemented in Northern Ireland through Order in Council after a delay of two or three years. Bamford points out that the level of 'per capita' spending on health and social services is around 25 per cent higher in Northern Ireland than in the rest of the United Kingdom. He explains this in terms of a higher level of morbidity reflected in more hospital admissions and a higher percentage of long-term patients in hospitals. Historically, there has also been a higher level of home help provision.

Conclusion

This chapter has provided some material for considering the modern relevance of Kahn and Kamerman's conclusions on international social services in their 1976 study.

It does appear, for example, that some of the EU countries with the highest standards of living, such as France, Belgium and Denmark, do have more highly developed social care services than do the poorer countries, such as Ireland, Greece and Portugal. More interesting was their view that political and economic ideologies are less important determinants of social welfare policies and provision than are countries' levels of economic and industrial development. Since 1976 right-wing political and economic ideologies have taken a powerful hold in some European countries – particularly Britain – with consequent changes in policies towards social welfare. The precise effect on social care provision of ideological shifts has been difficult to assess because of major economic recessions since 1976, their effects being arguably greater determinants of changes in social welfare policies.

As discussed earlier in this chapter, a further factor impacting on social care policies since Kahn and Kamerman's study is demographic change, particularly the increasing proportion of elderly people and the strong European trend towards smaller families with the implications for the future of care by families.

There is limited evidence in the review of social care in the member states for the view that as societies become more affluent and their social sectors more elaborate, so social services focus more on developmental and socialisation tasks, moving away from their earlier emphasis on substitute care, direct help and social control linked to provision of material help. Belgium in particular and to some extent the Netherlands provide this more open, preventative social care facility that does not require users to fit into a defined client category. But elsewhere, such as in the United Kingdom, social care is increasingly targeted (i.e. rationed) on those in greatest need, with first-stage preventative social care work seen as a scarcely affordable luxury.

Kahn and Kamerman found more similarities than differences in the social services of the countries they studied. Similarly there is a clear trend towards *convergence* in European social care systems. As chapter 4 illustrates, faced with increasing need and strictly limited state resources, all countries are rapidly adopting policies of welfare pluralism in social care, emphasising the contribution of families, independent organisations and volunteers, while reducing the role and direct contribution of central and local government. This trend is intensifying in countries such as Germany where the principle of subsidiarity has always ensured a central place for the independent sector, and emerging in Denmark, where this sector's contribution has been very modest until recently.

Less marked but still part of this convergence in Europe around policies and programmes of welfare pluralism is the gradual emergence of for-profit enterprises in social care. This is evident in Britain, Greece and Italy, for example. Likewise there is a tendency to introduce, widen or increase charges to social care service users to help address governments' financial problems in this field. The role of local government in social care is shifting in some countries from the traditional one of provider of services to that of 'enabler', retaining legal responsibility for services but moving progressively into a contractor, purchaser role. This shift is likely to spread to most, if not all, EU countries before the end of the century, intensifying the convergence of European social care systems as part of European integration and the adoption of similar solutions to common problems and needs.

References

Batley, R. and G. Stoker (eds) (1991) *Local Government in Europe*, Basingstoke: Macmillan Education.

Bekke, H. (1991) 'Experiences and experiments in Dutch local government', in Batley and Stoker (eds).

Blair, P. (1991) 'Trends in local autonomy and democracy: reflections from a European perspective', in Batley and Stoker (eds).

Casado, D. (1993) 'Spain', in Munday (ed.).

Casado, D. (1994) *Introduccion a los servicios sociales*, Madrid: Editorial Popular, SA.

Cinneide, S. and C. Corrigan (1992) *Personal Social Services and Social Exclusion: Report for the EC Observatory on Social Exclusion*, Maynooth, Ireland.

Commission of the European Communities: Directorate-General for Employment, Industrial Relations and Social Affairs (1993a) *European Social Policy: Options for the Union*, Luxembourg: Office for Official Publications of the European Communities.

Commission of the European Communities: Directorate-General for Employment, Industrial Relations and Social Affairs (1993b) *Social Protection in Europe*, Luxembourg: Office for Official Publications of the European Communities.

Commission of the European Communities: Directorate-General for Employment, Industrial Relations and Social Affairs (1994) *European Social Policy: A way forward for the Union*, Luxembourg: Office for Official Publications of the European Communities.

Ely, P. and R. Saunders (1993) 'France', in Munday (ed.).

Eurostat (1992) *Europe in Figures*, Luxembourg: Office for Official Publications of the European Communities.

Eurostat (1993) *Demographic Statistics 1993*, Luxembourg: Office for Official Publications of the European Communities.

Fassolo, E. (1993) 'Italy', in Munday (ed.).

Hansen, F., H. Hansen and C. Olsen (1992) *Social Services in Denmark: Report for the Observatory on Social Exclusion*, Copenhagen: Centre for Alternative Samfundsanalyse, a.m.b.a.

Hartmann-Hirsch, C., C. Welter and M. Neyens (1993) 'The Grand Duchy of Luxembourg', in Munday (ed.).

Kahn, A. and S. Kamerman (1976) *Social Services in International Perspective*, Washington: US Department of Health, Welfare and Education.

Karantinos, D., C. Ioannou and J. Cavounidis (1992) *The Social Services and Social Policies to Combat Social Exclusion*, Athens: National Centre of Social Research.

Kavanagh, L. (1993) 'Republic of Ireland', in Munday (ed.).

King, J. (1989) 'The poor relation', *Community Care* 23 November.

Landwehr, R. and R. Wolff (1993) 'The Federal Republic of Germany', in Munday (ed.).

Marques, C. and V. Bras Gomes (1993) 'Social action and local government in Portugal', unpublished lecture for Kent County Council, Maidstone, Kent, UK.

Mostinckx, J. (1993) 'The Flemish Community', in Munday (ed.).

Munday, B. (ed.) (1993) *European Social Services*, University of Kent at Canterbury: European Institute of Social Services.

Pereira, A. (1991) 'The system of local government in Portugal', in Batley and Stoker (ed.).

Pereirinha, J., M. Arcanjo and C. Pinto (1992) *Social Services in Portugal: Report for the European Community Observatory on National Policies to Combat Social Exclusion*, Basingstoke: Macmillan Education.

Philpot, T. (1989) 'Bringing home the bacon', *Community Care* 16 November.

Pijl, M. (1993) 'The Netherlands', in Munday (ed.).

Rossell, T. and C. Rimbau (1989) 'Spain: social services in the post-Franco democracy', in B. Munday (ed.), *The Crisis in Welfare: An international perspective on social services and social work*, Hemel Hempstead: Harvester Wheatsheaf.

Sokoly, L. (1993) 'Greece', in Munday (ed.).

Warner, N., C. Humphreys, C. Lyon and T. Bamford (1993) 'The United Kingdom', in Munday (ed.).

Wanlin, P. (1993) 'The French Community of Belgium', in Munday (ed.).

CHAPTER 3

The European Union and social care

Andrew Swithinbank

Introduction

This chapter discusses the role of the European Union in social care, including policies, legislation, major programmes and other involvements in this field. A central issue is the extent and limitations of the European Union's power and influence over social care across the territory. The recent completion of the Single European Market has significant implications for social services users and agencies, the adverse consequences and opportunities of which will be highlighted.

A brief clarification of terminology is necessary. The term 'European Union' is used when referring to the geographic area covered by the twelve member states – fifteen from the beginning of 1995 with the inclusion of Finland, Austria and Sweden. 'European Union' will also be used when referring to actions involving more than one of the European institutions of the Council of Ministers, the Commission, the European Parliament and the Committee of the Regions. When referring to European activity prior to the Maastricht Treaty the term 'European Community' will be used. There are actually three European communities: the European Economic Community (EEC); the European Coal and Steel Industry Community (ECSC); and the Atomic Energy Community (Eur-Atom), but the term 'European Community' is commonly used to denote all three together. The Commission of the European Communities is the main policy-making body with exclusive power to initiate legislation and the executive body which implements policy. It is not intended that this chapter be used as a fully comprehensive reference guide for all EC programmes, funds and networks. There are other publications which do this (Harvey 1992; Davison 1993; Swithinbank 1991).

The role of the European Union in social affairs

The European Community was created in 1957 by the Treaty of Rome, its objective being to create a common market, with an accelerated standard of living and a closer relationship between member countries. The three European Communities listed above were created as entities primarily for economic co-operation designed to increase international trade between the member states and to support the industrial and economic development of the European Community. However, there are those with a vision of a 'social Europe' whose emphasis was on human rights and fundamental freedom as part of the common heritage of Europeans. It placed importance on the building of a European society in which individuals could thrive whilst maintaining responsibilities towards others in the Community. Jacques Delors, as president of the Commission between 1984 and 1994, was the key figure in this social Europe vision. The Cecchini report (Cecchini 1988) referred to the European Community as having a social as well as an economic dimension, directing resources to assisting groups such as the long-term unemployed and young people and assisting the backward regions of the Community.

As Cannan *et al.* (1992) point out, there were two tenets to Delors' vision of social Europe: first, the creation of a strong and united Europe with a clear identity, because this would be conducive to economic growth throughout Europe; secondly, a recognition that there would be losers as well as winners in this economic growth, particularly in the process of economic change. Protection would be required for those excluded from increased prosperity.

The links between the social and economic aspects of the European Union are very clear in an analysis of the meaning of the word 'social' in European terms. It typically refers to four areas of activity: tackling unemployment and creating employment; development and protection of the rights of workers; equal opportunities in access to employment and training; and the creation of partnerships in a social dialogue between employers and employees. The term is used to describe the aspects of work not directly related to production, so that much social legislation has been considered a burden to employers, adding a social cost to employment. Even in this rather limited sense there has been disagreement over the extent to which the European Union should interfere in subjects which other states consider part of their national sovereignty. The British government considers the European Union should only be involved in social action where it is concerned with the creation of employment as part of economic growth. Contractual matters on the terms and conditions of employment, for instance working hours and minimum wages, should be the business of employers and employees. 'Social' is rarely used to describe the provision of social care services for disabled and disadvantaged people or of cash benefits.

Policy and legislative landmarks for social care

Three major initiatives will be considered: the Social Charter, the Maastricht Treaty (or Treaty of the European Union) and the White Paper on European Social Policy.

The Social Charter

The Community Charter of Fundamental Social Rights for Workers is a solemn and political declaration signed by all heads of states and governments of the members of the European Community – with the exception of the United Kingdom – at Strasbourg in December 1989. It comprised principles and rights which the signatories believed should be common throughout the European Community. It was both a statement of progress made until then in the social field and a preparation for new advances. The Charter recognised differential rates of development throughout Europe, setting minimum standards for some members, whereas for others it was a statement of high principles to strive for. It was not a binding legal instrument for any member state, although many of the directives which followed it were. The Charter referred only to the rights of workers, not of all citizens. Sections on disabled people, elderly people and children and adolescents referred only to them with regard to the work in which they are, have been or will be engaged.

To turn the dream into reality the Commission set out a Social Action Programme of about fifty proposals under the twelve groups of rights or principles. The Commission's role was to submit proposals for directives, regulations and recommendations and to clarify for member states, or agencies within them that are responsible for the management of social policy, how the Social Charter might be implemented.

The Maastricht Treaty

At the Maastricht summit social affairs emerged as a major issue, although the focus of the meeting was on economic and political union. Social policy was moved up the agenda as it became used as a bargaining chip for negotiation and compromise. For the twelve member states to agree on greater economic and political union the controversial question of the level of the European Community's involvement in social policy had to be resolved.

The twelve member states signed the EU agreement on the basis of Britain having the opportunity to opt out of the monetary union and maintaining its right to decide whether to join a single currency. The other countries did not want Britain to opt out of the social legislation part of the treaty, the social chapter. Finally, it was agreed that the social chapter would be dropped from the Maastricht Treaty altogether because of Britain's refusal to sign with its inclusion. The other eleven countries agreed to opt in to their own arrangements on social affairs through the so-called social policy protocol or 'agreement of the eleven'.

The social chapter of the proposed treaty would have expanded the areas of social policy for which majority rather than unanimous voting would ensure the passage of legislation. Areas of social affairs which, under the Treaty of Rome as amended by the Single European Act, require all countries to agree would have been passable if supported by a qualified majority. Thus Britain would have lost its power of veto.

The aim of the social policy protocol – or agreement of the eleven – was to take forward the Social Charter. It was primarily concerned with future development of social policy and the introduction of new legislation. Previously existing social legislation remains protected under the Maastricht agreement and applies to all member states. It extended majority voting to European

Commission directives covering working conditions, information and consultation of workers, equal opportunities for men and women at work, protection of pensioners and the unemployed, the improvement of the working environment, equal rights for more part-time workers and the legal basis for employee organisations to propose social directives.

After Maastricht, without the restraining influence or blocking by the British government, the European Union pushed ahead with a more ambitious programme of social legislation. The protocol allowed for agreement on a series of measures previously vetoed by Britain. This was illustrated in September 1994 by the directive giving a mandatory right to three months' paternity leave in the eleven member states. Further developments may cover social security, redundancy terms, collective representation and bargaining, employment conditions for non-EU workers and job creation schemes.

Britain's perceived intransigence on social affairs has left the impression in Europe of a Britain which sees the European Union as merely a huge free-trade area. The image will persist despite the fact that Britain has signed up to and is implementing many aspects of the social dimension of the Union. The British government may find itself excluded from a major influence on the development of European social policies.

The White Paper on European Social Policy

As one of his last acts as president of the European Commission, Jacques Delors launched the Commission's statement on the future of EU social policy. The White Paper (1994) is a policy document setting out the framework for action by the European Union. Implementation will be in the form of directives, regulations, action programmes, observatories and the all-important funds.

The *raison d'être* for the White Paper is a recognition that Europe will face enormous and often painful changes in an increasingly competitive world market. There will be detrimental consequences for those who are not economically active and socially marginalised.

Social policy is designed to underpin economic changes and ensure a more equitable distribution of the benefits. The White Paper breaks new ground in acknowledging that social policy goes beyond employment, affecting family life, health and old age. The section 'Social policy and social protection – an active society for all' recognises that the welfare state needs to be maintained; greater assistance needs to be given to ensure the social and economic integration of the excluded by a 'trampoline safety net' – a 'hand up' rather than a 'hand out'; and that those not in the labour market also have a useful role to play in society, for example the active elderly.

The White Paper is high on rhetoric but low on the specifics on what the European Commission will do. It does promise more action on tackling poverty and to target resources on areas of urban deprivation, rural communities and disabled people. It will continue the approach of the Horizon programme to enable disabled people to enter or re-enter the labour market – see chapter 6 in this book.

Tackling poverty amongst all socially excluded people requires a multifaceted approach, requiring a new EU programme to cover social as well as economic dimensions of integrating excluded people into mainstream society. This is considered important not just as a matter of social justice but because Europe can benefit from their future economic contribution.

There is no direct reference to social care services in the White Paper and little on health. However, the Commission will cautiously use its powers to affect social care services in member states in two ways. First, it will recommend and provide the legal framework to underpin minimum standards in each country for policies and resources to help groups such as those seeking employment and those excluded from the labour market. Secondly, it will aid the spreading of new ideas on best practice and support innovation and experimentation of a transnational character through European funded programmes.

What would have been welcome is a clear indication that the Commission recognises the important role of social care services in aiding the integration, independence, freedom of choice, opportunities and quality of life of young, disabled and elderly people.

Extent and limitations of European Union power and influence over social care

The Treaty of Rome and subsequent acts have given the European Union only very limited competence in the field of social care, its competence being guided by the following key principles.

Subsidiarity

The principle of subsidiarity sets the limits of community action. The Maastricht Treaty added a new article to the Treaty of Rome, limiting the Union's powers to act only in circumstances where the objectives of the proposed action cannot be adequately achieved by the member states. Policies should always be made at the lowest possible level of government. Adherence to this principle of subsidiarity has made the European Union reluctant to over-ride national sovereignty by introducing any radical action in the field of social services. It will only become involved in areas in which member states cannot or will not act or where pan-European action is absolutely necessary. However, it is not clear who decides whether pan-European action will more effectively achieve the European objective. This was illustrated recently by the debate between the European Union and the German *Länder* over competence for anti-poverty programmes. The start of the Poverty Four programme has been delayed as the German *Länder* consider anti-poverty drives are their own rather than European responsibility and best achieved by them.

Additionality

The principle of additionality means that the European Union only has competence to support activities which are additional to the normal operations of a national government; and member state governments may only use European funds for these additional activities. This is open to differing interpretations, seen in the debate between the British government and the European Commission over the use of the European Social Fund for vocational training.

Transparency

The European Union has affirmed its commitment to a more open form of government. The European Commission now produces an annual work programme, Green Papers, and Commission documents for the public in all community languages to facilitate wider consultation. The Commission is gradually changing to a more transparent approach in the allocation of funds for social programmes, but has a long way to go in ensuring its national agents in the member states do likewise.

Because of these principles the European Union has strictly limited competencies in social care and is even more limited in its operation of those competencies. This is either because it must operate through national governments and can only act where they do not, or it must make its procedures so open that it is hard to circumvent subsidiarity and additionality. The common impression of the European Union – and especially the Commission – as a huge bureaucracy over-riding national sovereignty and imposing European-wide legislation against the member states is an exaggerated and prejudiced view.

Several items of legislation adopted by national governments are derived from European objectives and directives affecting social care. The European Union seeks to influence protection measures for workers on such issues as working hours and health and safety. The social action programme, following the social charter, the Single European Act and the Social Chapter of the Maastricht Treaty all introduced new employment legislation. These affect the health and welfare of all workers but have a special significance for social care agencies employing a high proportion of women, part-time workers, night workers and people in vulnerable positions. For example, in attempts to improve the working conditions of people in the member states European legislation has included a minimum daily rest period (eleven hours), a maximum working week (forty-eight hours), a ban on individuals working two consecutive shifts, a ban on night work for people under the age of eighteen and pregnant women, and a maximum working night time of eighteen hours. As social care work requires people to provide round-the-clock cover, social service agencies will have to ensure adequate rest periods and limited hours. This applies especially to residential care staff, after-hours and emergency staff cover and attendance at evening meetings. Any junior staff or pregnant women will be unable to provide night care or be on call. Social services departments in Britain will need to ensure that contracted private and voluntary residential homes abide by these requirements.

The single European market

Despite the marginality of social services in the European Union since 1957, changes are under way in the 1990s. Some changes stem from the adoption of the Single European Act by the heads of government of the member states which came into force in 1985. Although this Act was primarily concerned with the economic union of the European Union many of its provisions have implications for social care organisations in Europe. These implications will particularly affect statutory agencies as service providers, employers and enabling authorities, particularly in co-ordinating, regulating and purchasing services from the independent sector.

The main intent of the Single European Act was to establish by the end of 1992 the European Community as a single entity without frontiers, where people, money, goods and services would be free to pass between member states without restrictions. The Act aims to enable the European institutions to take more action to stimulate international trade and commerce, and to provide a boost to European industry, creating jobs and wealth. Although the single market is predominantly an economic phenomenon, there is some evidence that it is having far-reaching social consequences. Some provisions of the Single European Act relevant to social services provision are now considered.

Freedom of movement of people and services

Workers are now entitled to social security benefits accumulated from eligible periods in each EU country in which they have worked and contributed to that country's social security system (Article 51 of the Single European Act). This has great implications for the work of welfare benefits advice agencies who need to ensure that EU residents are aware of their entitlements and receive benefits to which they have contributed in their home state.

The extension of Regulation 1408/1 means that this applies not only to private sector employees and self-employed people but also to workers in the public sector (including social services staff) students and 'non-active persons'. People with disabilities, mental health problems, elderly people and others unable to work due to illness or infirmity may move between countries and take with them entitlements for benefit.

Articles 52–58 of the Single European Act give the right to any EU national to establish him- or herself as a self-employed person and to set up agencies, branches and subsidiaries in any member state. This provides social care enterprises the opportunity to expand their services throughout Europe. A UK social services department may wish to explore the possibility of services being delivered by a provider from outside their own country, particularly to fill a specialist niche where there is an undersupply. Organisations which have been established by local authorities at arm's length, such as housing trusts, training agencies or occupational therapy and other bureaux, may wish to expand into the European market. In Denmark social care organisations from several sectors collaborated to market in Europe Danish expertise in services for young children and people with disabilities.

The Single European Act encourages the movement of professional people between member states of the European Union. It gives the right to individuals to pursue their profession in any member state, subject to the entrance requirements in that particular state. The Commission has sought for some time to encourage the mutual recognition of professional qualifications across the European Union. Early directives ensured the recognition for certain occupations in higher echelons of the professional hierarchy, such as doctors, lawyers and dentists. In 1988 a directive on higher education diplomas required that all professional qualifications meeting certain criteria were to be mutually recognised. These professional qualifications should involve three years of further or higher education training followed by the award of a diploma from an institute of higher education. Further, admission to the profession should be legally restricted to practitioners entered on a professional register. In Britain personnel with degrees and postgraduate qualifications in social work will meet the first two requirements, but Britain is in a very small minority of member states where 'social work' is still not a legally protected title. Many British social workers could be at a disadvantage should they wish to work in other EU countries.

The principle of the free movement of goods, services, personnel and capital applies to all sectors involved in purchasing, selling or providing services. It has opened up the area of public procurement (which accounts for 15 per cent of total EU gross domestic products) to non-national enterprises. Directives are designed to allow all companies within the Union a fair chance of seeking public contracts and to ensure public authorities buy from sources which offer best value for money. A local authority will be obliged to ensure that any service agreements with voluntary sector organisations or contracts with private companies do not distort conditions of operation and do not go against the spirit of free competition throughout Europe.

Child protection and child care

See chapter 5 for an extended discussion of this subject in European social care. There is no European-wide definition of the concepts of child neglect or abuse. Different cultural traditions in the treatment of children may make an acceptable practice in one country a criminal act in another. The level of identification and recognition of the problem varies enormously throughout Europe with taboos ensuring that abuse, particularly sexual abuse, is not revealed. Free movement makes it potentially easier for abusers to operate in more than one country and for 'sex-rings' to spread. Entry points should be particularly concerned to obtain information about EU nationals entering from other European countries who are on the Child Protection Register (or equivalent) of their home country.

Variations in the laws on marriage, divorce and child custody lead to complexities for the children of separated parents who are from different EU countries or who have moved throughout the European Union. Questions will arise over which laws apply – those of the place of marriage, the birth place of parents or children, or present place of residence.

There has been an increase in children moving across national boundaries between the custodial parent and the parent with the right to access, with the potential for an increase in incidents of abduction of children by non-custodial parents to other EU countries with laws more favourable to the abducting parent. Families have also moved across frontiers to avoid court orders.

Conventions and practices regarding the adoption of children from other countries may need re-examining. Restrictions on, lower priority given to or charges made for intra-EU international adoptions may be out of line with the spirit of free movement within a frontier-free Europe. EU members have different policies determining whether the child or the adoptive parent is the primary client.

Mental health

There is no European-wide definition of mental illness. A diverse range of policies and approaches varying from the very liberal to the punitive exist throughout Europe which may affect mental illness sufferers moving from one nation to another. There are attempts to harmonise laws, procedures and practices regarding the protection of people with a mental illness, particularly the compulsory admission of someone to hospital if they are a serious danger to their own health or safety, or the safety of others. This area is fraught with difficulty as one country's practice and criteria may, if applied to another EU nation, contravene their home country's definition of civil liberties. It is the United Nation's Commission on Human Rights and the World Health Organisation rather than the European Union who have encouraged moves for a common declaration on the rights of people with a mental illness.

Diversity in service provision and uses

Increased mobility should lead to a richer mix of nationalities, cultures and languages, with implications for access to existing services, the type of new services that need to be developed and the training and recruitment of staff to understand the needs of clients of the social care services. Agencies and their staff will also need to understand governmental and administrative structures in other EU countries, as well as the operation of their welfare systems.

Many people moving across frontiers into the European Union are from outside the twelve member states and are of refugee status. The ethnic conflicts and turmoil of eastern Europe – particularly former Yugoslavia – have forced the largest movement of people since 1945. This has created demands for social care in both the immediate emergency provision and long-term resettlement. The slow but steady harmonisation of immigration and asylum policies has led to the exclusion of third-country nationals from entering the European Union and the creation of a 'fortress Europe' with free movement for EU citizens but no entry to those outside. Estimates suggest that half of the world's 15 million refugees are children. They – particularly unaccompanied minors – are most likely to be turned away or need greatest social and psychological as well as practical support. In fortress Europe refugees suffer from the xenophobic attitudes and the rise of extreme right-wing racist movements, particularly in West Germany which received 140,000 asylum seekers in 1989.

European Union social care programmes

In addition to its varied involvement in the broad field of social affairs the European Union also uses the instruments of *programmes*, *networks* and *observatories* to tackle the range of needs and social problems more central to social care. These are the incentives offered to member states compared to directives and legislation which require sometimes reluctant compliance. In the 1970s those seeking a strong social role for the then European Community wished to see a harmonisation of social protection systems in Europe, with minimum standards across the Community and a levelling up of all systems to that of the most generous and progressive. This view is now less prominent for reasons discussed earlier.

The emphasis now is on *convergence* of the different national systems, to be achieved through four different but inter-related means. First, to encourage each member state to adopt similar policy objectives for its social care system. Objectives include the eradication of poverty, the improvement of living conditions of the most disadvantaged citizens, the integration of disabled and disadvantaged people into mainstream society and the provision of good-quality cost-effective services to people in most need. If member states can agree on the purpose of social care and the priorities for its provision then there will be increasing similarity in provision across Europe, as discussed in chapter 2. Secondly, convergence is to be achieved through encouraging countries to share information, experience and expertise about their own systems. The best features of each system will be selectively adopted by others, leading to an improvement of social care across the Union. Thirdly, by encouraging member states to co-operate in addressing major European social concerns such as poverty, the needs of the family and the increasing proportion of elderly people. This may be achieved by creating an observatory of experts from the twelve countries, such as observatories on social exclusion and elderly citizens. The Commission also concentrates attention and action on, for example, elderly people or the family through 'special years'. Fourthly, to redistribute the resources available for social care to the most economically disadvantaged areas of the European Union, namely the designated Objective 1, 2 and 5b areas.

Objectives of European programmes

There are various EU programmes, funds, networks and observatories of direct relevance and value to social care agencies. But because the term 'social' is used in a different way from that adopted by most social care agencies it is important to understand the objectives of these programmes. Any social care organisation wishing to participate in the programmes must demonstrate how they will contribute towards these European objectives. The following are the most frequently found objectives:

1. To tackle unemployment.
2. To encourage the free movement of goods, people and services within the European Union.
3. To alleviate the adverse social effects of the Single European Market.
4. To assist less-developed European nations, especially in southern, eastern and central Europe, through redistribution of financial resources and the transfer of expertise from richer to poorer countries.
5. To facilitate the social and economic integration of marginalised groups.
6. To provide information on rights, jobs and services to European citizens.

Few social care agencies would have a similar list of objectives, so social care staff need to think imaginatively about possible involvement in European programmes.

Target groups and issues

Key issues in EU programmes include poverty, unemployment and the imbalance between economically active people and those who are dependent on their support. The concept used to encapsulate the effect of these conditions is 'social exclusion'. This is a peculiarly European concept that states there are groups of people who are excluded from and by mainstream society. These people are prevented from having access to the economic benefits and social support enjoyed by the rest of society. Their exclusion from jobs, housing, financial means and social support drives these groups further into a so-called underclass. A major purpose of European programmes is to re-integrate those who are excluded or marginalised back into mainstream society.

A feature of most European programmes is their focus on specific groups of people defined according to a given set of criteria. These include young people, long-term unemployed people, migrants and ethnic minorities, women, drug and alcohol dependants, disabled and disadvantaged people. This categorisation enables the European Union to target its programmes. Inevitably, it leads to much discussion amongst interest groups about the extent of the list and whether other groups should be involved, for example the debate over the exclusion of homeless people from the community initiative programmes.

The nature of European programmes

Several means are used to address the priority problems and groups identified above. First, the use of training in specific vocational skills or retraining of people whose current skills are no longer needed in the labour market. Secondly, the creation of new jobs particularly through the development of small and medium-sized enterprises of under 250 employees. Thirdly, the provision of support mechanisms to aid entry or re-entry into the labour market. This recognises that vocational skills and the creation of a job are only useful if the socially excluded individual has the social skills, competence and necessary support to fulfil their new job. Fourthly, the facilitation of independent living for people who would otherwise have to live in residential care establishments or institutions.

The European Union favours certain approaches in line with the principle of subsidiarity: namely, that solutions should be found and action should be taken as close to the people in need as possible. As Cannan *et al.* (1992) point out, the Commission favours a grass-roots approach, leading to a plurality of methods involving statutory and independent organisations in different combinations and locations. A multidisciplinary approach is also favoured, involving consortia of local government, independent associations and community groups. Actors are brought together who are able to affect important aspects of the lives of the targeted groups, such as housing, education, health, employment and social care.

The European trend in social care is towards a community development approach once popular in Britain in the 1970s but replaced by a more reactive crisis intervention model, targeting resources on priority clients. Experimental methods are encouraged by the European Commission, who often require innovation in their social programmes. Proposed schemes must have clear objectives and outcomes for target groups, with requirements for monitoring and evaluation of the projects. Unfortunately, dissemination of the results and lessons from useful projects has been a chronic problem for the Commission, with much potentially valuable social care material largely unknown to the EU social care community.

The European Union has no competence to be involved with social projects of value only to the participants in a specific locality within one member state, unless the lessons learnt from that project are disseminated to and are of help to several states. It is concerned with the multiplier effect, that is, that the benefits of its programmes are multiplied across several countries. This multiplier effect will materialise through transnational partnerships between social care organisations in at least two member states. These organisations transfer different methods and share their experience and expertise, with two or more similar projects developing simultaneously.

The European Union supports the establishment and development of networks which can take various forms. Harvey (1992) describes European networks as reflecting on matters of concern to their members, collecting information about their field of work in different European countries and lobbying the European institutions for improved social policies. The first two activities encourage the multiplier effect particularly when the networks exist to share models of policy and best practice. Some networks are designed for local government, such as the International Union of Local Authorities. Others bring together organisations providing services for a particular client group, such as Rehabilitation International, the European Federation for the Employment of Handicapped People, which encourages policies and models of good practice in their field, and the Forum for the Reintegration of Ex-offenders, which concentrates on the exchange of information and good practice with ex-offenders throughout Europe. One of the longest-established and most successful networks is Eurolink Age, which was particularly instrumental in encouraging events and programmes for elderly people during the European Year of Older People. HELIOS and HORIZON programmes concerned with disabled people in Europe are considered in chapter 6.

No European programmes are specifically designed to support the provision of social care services. Many can support social care if applicants are creative in the way they think about their organisations' purpose and activities. Several guides and specialist organisations provide information on European grants and programmes, such as Davison's (1993) publication for the National Council for Voluntary Organisations; the Scottish Community Education Council produces 'Eurodesk' with information on youth and community programmes; the European Institute of Social Services at the University of Kent disseminates information on funding relevant to statutory and independent social care agencies. The major programmes are now outlined.

Vocational training

The European Social Fund (ESF) has the been the major source of finance in the field of vocational training. It is one of the three structural funds, the other two being the Agricultural Guidance Fund and the European Regional Development Fund. Objective 3 of the ESF is to tackle long-term unemployment with special measures for long-term unemployed people who are either disabled or disadvantaged. Whilst it does have a transnational strand, it is one of the few European programmes where it is not essential to have any links with other European countries. The ESF's purpose is to improve employment by training workers in new skills or unemployed people in skills which will enable them to enter the labour market either for the first time or to return after a lengthy absence.

It has been used by social care organisations to support vocational training schemes for disabled people and people with mental health problems as part of their rehabilitation and re-integration programme. The European Commission has recently emphasised the obtaining of recognised qualifications, making it difficult to provide training for the most vulnerable and dependent people and favouring those who have a higher chance of gaining qualifications and are more employable. Other difficulties have been that the ESF is notoriously slow in providing the money, so small organisations find it difficult to underwrite projects which will be funded retrospectively.

People with disabilities

Please see Chapter 6 for details of special programmes in this field.

Women

As part of the European Commission's work to promote equal opportunities amongst men and women they have developed several programmes specifically targeted at women. The Community Initiative NOW (New Opportunities for Women) is designed to update and develop women's qualifications, help them to establish enterprises or re-enter the labour market. It is intended to aid women in responding to the changes in the organisation of work and new job requirements. Social services have used this programme to retrain traditional care workers or heads of old people's homes to become care managers or managers of new business-style enterprises.

This topic is mirrored in the 1994 theme of the IRIS Network Programme 'equal opportunities, socio-economic change and new forms of work organisation'. IRIS is a network of organisations carrying out women's training which sponsors model projects to celebrate women who are at the pinnacle of their profession, with the HELENA prize as an award for service in the public or independent not-for-profit sector.

At the other end of the spectrum the Women's Local Employment Initiatives (WLEI) programme enables women to start up and develop their own businesses, preferably employing other women who are in groups often excluded from the labour market. This programme might be used, for example, to establish a private domiciliary care business by women employing other women. Given that the vast majority of social services employees are women and that they tend to be under-represented in the senior management level, social care agencies should look particularly at how they could benefit from these European programmes.

Young people

There is a plethora of programmes for young people. The newest and most major of these is the community initiative on employment, YOUTHSTART, whose objective is to promote the labour market integration of young people, in particular those who have basic qualifications and training. The original aim of YOUTHSTART was that in the long term there would be a youth 'guarantee' that any young person under the age of twenty would be guaranteed either access to full-time employment or some form of education or training. The language of this programme has subsequently been toned down as it was considered that this was an impossibility. The *European Official Journal* text specifically mentions employment in care services but the trainees could also be young people who had been in care themselves. The programme, which is expected to start in 1995, will support training and placement programmes for young people to reinforce their personal, vocational, entrepreneurial and linguistic skills. It also encourages young entrepreneurs to exchange ideas with their counterparts from other member states through transnational trading agencies and self-help networks. The programme foresees an army of young peripatetic care workers crossing frontiers providing care for elderly and disabled people.

An older, more established programme is YOUTH FOR EUROPE, which will enter its third phase in 1995 once agreement is reached in the European Parliament's second reading. The programme aims to promote a sense of European citizenship and mutual understanding among young Europeans through youth exchanges (15–25 years old or up to 29 for disabled people) and between the European Union and external states. It also sponsors voluntary work undertaken by young people, exchanges between youth workers to promote the transnational exchange of good practice in youth services and the training of staff who work with disadvantaged young people.

Elderly people

At the other end of the age spectrum the European Union operates programmes for elderly people. The year 1993 was designated a European Year of Older People and Solidarity between the Generations. During this year thousands of events were organised at local, regional and national levels throughout the European Union for and by elderly people. The focus was on encouraging a positive attitude towards ageing, a healthy and active life for retired people, displaying examples of elderly people's contribution to the community and thus reducing stereotypes of elderly people as dependent on younger generations. In language typical of the European Union but rather peculiar in English the 'solidarity between the generations' aspect was added to encourage events, projects and incorporated partnerships between young and older people, for instance elderly people using their experience for the benefit of school children and school children assisting elderly people. Following the year's success, the Commission proposed a five-year programme of community actions for older people. These include actions to support people still at work but approaching retirement, retired people able to lead active and independent lives and, contrastingly, the very old whose ability to live independently is diminished. The Commission intends to use this programme to promote innovative approaches to the challenge of an ageing population, care for dependent older people, the role of actively retired people and the prevention of age-related illnesses. In line with the European Union's concern on the rights of workers the theme of older workers and older job seekers is included.

Several key principles emerge from this proposal and previous Commission work with elderly people. There has been a gradual widening of the gap between generations in their understanding and tolerance of each other, so that solidarity between the generations needs to be promoted to counteract this tendency. Elderly people are in great danger of being isolated, particularly older women, older migrants and older people in remote areas, with integration again seen as the necessary antidote. Crucially, elderly people should not be considered primarily as a burden on the state but their capacity to participate in and contribute to society is immense and this should be enhanced by European measures. The Commission implements these principles not only through major programmes but also by sponsoring research studies. For example, the European Institute of Social Services has recently completed a six-country study of 'Third Age Volunteering in Social Care' for the European Commission, concentrating on the involvement of statutory, independent not-for-profit and commercial organisations in this activity.

Poverty

The problem of poverty has been of over-riding concern for the European Commission for the last two decades. There have been three poverty programmes, their purpose being to prevent and reduce poverty across the European Union by funding experimental schemes to combat poverty at a local level, followed by widespread dissemination of the lessons. Each programme has received a substantial budget, with many questions asked about the cost-effectiveness of the programmes.

Poverty three concentrated on twenty-nine local model action projects. The Brownlow Community Trust project in Northern Ireland has been a prototype for projects proposed as part of the province's Objective 1 submission. Objective 1 is concerned with promoting the development and structural adjustment of the regions with underdevelopment. All the projects were in clearly defined areas of mostly urban deprivation, involving community outreach work tackling factors instrumental in social exclusion. Duffy (1994) illustrates how projects developed an entrepreneurial approach to combating poverty and developing partnerships for change, with examples from Antwerp and Utrecht which involved social enterprises and local business.

Three basic principles underline the new Poverty Four programme. First, a recognition that social exclusion is a multifaceted phenomenon, requiring projects to be multidimensional. One aspect of poverty, such as housing, must not be considered in isolation but rather there should be an integrated, coherent approach to the many facets such as health care, child care, public transport, unemployment, training and counselling. Secondly, in order to implement a multidimensional approach a partnership is needed between local authorities, community groups, employers, trade unions and independent organisations. Thirdly, for these partnerships to operate effectively the socially excluded recipients must be included in the process.

At the time of writing a decision on the future of Poverty Four has been deferred. The delay is because Germany objects to the programme on the basis of subsidiarity, believing poverty is within the responsibility of national and regional (*Länder*) governments and should not be in the realm of EU activity.

Offenders

One of the few funds initiated by the European Parliament is a fund to improve approaches to the integration and re-integration of offenders into the labour market. A typical project funded under this programme is in Kent, where a project links a scheme for diverting young offenders from a life of crime by a programme of training, counselling and job placement, including motor mechanic skills for car thieves, with similar schemes in Germany, France and Spain. Policies and practices in this field in the four countries are being compared and contrasted, the aim being that each country's work in this field will benefit from comparative study.

Health

A proposed action programme to combat drugs will support national governments working together to try to eradicate international drug trafficking, multidisciplinary programmes to prevent vulnerable people misusing drugs, and innovative rehabilitation work with drug addicts. This programme is in response to the recognition that the Single European Market, with its limiting of frontier checks, has made drug trafficking easier across international boundaries within the European Union and therefore that single-country approaches will no longer be successful.

The Commission has recently proposed an action programme on health promotion, information, education and training. Whilst its concern is for health promotion amongst all EU citizens, it focuses on preventing vulnerable people from needing health and social care. It aims to improve the standard of health, particularly amongst disadvantaged groups; to increase life expectancy without disability or sickness; to avoid chronic or disabling conditions; and to minimise the economic and social consequences of ill health. The programme will provide information on health to EU citizens, professionals, administrators and decision-makers, encourage health education programmes tailored to different target groups such as children and adolescents, encourage specific prevention and health promotion activities involving vulnerable groups in inner cities and isolated rural areas, and encourage co-operation on these schemes between member states.

Social and health care are closely linked, increasingly so in some European countries. For a useful overview of health systems and services in the European Union readers are referred to the European Health Services Handbook (Leadbeater 1992).

Social businesses

As explained earlier, social affairs is a minor part of the Commission's work so that programmes in this field are limited. However, other programmes primarily designed to encourage economic activity and to increase international trade can sometimes be relevant to social services.

Another programme designed to support the creation of other smaller medium-sized enterprises and their trade across Europe is concerned with Europe Economic Interest Groups. Many social care organisations are involved in economic activities through the production and the sale of products made by disabled and disadvantaged people. In order to maximise the income generated from these goods a trading arm is established through which the goods can be sold. Using the growing network of partners in other European countries, an import/export business is being developed for Kent social services department and its partners to transfer the goods across frontiers for sale in one another's countries. The ideas on how to establish and manage enterprises for disabled and disadvantaged people – and particularly how to include these people in the planning and decision-making processes – will follow the transfer and sale of goods.

Eastern and central Europe

The above programmes are designed for the benefit of member states of the European Union. In addition, there are programmes designed to help the emerging democracies of eastern and central Europe to develop their economic and social structures and to establish democratic institutions. Social care organisations in the European Union can assist eastern and central European countries to develop their social care systems, learning from member states' experiences. No social care organisation should enter into this type of programme believing it can simply transfer its approach to provision of social care to a central or eastern European country. Rather, it should plan for a long and complicated process in which it aids eastern European countries in relation to their situation and needs, using methods appropriate to their own cultural and political reality.

The major European programmes supporting east/west co-operation are OUVERTURE, ECOS, and PHARE. OUVERTURE and ECOS (European Cities Co-operation System) are both intended to promote co-operation between regional and local authorities respectively in the European Union and central Europe. Projects cover a wide range of spheres of co-operation – local and regional development, urban planning and the environment. ECOS particularly covers urban, social and health policy and the social impacts of unemployment and housing. It can pay for the training of social services staff in the partner country.

Unlike the ECOS and OUVERTURE programmes, PHARE (Poland, Hungary Assistance for Restructuring the Economy) is designed not for local governments but primarily for the private sector. Its aim is to assist the transformation to market economies in countries moving towards a democratic system away from centrally planned economies. It was established originally to assist Poland and Hungary and has since spread to eleven former communist countries. The emphasis has been on private sector institutions in the west aiding the east to develop its banking system and business structure. It has now changed its emphasis to building supports for eastern countries to improve their business performance, reduce unemployment, create a better environment in communities and reform institutions. The PHARE programme is led by eastern European countries, with countries consulting with the European Commission in determining priority programmes and projects. Outside consultants are then chosen through competitive tendering.

Beaumont (1994) indicates how local authorities are beginning to enter the PHARE programme by establishing partnerships with specific countries. The partnership programme is particularly concerned to promote social and economic development via the institutional framework of central and eastern Europe. This can include helping the partner country in eastern Europe with social services management training, launching new social care organisations, and the reform of the social care structure. Civil society and democracy programmes have managed to increase co-operation between non-governmental organisations in eastern and central Europe.

A welcome trend in these programmes is that eastern European contenders for the work are considered as appropriate as western ones, resulting in cross-eastern Europe assistance taking place, for instance with Polish experience and expertise being made available in Albania.

Transnational partnerships in social care

The final example of the European Union's support for the development of social care in member states is the Commission's work in furthering transnational partnerships. The growth of formal links and joint work between social care agencies in two or more member states was referred to early in chapter 1 and at points in this chapter. It has been emphasised that applications for most European funds require agencies to collaborate with partners in other countries.

In addition, the Commission has initiated and financially supported several large European programmes concerned with regional and urban development that incorporate a social care component. Two examples are the Second Cities programme and the Four Motor Regions of Europe initiative, the latter involving France, Germany, Italy and Belgium. Their work programmes concentrate on economic and social development but include subprojects concerned with subjects such as care for elderly people and volunteering.

The following are the main reasons why transnational social care partnerships in Europe are formed in increasing numbers:

1. With the accelerating movement of social care users across a 'frontier-free' Europe it is necessary for agencies in border areas especially to understand one another's systems and establish working relationships with their counterparts in neighbouring countries.
2. There is a trend in the European Union to plan a wide range of services in regions spanning national boundaries. For example, there is a European region comprising Brussels, Kent, Nord Pas de Calais, Flanders and Wallonia. The region has formed a strategic planning and infrastructure group concerned with population change, economy and employment, transport and the environment. Regional social care issues are included within this work.
3. The necessity to make joint applications for EU funds with partners in other EU countries has already been referred to and is a major motivation.
4. Also referred to earlier is the increasing interest in learning from the different ways in which other EU countries tackle similar needs and problems in their social care systems. This is strongly supported by the European Commission as part of their policy to work towards convergence as opposed to harmonisation in social policy generally and social care specifically.

There are encouraging examples of how transnational partnerships can enhance the quality of life of service users. Elderly people in an old people's home, some of whom had little to look forward to and were deteriorating rapidly both physically and mentally, participated in a transnational exchange and gained a new lease of life. They began planning and anticipating the next foreign trip and enjoyed telling their friends and relatives about it for months afterwards. People with learning disabilities who had restricted lives suddenly had the opportunity to broaden their horizons through a visit to another European country, learning something of the language and the culture. Because of the increased quality of life which they have achieved for service users these projects are now an integral part of the operation of services for the groups concerned.

Two short case studies of transnational partnerships in social care will illustrate some of the points above. The county of Kent is a large local authority (population about 1.4 million) in the south-east corner of England, some 40 minutes away from northern France using the new tunnel. Kent's social services department has a partnership programme with the corresponding department in the Pas de Calais in France. Both areas have had to prepare for the effects of the channel tunnel, including an increase of service users crossing to either country; both serve similar-sized populations and have similar-sized social services budgets; and both had areas of high unemployment and social deprivation resulting from the closure of mines and ports.

The Kent–Pas de Calais partnership was negotiated at a high level in the departments with a joint committee deciding on the policy and strategic direction of the partnership. Joint task groups were established, focusing on subjects such as child protection, mental health, and service implications of users crossing the channel. There have been exchanges of both staff and service users, with joint seminars on topics such as child protection. The partnership is firmly rooted and supported by both large local authorities.

The second example is rather different as it involves work with eastern and central European social care agencies. A consortium of statutory and independent not-for-profit social and health care agencies in the south-east of England have formed a Joint Committee on Social and Health Care Initiatives. Its explicit purpose is to help eastern and central European countries to establish or re-establish social care provision in their new political and economic systems. Initial work has concentrated on the Czech Republic to help providers there identify their needs and offer technical assistance and training. Identified needs included management training, the development of joint working between state and independent sector organisations in social and health care, and the planning and provision of mental health services.

A formal partnership was made with an umbrella organisation for independent organisations in the Czech Republic and funding acquired from the Charity Know-How Fund in Britain to support the first training in June 1994. The difficulties involved for all sides in this type of partnership should not be underestimated. Progress is inevitably slow and frustrating as differences in systems and cultural norms have to be assimilated and accommodated. For example, the participatory approach to training taken for granted in the United Kingdom was initially confusing and unacceptable to the Czech social care staff. Differences were worked through patiently, resulting in such satisfaction with the training programme that others are being planned and funding sought under the European Commission PHARE programme.

Conclusion

It is clear that the European Union rarely imposes restrictive legislation on member states. In social policy *convergence* is preferred rather than a Brussels-directed *harmonisation* of member states' policies, legislation and provision in social affairs. Those regulations the Union does initiate are often already undertaken by the more progressive member states, with the Commission preferring the facilitatory approach of using programmes and funds to encourage member states to introduce progressive and enlightened practice, for example in policies and provision for disabled and disadvantaged people.

The present system of European programmes and networks is far too complex and bureaucratic. There are recent attempts to rationalise and streamline the system, such as the introduction of the new Leonardo programme to replace four other programmes – Petra, Eurotechnic, Technet and Comet. There have been moves through individual member states to combine European programmes with national programmes. Britain's Single and Regeneration Grant will combine British and European funds designed to revitalise inner cities.

As a result of Maastricht the European Parliament has increased its power to influence and initiate European programmes and policies. As the only democratically elected major institution of the European Union, it may be more responsive to the needs of the European electorate, leading to the introduction of more social programmes – including social care. The recent creation of the Committee of the Regions made up of the representatives of local government throughout Europe could encourage the European Union to engage in programmes which more closely reflect the responsibilities of local government, including social care provision.

The expansion of the European Union in 1995 will bring a new and welcome dimension to social care provision in Europe. Finland and Sweden are leading representatives of the Scandinavian model of social care with their tradition of extensive state provision based on taxation. Although these countries are now seeking to diversify the financing and provision of social care, they should act as a brake on any right-wing attempts to decimate state support for social care in Europe.

This chapter has shown that, despite its very limited mandate for involvement in social care policy and provision across the European Union, the Commission has sponsored many programmes and other activities within the broad field of social care. Social care interest groups across Europe should continue to press for greater European Union involvement as properly funded and high-quality social care provision in all member states is central to the realisation of the vision of Delors and many others of a true 'social Europe'.

References

Beaumont, S. (1994) 'How to tackle TACIS and Phare', *European Information Service* 152 (August).

Cannan, C., L. Berry and K. Lyons (1992) *Social Work in Europe*, Basingstoke: Macmillan.

Cecchini, P. (1988) *The European Challenge: 1992 – the benefits of a Single Market*, Aldershot: Wildwood House.

Commission of the European Communities: Directorate-General for Employment, Industrial Relations and Social Affairs (1994) *European Social Policy: A way forward for the Union*, Luxembourg: Office for Official Publications of the European Communities.

Davison, A. (1993) *Grants from Europe: How to get money and influence policy*, London: NCVO Publications.

Duffy, C. (1994) 'Poverty 3, the final meeting', *EISS News* (Canterbury) 2, p. 4.

Harvey, B. (1992) *Networking in Europe*, London: NCVO Publications.

Leadbeater, N. (1992) *European Health Services Handbook*, London: Institute of Health Services Management.

Swithinbank, A. (1991) *Audit of the Implications of Greater European Integration for Kent Social Services*, Canterbury: European Institute of Social Services.

CHAPTER 4

The mixed economy of welfare

Peter Ely and Antonio Samà

Introduction

The 'welfare' of an individual is commonly held to derive from three main sources. First is the 'informal' care which comes from his or her family, surely the most influential source of welfare and one which exhibits the greatest individual variations. Less important sources of informal care such as the help of neighbours and of voluntary organisations in the community, the 'civil society', should also be mentioned. Second is the welfare which the individual or their families may be able to derive from participation in the labour market. Employment provides income: it also commonly provides membership of collective insurance arrangements in which compulsory contributions by both employer and employed build up entitlements to financial protection in sickness, disablement and old age. The third source of the individual's welfare derives from the various services financed or provided by the state.

Our approach is that before commenting in detail on the mixed economy of welfare as it applies to social care systems in European Union countries it is necessary to set this in the context of the methods of financing services. This is because systems of social protection in nearly all continental countries are insurance-based. In the case of services which are generally welcomed by the recipients, such as domiciliary care for elderly people and day care for young children, it is the user's contribution record which will determine how the service to that individual will be financed, and the terms on which the service will be offered. Eligibility is recognised not by the direct provision of the service, but by the insurance fund's agreement to finance a certain amount of it. The service itself is almost always provided by an independent provider. This does not apply, of course, to services which are imposed on users, such as interventions on behalf of abused, neglected or delinquent children. These are initially carried out by state-provided services with the involvement of the courts.

Three groups of welfare states

Since 'the welfare state' is a multidimensional concept there are many different ways of classifying national welfare states. But by the criterion of their structure the welfare states of the countries of the European Union fall into three groups.

In the central group of Germany, France and the Benelux countries the individual gains access to social protection through participation in the labour market and its statutory insurance schemes. Through a long period of time these have been developed to cover most of life's common vicissitudes apart from long-term structural unemployment (a new problem for those countries) and long-term dependency in old age.

The four southern countries, Italy, Greece, Portugal and Spain, have systems which are based on similar principles but are less developed. Their statutory insurance schemes cover fewer risks and are extended to fewer sections of the workforce. The burdens on and the importance of the informal help of families and civil society are correspondingly greater in these countries.

In the remaining northern group of Denmark, Ireland and the United Kingdom, the insurance principle is not strong. For example, in Ireland and the United Kingdom there are extensive entitlements to unemployment assistance outside insurance frameworks. Denmark funds the bulk of its welfare provisions from general taxation, and Ireland and the United Kingdom do not seriously try to maintain an insurance-based organisation of expenditure.

The central group of countries, in contrast, while forced to subsidise their insurance-based schemes more and more from taxation because of the rising population of dependent people which the schemes support, frequently distinguish such taxation from that for other purposes. For instance, the *Contribution sociale généralisée* tax in France is devoted to providing for those such as retired subsistence farmers who have been too poor to develop an adequate contribution record. This is one aspect of these countries' determination to maintain the appearance of an insurance base to their systems, which is an important reason for popular support for welfare. Their populations have made significant financial investments in these systems for several generations and are greatly attached to them.

In terms of value orientation, the insurance-based systems emphasise equity, a concept of fairness based on skill and effort in the labour market, while the northern systems lean more towards equality, formal rights of every citizen to certain minimum provisions. But this is to greatly oversimplify the different ways of adjusting to the permanent tension between these two principles which is experienced in every country.

In the first place, it is in the interest of every country to maintain the work ethic. Without the work ethic, as Pinker (1992) pointed out, there would be no money for social services at all. In all of Europe, those not participating in the labour market tend to have their needs defined in less favourable terms than those who work, and to be provided not with social protection entitlements but with less favourable forms of social assistance. Social assistance is only available conditionally, as it may be means-tested or subject to the more general discretion of an official who makes a judgement on the merit of the application.

The extent to which a fit adult of working age and demonstrably seeking work would be entitled to social assistance if he or she had exhausted or never been able to build up insurance-based entitlements to unemployment benefit varies very markedly between the three groups of countries.

In the southern group there is no public assistance available for such a person (Commission of the European Communities 1994) except in certain Italian regions which finance and administer their own schemes.

As regards the central group of countries, in France obtaining the *Revenue minimum d'insertion* benefit is dependent on securing the co-operation of a social worker who will devise a rehabilitative contract. According to this the applicant agrees to undergo further training or similar measures during the time-limited duration of the benefit. In the other central countries, social assistance has to be financed from local, not central, funds. This creates acute difficulties where there is mass unemployment in a particular locality and there are thus heavy demands at the same time as revenue from local income tax is seriously reduced. In any case the majority of the central group countries have systems of family law which oblige descendants and ascendants of applicants, and their spouses, to assume financial responsibility for the applicant. If these relatives have resources, the cost of public assistance payments will be recovered from them.

While the United Kingdom's national system of entitlements is subject to much criticism both because of the inadequacy of its benefit levels and shortcomings in its administration, there may be something to be said for the principles behind it, at least in comparison with, say, Germany, where there is a long tradition of using volunteers to make social assistance assessments (Lorenz 1994). In certain *Länder* such work can be undertaken as an alternative to compulsory military service, and the provision seems somewhat unpredictable.

But though the insurance-based systems of the central group of countries disadvantage the long-term unemployed and those in marginal or precarious employment, they do provide excellent levels of social protection against other risks for the majority of the population. Social assistance recipients are in any case disadvantaged and stigmatised and subjected to numerous checks in every country. Both France and the United Kingdom, for instance, have experienced the same revealing phenomenon. The high levels of morbidity which develop among long-term unemployed people have resulted in a growth in the numbers claiming disability benefits. Apart from providing a slightly higher income, these confer a somewhat less stigmatised status. Abrahamson (1992) points out that some aspects of European policy tend to reinforce the division between the comfortable two-thirds of households with secure labour market participation and the marginal one-third of the population. For instance the 'Social Charter' is about the rights of *workers*.

The former communist regimes of east central Europe also faced the need to sustain state control of the work ethic, and the provision of universal employment was the main form of welfare. State employment provided direct access to welfare, and health, housing, pensions and other services were usually provided through or by the state-owned enterprise in which the individual was employed. Those not participating in the labour market, or in non-state sectors such as private agriculture, received very few welfare provisions. In the final decades of communist rule the provision of real universal employment was beyond the state's capacity and became the universal right to be physically present at a place of work, which increasingly damaged both productivity and the work ethic (Ksiezopolski 1987). Now that eastern European countries are experiencing mass unemployment for the first time since 1945, Konopasek (1993) argues for a better reconciliation between the status of 'employee' and of 'citizen' in both western and eastern Europe.

The underlying principles of social protection in each country are fundamental to the provision of personal health and social services there. The insurance-based systems of the central group of countries incorporate financial entitlements to services providing the qualifying conditions are met. For example, in France dependent pensioners have rights to a fixed number of home help hours per month funded by their pension schemes. While such arrangements introduce an element of inflexibility (for instance, it may be difficult to provide more than this entitlement), they do provide an uncontestable right to the service. In the United Kingdom there is more flexibility but no guarantee that services will be provided at all.

Financial pressures on European welfare states, inclusion and exclusion

In each country of the European Union, whether welfare provisions are comprehensive or restricted, based on contributory insurance schemes or funded from general taxation, they are all coming under pressure for identical reasons.

The main pressures are the financial ones caused by the economic recession and the restructuring of the European economy. The partial dismantling of internal trade barriers has given rise to complex developments. Certain industries in some countries have extended their markets beyond national frontiers, often in partnership with similar companies in other countries. Other industries have responded with anti-competitive policies such as the formation of cartels and have obtained increased government subsidies, in spite of the legislative rules.

These developments and efforts to slow them have doubtless contributed something to the restructuring process, but only within the context of the globalisation of the world economy. European manufacturers now face high-technology competition from the Far East, and the worldwide trend to relocate manufacturing processes to countries with lower wages and fewer social protection obligations to add to employers' labour costs. Consumption, not production, now accounts for an expanding proportion of employment as Europe develops into a 'mature economy' where services, and the creation of images and styles, become more important at the expense of mass manufacturing. At the same time, the mechanisation of nearly all heavy manual jobs, the computerisation of routine administrative work, robotisation and other developing technologies have reduced demand for labour, as have changing employment practices which require reductions in costs through employing as few workers as possible while making far greater demands on those who are employed.

The resulting rise in unemployment in all EU countries has meant that there is a shrinking income tax and insurance contribution base from which to fund welfare provisions. And structural unemployment frequently entails long-term unemployment in which insurance-based unemployment benefits, which are now time-limited in all European Union countries, become exhausted. Thus greatly increased expenditure on social assistance is required. In countries with insurance-based welfare regimes, unemployment is also storing up difficulties for the future as larger proportions of the population will eventually reach retirement age without having had an opportunity to build up an adequate contribution record. And a large and growing sector of the European economy is now based in multinational companies operating in a global market outside the control of nation states, which have a declining ability to raise tax revenue from them partly because of the fear that they will relocate. European employers' associations, most prominently those in France, are now demanding that in order to compete they will need to be relieved of their obligations to contribute to employees' social protection, which they propose should be funded from general taxation.

As a result of the rise in unemployment, many unemployed people who could formerly have reasonably expected to be potential beneficiaries of social protection entitlements based on their insurance contribution records now find themselves excluded and obliged to rely on means-tested 'social assistance' provision. This places them alongside groups who have long been marginal to the labour market but which were formerly separated from them by a degree of social distance.

At the same time, states face the prospect of a rising population of potentially dependent people, partly because of unemployment and partly because of the rising proportion of children in mono-parental families, but mainly because of the ageing of the European population. While the numbers of old people grow, the numbers of people of working age whose taxes and insurance contributions support them are not expected to expand significantly. Increasing longevity and mass survival into old age entail increased health expenditure. It overwhelms the insurance base of statutory old age pension schemes, as these are everywhere based on the principle that those currently in work pay insurance contributions to support those currently retired. To maintain even the existing level of such schemes, direct subsidies from general taxation will be increasingly required.

Ideological pressures on the welfare state

As the tax base of the state shrinks because of unemployment and globalisation and while calls on its resources increase because of growing numbers of dependent pensioners, unemployed people and monoparental families, ideologies concerned with reducing the size of state expenditure succeed on the ideological market.

The European countries engaged in a long struggle to sustain mass production manufacturing as the basis of their economies, and hence maintain full employment, through state subsidies intended to counteract the operation of market forces. Though sustained for several decades for humane reasons as well as in the defence of vested interests, its universal defeat during the 1980s called into question the prestige and the competence of state management. In eastern Europe, where state management was most pervasive, communism did not survive the accompanying economic crisis. The ideas of Hayek (1944), once considered of marginal interest, seemed to have been vindicated. In their essentials these are that the state's attempts to manage the economy in defiance of market forces results in unforeseeable economic consequences. To correct these, further state controls are required, resulting in increasingly grave distortions to economic activity. Extensive state management of the economy will ultimately prove too complex to be practicable. At the same time state management of the economy is a threat to democracy, as more and more people would become either direct employees of the state or have their employment subsidised by the state. This fosters dependence on the state while restricting the freedom of the employee to criticise the state. To Hayek's free-market criticism of Keynesian state management to sustain full employment, Friedman (1962, 1970) added a monetarist critique.

Thatcherism and Reaganism established an ideological hegemony in the 1980s based in theory on ideas of the residual or *laissez-faire* state whose core tasks were defence, the maintenance of law and order, and sustaining the conditions within which market forces could operate relatively freely, which include the free circulation of information. The state was alleged to be overloaded with functions which individuals and families should undertake for themselves. The frontiers of the state were to be rolled back to concentrate on its core functions, while the citizens were to be freed from unnecessary regulations which hindered them from becoming more self-sufficient.

While these ideas have had a variable degree of impact on the generally collectivist welfare philosophies and corporatist welfare policies of different European countries, the reduction in protectionism and state subsidies required by the removal of internal economic barriers in the European Union has made them a guiding influence in the economic field and has increasingly led to their incorporation in plans to reform welfare provisions to take into account changed economic and demographic circumstances.

Declining public support for the welfare state?

In the 1980s it was fashionable to speak of a 'crisis of legitimacy' in the welfare state. The traditional welfare state was felt to be no longer suited to changed economic and demographic conditions, greater family instability, the desire for equal opportunities for women and other developments. From the Marxist tradition there was an attack on the welfare state for serving to legitimise the interests of capital instead of being seriously concerned with redistribution between social classes, and from the communitarian direction for being directed from above instead of by the local community. Organisations of users criticised the state bureaucracy for providing services which were rigid, unimaginative and unresponsive to the needs of individuals and local communities. Those concerned with equality of opportunity for women criticised the basic assumptions of the provisions that the kind of family to be supported was to consist of a male breadwinner with a dependent wife and children. Criticisms from the New Right centre on the presumption that the welfare state restricts the public's choice of how to spend their income because of the high tax burdens necessary to finance it, and encourages a culture of dependency among those in need. It creates waste through poorly targeted services and requires a large unproductive bureaucracy to administer it. No matter from what direction the criticism came, there were common elements concerning the remoteness, unresponsiveness and lack of flexibility in state provisions and the difficulties of tailoring services to the needs of any particular individual.

During the 1980s there was no Europe-wide survey of public attitudes to the welfare state to ascertain the extent of support for the various policy-making constituencies listed above. But in 1992 the Commission promoted a Eurobarometer survey (Ferrera 1993) which provided information on citizens' feelings both about social protection in general and about specific programmes.

This revealed substantial differences both between different occupational groups within the same country and between countries; but the conclusions were that popular support for social protection was 'wide and robust': 'the broad normative objectives and basic institutional instruments of social protection meet with almost universal approval at the mass level' (Ferrera 1993, p. 9).

The public was aware of the multiple problems which currently confront social policy, especially the financial strains on the health care and pensions systems, and the risk of cuts in these sectors. But a majority expressed themselves in favour of the maintenance of a broad range of provisions, even if this entails increased taxes or contributions. In no country was there a majority for drastic reductions due to resentment at the tax burden, though there was a minority which favoured contraction, which 'will constitute a significant and lasting component of the attitudinal landscape of the 1990s' (Ferrera 1993, p. 23).

In terms of differences between countries, in general the citizens of northern and central group countries showed themselves more satisfied with the benefits and services they receive, whereas southern Europeans expressed more discontent. This is partly an objective reflection of the levels of provision available. The four southern countries showed most support for the proposal that the Commission should assume responsibility for social protection, whereas opposition to this proposal was strongest in Denmark because of justifiable fears that 'convergence' on social protection issues would result in a levelling down of that country's well-developed welfare provisions.

Ferrera (1993) also suggested that there is no country with a majority in favour of excluding non-nationals from welfare provision, even in Luxembourg, which systematically excludes them. France (29 per cent), Belgium (28 per cent), Germany (22 per cent) and the United Kingdom (21 per cent) were the countries with the biggest minorities in favour of exclusionary policies. This is an interesting finding, since some political parties which have historically emphasised the rights of citizenship rather than the concept of equity, notably the SDP in Germany, have not fared well in recent years, and hostility to ethnic and racial minorities has been suggested as one possible reason.

Changes in the mode of production, and accompanying cultural changes, in relation to the welfare state

Changes in the mode of production have contributed to changes in the climate of opinion. As production becomes robotised or relocated in parts of the world with low labour costs, relatively few European workers now produce in the old manner, with hundreds or thousands of employees working at the same site in centrally controlled and hierarchical structures, with strong trades union loyalties and mass participation in organised leisure activities.

In many industries this employment pattern was associated with vertical integration, where the same company owned the raw materials production, power production, means of transport to the factories, the factories themselves and distribution networks for the finished goods. The Ford Motor Company is always cited as a prime example of vertical integration.

Vertical integration has now given way to 'post-Fordism', a mode of industrial organisation where companies prefer to concentrate on the core activity which they do best. Developments in information technology have made it unnecessary to control all aspects of production through ownership. Now firms tend to divest themselves of ownership of peripheral activities, as a more cost-effective way to exercise the necessary control is through contractual agreements with independent suppliers. This gives the company the flexibility of choice of supplier, distributor etc. and the price benefits of competition among these. And it gives the company the freedom to restructure without bearing the full costs of this process itself. The change can be summed up as Fordism requiring enterprises to make more than they buy, while post-Fordism requires enterprises to buy more than they make.

Relative increases in the numbers of people employed in service-based as compared to industrial production, and the splitting up of formerly vertically integrated producers, have involved many incremental changes in the mode of production. In the first place, many more individuals now have, as managers, to act as customers in the markets among their potential suppliers. And many more individuals now have to 'attend to the wants of the customer' in various ways, and join in making their activities attractive to the market, both the market for their companies' production and the market for their own labour; gone is the expectation of secure lifetime employment in one occupation or with one company.

These changes in the means of production have been reflected in new climates of opinion, in particular the worldwide rise in consumerism. This movement has many strands, one of the most important being the drive to keep the supplier to the terms of the contract as regards the specification which is advertised compared to the reality of what is provided. A more questioning attitude to suppliers is an inevitable result of a better-educated population experiencing the changes outlined above. But it is also an element of a much broader process of cultural change involving a general diminution in the power of existing power-holding élites and 'policy communities' due partly to the intellectual challenge from the New Right, but also to the improved quantity and quality of information and hence the greater transparency of all institutions and the growing power of an intrusive and independent media. There has been a Europe-wide diminution in support for the traditional political parties. A multiplicity of individuals and groups now have or can get access to information and hold power alongside traditional power-holding élites and institutions.

A second, more diffuse influence has been the increasing importance of the home as the major site of private investment and consumption, and now of new leisure activities, shopping and employment. At the same time the home is targeted both for commercial advertising and by governments hoping to influence or manipulate its production of informal welfare in ways which will avoid the need for government expenditure. The home is now seen as the appropriate site for the delivery of most welfare services, where the service user can exercise control, or at least influence, to ensure that they meet their individual needs. Standardised services are no longer acceptable.

The need to control expenditure

Above all, however, new developments have been driven by the common need to control rising welfare expenditures. There has been a realisation that simply devoting more money to existing forms of near-monopoly services produces only marginal increases in welfare. The requirements of the staff of these services for enhanced service co-ordination, training, conditions, pensions, and so on are considered to absorb an unduly large share.

In nearly all the countries of the European Union, governments have moved to control health expenditure by centralising responsibility at the national level. With social services, in contrast, the tendency has been to decentralise responsibility to local governments. The sole exceptions to these patterns are Italy, where health is a regional responsibility, and Denmark, where local government holds responsibility for both health and social services budgets.

Health services involve highly trained personnel, increasingly expensive treatments and high-technology equipment. Local democratic participation in health service policy has seldom been enhanced. Governments are, on the contrary, keen to increase their control over the semi-autonomous health professions and to impose ceilings on health expenditures. Even in the United

Kingdom, the decentralisation of responsibility to hospital trusts and groups of family doctors leaves them dealing directly with the central civil service, since the former health service bureaucracy has been abolished.

In the social services field there is little prospect of the new technical developments which periodically shed the warm glow of favourable publicity on the health services and their associated government department. There is little that is attractive for central government in social services, which carry out most of their work out of sight in private homes and which are associated mainly with various kinds of intractable personal difficulties. The preferred method for containing expenditure in social services has been by decentralisation, by delegating responsibility for them to lower levels of government. These local governments are typically allocated a finite budget and told that within central government guidelines the services are their responsibility.

Welfare pluralism

Faced with the current developments and difficulties, many countries have seen 'welfare pluralism' as an acceptable way forward. There are two main aspects to this concept. The first entails a perceptual shift away from the previous exclusive concentration on state-provided services in which the state was seen as the creator and controller of welfare provision. The resources needed for welfare were seen as financial, and the state was seen as the only significant provider.

Now non-financial resources for welfare are given increasing recognition in policy and practice. These include particularly the help of the individual's family and social network, assistance from the not-for-profit sector (with its ability to attract voluntary labour) and that which comes from membership of self-help groups. Policy-makers in several countries have also re-evaluated the potential contribution of the commercial sector though its acceptance as a component part of the total field of policy-making along with the informal, not-for-profit and state sectors meets considerable resistance.

The second important aspect of the 'welfare pluralism' concept is the idea that the state, rather than aiming to be the eventual monopoly provider of services, should draw upon the resources of all sectors, regulating the overall system so that the various providers behave responsively and efficiently. Informal care should be recognised and cherished and carers given every possible assistance to continue, the work of not-for-profit organisations should be extended by making contractual arrangements for them to provide specified services, and the potential of the commercial sector to provide cost-effective and customer-orientated services should also be utilised. In some countries it is envisaged that the economy and effectiveness of the overall welfare mix will be secured through competition between different providers, state regulation producing a 'market' in provision. In other countries this element is absent.

There are a large number of reasons for the widespread adoption of such ideas apart from the significant influence of right-wing ideology and the need to save money. It brings the production of welfare closer to general post-Fordist modes of production, which entails contracting out parts of the process to lower-cost producers. It responds to consumerism with the prospect of a choice between providers and the hope that competition will make them more consumer-orientated. It is very compatible with the decentralisation of responsibility to local government which has taken place in every state of the European Union except the United Kingdom. And it can also be seen as a response 'to demands of citizens to be seen as co-producers of welfare not as passive recipients' (Evers 1988, p. 20). Such demands have been made particularly by groups of young physically disabled people, the parents of learning disabled people and newly retired elderly people, many of whom have been keen not only to increase their influence, as service users, over service delivery, but to assume responsibility for the services.

Opposition to the 'welfare pluralism' concept derives mainly from suspicion of the motives of governments driven by right-wing ideologies. Perhaps ultimately they will reduce the role of government as the funder of welfare and, in line with the general model of the proper functions of the *laissez-faire* state, will restrict themselves to maintaining the conditions for a free market in welfare. This would leave the poor without protection. But this would be for the future. At the moment, 'welfare pluralism' can be seen as a survival strategy for the liberal capitalist state. In a situation of reduced resources facing rising demands, governments find it attractive to involve a much wider range of social actors in the provision of welfare in order to spread responsibility and the blame for the inevitable frustrated expectations.

Governments have only to look at the fate of communist east Europe, where self-reliance was not encouraged, voluntary groups were suppressed or incorporated into official movements, and market activity was generally illegal. The inability to adopt a welfare pluralist model hastened the collapse of the entire system. As described for Poland:

> Communism preached and practised the state monopoly of justice. Monopoly, however, meant unshared responsibility; anything conceived as injustice rebounded potentially as a complaint against the state; every disaffection turned into anti-state dissent. As a consequence, the communist state displayed an uncanny ability to attract divers strands of grievance which would hardly combine in a type of society in which the satisfaction of desire is sought in the market-place.
>
> This process, however, was deeply paradoxical. . . . It was prompted by the system's malfunction, more precisely by the feeling that the state does not function the way it should according to its own promises. Most groups opposing the practice of the state wished to press that practice closer to the ideal the self-same state had preached. At the height of popular disaffection . . . research after research found that a large (and growing!) majority of the population wanted the state to deliver more of its, specifically communist, promise. . . .
>
> Disaffection had to do not with the *content* of demands . . . but with the *volume* of demands that exceeded the performative capacity of a rigid, centralised system of production and distribution. . . .
>
> Under the circumstances, the only hope of 'salvation' for the system was to . . . shift some of the 'caring responsibilities' of the state to the market and, more generally, to private or group initiatives . . . one that only the most naive among the communist rulers could hope to contain once they had set it in motion. (Bauman 1994, pp. 19–21)

The macro-economy of the welfare mix

The different resources of the welfare mix, welfare pluralism or the mixed economy of welfare have traditionally been listed as four: these are the informal sector, the not-for-profit sector, the for-profit sector and the state. But in our opinion, changed circumstances now require that the individual's own resources should be distinguished as a component of the welfare mix which is of increasing interest to policy-makers. We shall consider each sector in turn with respect to financial, organisational, professional and ethical resources, in so far as they are relevant to each sector.

Individuals are now being exhorted to take greater responsibility for securing themselves against the risk of dependency by taking out personal pensions and insurance schemes, and to rely less on collective schemes mediated by the state. The problematic future of statutory schemes in which current contributors finance the benefits of current pensioners have had an influence on this development; greater longevity, and mass unemployment resulting in fewer employees' and employers' contributions have undermined the viability of these arrangements. Statutory schemes will face their severest crisis during the second decade of the next century, when the 'baby boomers' born during the era of high birthrates which followed the Second World War start to retire in substantial numbers. But rising levels of unemployment mean that fewer individuals are able to make personal pension and insurance provision, which without an employers' contribution is relatively much more expensive for the same level of pension. And a greater reliance on individual provisions will exacerbate the disadvantages already experienced by women. The traditional welfare state was based on the assumption that women and children were dependent on a male breadwinner in secure lifetime employment. Changing family patterns, the greater propensity of women to enter the labour market, their greater longevity, together with their generally lower earning power and the greater likelihood that their employment will be interrupted by childcare and caring for elderly parents, give rise to a number of inequities which reduce their capacity to purchase their own protection. There would be a similar effect for other disadvantaged groups.

Additionally, to associate independence exclusively with individualism is an ideological construct which denies the power of *collective* arrangements to maintain the independence of individuals (Oliver 1990). The individualist road to independence is available only to the more affluent sections of the population.

Of more practical interest are the financial resources of the individual as a component of his or her own welfare mix. Even the most collectivist of European Union countries have been developing 'cost-sharing' arrangements in which users are charged for services according to their means. Capital resources as well as the income of the user are commonly taken into consideration, which affects particularly elderly people who own their own house, raising an issue for informal carers who could have expected to inherit.

We have already described how several EU countries (for instance Belgium, France, Germany, Spain) have codes of family law which make relatives collectively responsible for the financial support of a family member who is without sufficient resources. This legislation commonly comes into play when the family member is admitted to residential care: domiciliary services are charged for solely according to the individual's own resources, or the household's own resources. While there are historical reasons for this distinction, it may now be intended to act as a financial incentive for families to provide informal care.

Informal care (i.e. care by a family member, partner or friend) is in the opinion of most authors more important for the individual than the other sectors combined. The carer's willingness to care is a unique ethical resource, and policies are now generally intended to support informal care rather than replace it.

Numerous feminist writers have pointed out that policies could prevent the current situation, where much caring takes place in poverty, by protecting carers from loss of income and pension rights and compensating them for the additional expenses like extra heating, transport or laundry.

To develop personal social services which support informal care has proved no easy matter, raising acute ethical problems and problems of targeting (Twigg 1993). Service practices aimed at maximising the quantity of informal care are unacceptable if they neglect the strain on the carer, and have been compared to 'asset-stripping' in business practice (Johnson 1990). On the other hand offering help is a matter for skilled personnel if it is to be acceptable to both the carer and the person cared for. It requires a delicacy and responsiveness which not all service providers will be able to deliver with consistency. The provision of even concrete services like respite care (short-term admission of the dependent person to provide a respite for the carer) is very variable across Europe, particularly as financing it is not often covered by insurance provisions. On the other hand receiving frail elderly people living in mountainous areas into residential care for the winter months does take place extensively (e.g. in France) as it has proved cost-effective in terms of savings to other service entitlements.

Women within the nuclear family or partners in the same household are the major providers of informal care. Their social network and community seldom do more than provide social contact and encouragement to help with the carer's isolation and loneliness. Where neighbours are willing to do more, experiments have taken place in the United Kingdom with the intention of making this help more reliable by using contracts in which the 'volunteer' formally undertakes with a formal care-giving organisation to provide a service (for instance, exercising surveillance on two occasions daily) in return for a small expenses payment (Challis and Davies 1986). Thus 'voluntary service' has been disaggregated from 'unpaid'. In less cumbersome fashion, elderly French people in rural areas routinely pay their neighbours to perform services for them, as up to a point this is less expensive than the means-tested official services. In Germany too a substantial proportion of those entitled to domiciliary care following an acute medical episode, rather than accept the service, prefer to make their own arrangements with an entitlement to a much-reduced cash equivalent. This is due to the perceived unreliability of the service.

The blurring of distinctions between paid and unpaid, volunteer work and employment is widespread. Research by the Commission of the European Communities (1984) showed how in some countries, expenses and other payments to 'volunteers', the work expected of them, and the training they receive are so substantial that it provides a cheap labour force who maintain their volunteer activity in the hope that they will eventually find employment with the same organisation.

The nature and hence the resources of the not-for-profit sector of the welfare mix vary substantially between different European Union countries (Ely 1992), to the extent that few generalisations can be made about it. The not-for-profit sector is usually praised for its flexibility and ability to point the way in providing for populations in need who are not well catered for by the state services, and for embodying the enlightened self-interest of concerned citizens who act on their own initiative. This is most true when not-for-profit organisations are first set up. The largest ones in particular are not immune from the bureaucracy, inflexibility and other accusations levelled at the state sector, which they come largely to resemble, with the additional weakness that the operations of not-for-profits are not directly accountable to the electorate.

As regards financial resources, though not-for-profit organisations can raise their own money through fund-raising activities this seldom produces funding on the scale necessary to provide substantial services with qualified staff. Not-for-profits are generally dependent on the state and service charges for their running costs. Their resources in terms of professional staff are also less than those of the state or the for-profit sector. Their organisational resources are likewise frequently weaker than those of these other two sectors. Their ethical resources are their strength. They can assume an overtly altruistic purpose which attracts both state funding and the free labour of volunteers. As Evers (1988, p. 24) observes concerning the intermediary role of not-for-profits:

> Many of these new innovative groups and projects are visibly state dependent, but not part of the state. . . . Consequently, this leads to a questioning of the inherited concept of 'civil society'. First of all, it becomes clearer that it is not constituted solely through political, cultural and social protest organisations and their discourses, but also through organisations representing work, production and economies beyond markets and formal economies. Secondly, freedom is to be guaranteed by the state, not as a question of distance but of functioning types of more and better intermediation between state and social actors.

The state sector has strong financial resources, professional resources and organisational resources. But its ethical resources are ambiguous due to its multiplicity of objectives including the satisfaction of political and bureaucratic interest groups. The agents of the state can behave in ways ranging from acting in the public interest to bureaucratically limiting their responsibility to ensuring that public money is spent according to the regulations. Recently weight has been given to complaints of the irrelevance, inflexibility and remoteness of many government services. On the other hand its services are likely to be provided equitably and consistently across its geographical area. Other disadvantages relate to high labour costs and the difficulty of changing its workforce's behaviour to meet new needs when state services are monopoly providers.

Countries vary widely in the extent to which the for-profit sector is accepted as a component in the planning of their welfare mix, though it exists everywhere to cater for the better-off. This sector has similar resources to those of the state sector as regards strong financial resources and organisational resources and it can purchase strong professional resources. Its ethical resources would consist of its reputed cost-effectiveness and the degree of orientation to the consumer in its service delivery. Its main difference from the not-for-profit sector is that the for-profit sector is more independent of the state and is the sector with the largest capacity to replace the state, as described in the final section.

The micro-economy of the welfare mix

Managers and practitioners are now in a new situation in which the importance of hierarchy as a means of co-ordinating provision has declined in relation to networks and (to a degree) markets (Thompson *et al.* 1991). They must behave less as members of a bureaucracy and more as entrepreneurial workers with financial responsibilities. How is this change to be achieved? An investment in training and in information technology is required.

Middle- and front-line management need information on all the resources available in the area, the potential of each for-profit and not-for-profit organisation. Service standards must be promulgated by the local authority to help its managers identify and control potential partners, and this information must be made available to organisations to whom service provision may be contracted out to clarify what is expected of them. Standard contracts must be produced which are available off the shelf in order to reduce the transaction costs of contracting out. Better financial information is needed about the true costs of existing state-provided services and the likely costs of contracted-out services. At the same time the local authority has to make more use of working parties called together to achieve a specific objective and then disbanded. The memberships will frequently include managers and practitioners from the non-state sectors as well as representatives of organisations of service users.

The welfare mix and the market – separate or together?

To what extent does a 'welfare mix' now exist in each European Union country, and how does its character vary from country to country? Much will depend on what existed in each country before the current economic difficulties.

As regards the broadening of perceptions to take into account the resources of all sectors, no change is required here for the southern group of countries, whose relative lack of state provisions has always left the other sectors a prominent role. In Italy in particular, while the state is the principal provider of services, there is a well-developed system of contracting out (the *convenzione* system) to not-for-profits and also to co-operatives, which have more prominence than in northern countries. For-profit provisions are mainly confined to certain forms of residential care. Contracting out to not-for-profits avoids further growth of employment in the public sector. It extends to domiciliary care, rehabilitation services, projects which counter social exclusion and work placement and employment schemes.

As regards changing the overall structure of state regulation to introduce market disciplines and competition between producers, this is most unlikely within the Italian and other southern European contexts, where there is little tradition of strong state leadership. In Italy new developments in either the economy or the field of welfare have seldom been led by the state, but overwhelmingly have been produced by private initiatives to which the state has acquiesced. In this context overall policy formulation is the product of continuous discussions between the many actors and interest groups, a fundamental difference to the situation in, say, the United Kingdom.

In the Netherlands services were also built up by not-for-profit activity based on the different religious denominations in the country and on certain political parties. Thus adherents of each denomination or party could pass their lives in encapsulated social worlds each equipped with a complete set of services (social protection, health, education, etc.) providing only for their fellow adherents – systems not just of welfare but of social control. Government regulation developed late, only during and after the Second World War. These provider organisations survive although advancing secularisation and new political allegiances have resulted in the abandonment of the segregated living patterns ('consociation') which they once represented. The three largest confessional parties merged to form the Christian Democratic Appeal party in 1980. And the appeal of the traditional groupings as a source of values or communal feeling has greatly reduced for most people (Hupe 1993).

In 1987 the government-sponsored Dekker report put forward radical proposals which are an outstanding example of how an insurance-based system of financing and providing health and social care might be modernised. The report pointed out that there were few financial incentives for consumers, insurers or producers to act efficiently. Insured consumers benefited from virtually free health care and had no incentive to restrain their demands. The sickness funds had no incentive to seek efficient providers, since all claims were reimbursed from a central fund. Private insurers were more cost-conscious but maintained their competitive position by avoiding enrolling individuals who represented poor health risks rather than by choosing cost-effective providers (Pijl 1991).

Under the proposed new arrangements there would be one central fund covering nearly all health risks, into which the population would pay income-related premiums. The fund would then pay the private insurer of the individual's choice a risk-related premium. These insurers would be obliged to enrol all applicants, and would charge subscribers a flat-rate premium. This would eliminate incentives for insurers to compete on the basis of the individual's risk. Insurers would compete on the level of the flat-rate premium they charged subscribers, and this would promote competition between providers as the insurers sought out the most efficient. There would not be competition between consumers: contributions would be based on ability to pay while retaining treatment according to need. Long-term health and social care would be included in the basic insurance package, though there is continuing debate about this.

While introducing market disciplines the report spelled out that the role of such mechanisms should be limited by social, ethical and cultural considerations. Government regulation would still be required to safeguard the quality of care, cost control and equity, and to prevent the formation of monopolies and cartels. Tacit and overt agreements among associations of providers in restraint of trade are not uncommon.

The reforms have been introduced gradually and there is as yet little accumulated experience of managed competition in practice.

To what degree is it possible to speak of a quasi-market for welfare in France? Not at all perhaps, as everything is closely managed by the state at every level of government. Most of the burgeoning not-for-profit sector in social welfare developed during the last twenty years under the aegis of local governments, and to some degree is an aspect of and a response to decentralisation. Not-for-profit associations located within one *département*, often presided over by the deputy mayor for social affairs, are mandated with responsibility for a service or services to a particular client group, but can draw on varied financial resources to do this, using, for example, financial benefits granted to an individual by the state, statutory pension fund entitlements and locally provided benefits to finance services. The different funds and levels of government find it easier to co-operate through an association than to attempt to do so directly.

Associations also provide additional points at which decisions can be made, making the service more responsive to and accountable to the needs of users instead of to the rules of government organisations. They provide a less expensive and less rigid workforce than the government bureaucracies and their financial cost is more transparent. They largely form a kind of adjunct to the state.

Not-for-profit associations' services have sometimes been substituted for formerly state-provided services, for instance in the accommodation and supervision of delinquents, but this has been a national policy decision and not a result of direct competition at the local level. Associations providing domiciliary services for elderly people each have their own local area in which they are monopoly suppliers, and a new provider would not be permitted to receive *departmental* funding unless it was initiating some new form of service (for instance, home nursing) which did not yet exist in the locality. There is no evidence of competition or the desire for it.

Germany has a different pattern, where most welfare services are provided through six large not-for-profit organisations linked to religious denominations and political parties, the 'Big Six'. They are best described as incorporated in the state, and the language recognises this: all other not-for-profits are described as 'self-help organisations', or 'citizens' initiatives', whether they are self-help in the English sense of being organisations of users or whether they are actually created by paid professionals. During the 1970s there was a burgeoning of these *Bürgerinitiativen* as there was of voluntary action generally. This was an aspect of the general decline in authoritarianism in German culture at that time, but occurred more specifically as a response to criticisms of the quality of care provided by the Big Six, which resembled complaints about state services made in other countries. The new initiatives posed a threat to the monopoly position of the Big Six which the latter countered by deputing one of their number to offer an 'umbrella' organisation with which new organisations could federate and receive advisory and mentoring services. And in most localities, Big Six representatives have the dominant voice on committees which act as gatekeepers to the health insurance funds. These are the key source of finance for services and new applicants are excluded if it is alleged that they will compete with existing services or have connections with for-profit interests. Existing providers thus form a cartel restricting access to these funds in their own interests.

The health-related basis of German provision for domiciliary care has distorted the response to consumers' needs. There has been good insurance-based provision for a time-limited period of 'rehabilitative' care following acute health episodes like hospital stays. But domiciliary care for long-term dependency has historically been a neglected aspect of social protection, which has led to reliance on social assistance or to unnecessary residential care. National legislation in 1994 to remedy this deficit deliberately set out to introduce market forces by creating the structure for new providers, including for-profits, to enter the long-term domiciliary care field and for competition between providers (Igl 1994). But the effectiveness of the reforms has yet to be seen. Because of the subsidiarity principle the implementation of these innovations is in the hands of local *Kommunen* and *Länder* administrations who strongly criticised this aspect of the proposals, and whose planning arrangements and vested interests remain in place.

In Denmark, with its small population and collectivist traditions, there is little tradition of not-for-profit activity, which until recently was thought to be a sign of backwardness. The official description of care for old people (Ministry of Social Affairs 1992) makes no mention of non-state services. There are some church-based organisations who help marginal groups like alcoholics and immigrants, and self-help groups of clients who offer each other mutual support. 'Volunteering' has recently been rehabilitated but only to carry out such services as social visiting: qualified members of the appropriate professional associations exercise a strong monopoly over employment in the welfare sector.

Because of the very high participation of women in the labour force there are relatively few full-time carers of old or disabled relatives. It seems unlikely that in the near future the existing state monopoly of service provision will be significantly disturbed, not least because of the consensual style of policy formulation. The only tangible signs of 'pluralism' so far are decentralisation of responsibility for health and social services to municipal and regional government, and increasing charges to users, coupled with the strong recent development of collective but non-state supplementary schemes of social protection for the better-off wage earners. This leaves dependence on basic state provision to the most impoverished, and seems to presage an increasingly bifurcated welfare state (Abrahamson 1991).

The development of social services in the United Kingdom followed the Scandinavian model, with a near monopoly of services provided directly by the state. Near the end of the 1980s the UK government enacted a series of administrative changes to the management of education, health and social services designed to introduce the benefits of market competition to service provision in these fields. These benefits were intended to provide more choice for users, more attention to the needs of users, economy, efficiency and effectiveness. Thus schools were to be in competition with each other for pupils, hospitals and family doctors for patients, and different elements in the welfare mix for users. To create a welfare mix in social services provision, the local government services were to provide far fewer services themselves, and instead to purchase them from for-profit or not-for-profit providers, a practice commonplace in certain other EU countries with regard to not-for-profits, as described above.

These changes create a market, in that there is intended to be competition between different welfare service providers. But since one of the objects of the changes was to reduce the volume of services provided directly by the local authorities, these services will compete on less favourable terms. Emphasis has been placed on developing provisions in the for-profit sector.

As in the Dutch proposals, there is no competition between users. In the United Kingdom the state remains the main purchaser: but the money is not given to the users as a cash transfer. Instead the benefit is received in the form of services for which a local government care manager has acted as purchasing agent using public money on their behalf. The term 'quasi-market' or managed market has been coined for this state of affairs, which protects the user against the gross inequalities which would result if the kind and amount of service provided depended only on their own financial resources.

Le Grand (1993) suggests the following set of conditions for the success of quasi-markets in social care. In the market structure, both purchasers and providers must be competitive. They should be financially motivated, otherwise they will not be sensitive to the signals sent by the market. The purchaser needs information on the price and quality of services, and the provider also needs information on the cost of providing the services. The 'transaction costs', those of negotiating the contract and monitoring compliance with it must be low to both purchaser and provider, otherwise the new system will be less cost-effective than the traditional management hierarchy. In addition, the scope for providers (and indeed for purchasers) to indulge in 'cream-skimming' by choosing to service only the least troublesome clients must be limited, as otherwise the most services will be provided to those who need them least. Finally the entry of new providers into the market and the exit of failing providers from the market need to be carefully regulated in the public interest.

In the United Kingdom, the welfare mix had in many areas to be created before competition between providers could be said to exist, so that it is too early to say whether the benefits of competition and choice have been secured in the social welfare sector. There is competition within the for-profit sector between providers of residential care since in certain localities there is an excess of this provision over demand due to the new proposals' emphasis on the development of intensive forms of domiciliary care. This can be expected to lead to the elimination of less efficient providers. And it is a difficulty with the proposals for market competition in general that providers who fail to secure a contract with the local authority will cease trading, whereas apart from the residential care field, much of the 'business' on offer is on a local scale which would hardly admit of more than one provider.

No doubt because of the relatively more right-wing nature of the British government, the UK proposals included few of the qualifications about the role of market disciplines in the welfare field, the danger of monopolies and so on which were so prominent in the Dutch blueprint.

Conclusions

It seems likely that the Dutch and British experiments with market forces will continue to influence a number of European Union countries, but it is not likely that a common model of service provision will emerge. Underlying systems of social protection and of financing and organising service provision are too divergent, as are the expectations of the public in the different countries.

In addition the British plans, whatever their current form, are associated with an ideological preference for a completely free, uncontrolled market: a general economic doctrine which in the opinion of many continental observers has yet to prove its capacity to work to the public benefit in any economic sphere (Hutton 1995). This makes them unattractive to countries with more corporatist or consensual traditions of policy-making and long-term relationships of commitment between the partners involved.

Some UK commentators have foretold that service provision will steadily become concentrated into the hands of a few very large for-profit providers, often foreign-owned, who will in effect have captured the market and will reduce user choice and involvement in service provision. This forecast assumes that the welfare mix will turn into a near-parody of the nation's economic life. As we have seen, the operation of the existing welfare mix in a number of other European countries also mirrors their characteristic economic forms.

It is the future role of the commercial, for-profit sector which has given rise to most disquiet in comment on the UK proposals. Evers (1993) denies the right of the commercial sector to participate on the grounds that it has had a negligible historical role in welfare development, and its values make it unsuitable. He suggests that in countries with predominantly direct provision by the state, the welfare mix should be extended only to the not-for-profit sector – it should be limited to the historical German model.

There is general concern that while classical economists were well aware of the welfare resources which were not reducible to economic values, less of this awareness is evident in today's accountancy-based thinking, which sometimes tends to assume that the for-profit model is the dominant paradigm. There is a danger that in a competitive situation, the more that the different providing sectors are mixed, the more uniform the mix becomes. State services, large not-for-profit and for-profit organisations all adopt what they imagine is a commercial management style, leaving the informal sector in danger of being seen as a resource to be ruthlessly exploited (Johnson 1990).

Johnson, a supporter of state provision, has looked to the United States as a model for indications of the likely outcomes when market forces are given their head. The lessons are not encouraging, with fragmented provision, for-profit producers filing legal complaints that the tax exemptions of not-for-profits are unfair trading advantages, gross disparities in services between different areas and income groups, local administrations who have dispensed with their own direct services now held to ransom by for-profit providers, and neglect of those in poverty (Johnson 1990).

This is a situation where state policy-making has relinquished that universalistic frame which is concerned to some extent for the needs of all. The UK reforms are still seemingly taking place within this universalistic frame. Should the frame be abandoned under pressures from ideology, large for-profit producers and declining government expenditure and should the crude operation of market forces replace it, then the future of welfare is likely to be bleak, and the process would be extremely difficult to reverse.

Each European country has the responsibility for developing the mixed economy of welfare which it feels is most suitable to its own values and needs, including the appropriate role for market forces, if any. In countries with strong state organisation, as in the Netherlands, the managed market is less likely to get out of control. To use it to influence the behaviour of the actors in more progressive and economical directions is a creditable aim. In the same way, to use the threat of competition to influence the behaviour of welfare providers in more consumer-friendly directions, as in the new German arrangements for long-term social care, also has positive potential.

No sector can claim a monopoly of positive values nor of positive outcomes in service provision. Monopoly provision within any sector seems more conducive to inflexible and producer-orientated behaviour than to innovation and consumer-orientated behaviour.

References

Abrahamson, P. (1991) 'Welfare for the elderly in Denmark: from institutionalisation to self-reliance', in A. Evers and I. Svetlik (eds), *New Welfare Mixes in Care for the Elderly*, vol. 2, Vienna: Euro Social.

Abrahamson, P. (1992) 'Welfare pluralism: towards a new consensus for a European social policy?', in L. Hantrais, M. O'Brien and S. Manger (eds), *Cross-National Research Paper 6: The mixed economy of welfare*, Leicester: European Research Centre, Loughborough University.

Bauman, Z. (1994) 'After the patronage state: a model in search of class interests', in C.G.A. Bryant and E. Mokrzycki (eds), *The New Great Transformation?*, London and New York: Routledge.

Challis, D. and B. Davies (1986) *Case Management in Community Care: An evaluated experiment in home care of the elderly*, Aldershot: Gower.

Commission of the European Communities (1984) *The Extent and Kind of Voluntary Work in the EC: Questions surrounding the relations between volunteering and employment*, Brussels: Commission of the European Communities.

Commission of the European Communities (1994) *Social Protection in Europe 1993* COM(93)531, 26 April, Brussels: Commission of the European Communities.

Ely, P. (1992) 'Democracy, voluntary action and the social welfare sector in mainland Europe', in R. Hedley and J. Davis-Smith (eds), *Volunteering and Society: Principles and practice*, London: Bedford Square Press.

Evers, A. (1988) 'Shifts in the welfare mix: introducing a new approach for the study of transformations in welfare and social policy', in A. Evers and H. Wintersberger (eds), *Shifts in the Welfare Mix: Introducing a new approach for the study of transformations in welfare and social-policy*, Vienna: Eurosocial.

Evers, A. (1993) 'The welfare mix approach: understanding the pluralism of welfare systems', in A. Evers and I. Svetlik (eds), *Balancing Pluralism: New welfare mixes in care for the elderly*, Aldershot: Avebury.

Ferrera, M. (1993) *EC Citizens and Social Protection*, Brussels: Commission of the European Communities.

Freidman, M. (1962) *Capitalism and Freedom*, Chicago: University of Chicago Press.

Friedman, M. (1970) *The Counter-Revolution in Monetary Theory*, London: Institute of Economic Affairs.

Hayek, F. (1944) *The Road to Serfdom*, London, Routledge.

Hupe, P.L. (1993) 'Beyond pillarisation: the (post-) welfare state in the Netherlands', *European Journal of Political Research* 23, 4 (June), pp. 359–86.

Hutton, W. (1995) *The State We Are In*, London: Jonathan Cape.

Igl, G. (1994) 'La prise en charge de la dépendance des personnes âgées: les discussions et les solutions en Allemagne', in F. Kessler (ed.), *La Dépendance des personnes âgées*, Strasbourg: Presses Universitaires de Strasbourg.

Johnson, N. (1987) *The Welfare State in Transition: The theory and practice of welfare pluralism*, Hemel Hempstead: Harvester Wheatsheaf.

Johnson, N. (1990) *Reconstructing the Welfare State: A decade of change 1980–90*, Hemel Hempstead: Harvester Wheatsheaf.

Konopasek, Z. (1993) 'The welfare mix on the way to welfare universalism', *Czech Sociological Review* 1, 1, pp. 91–103.

Ksiezopolski, M. (1987) 'Polish social policy in a situation of economic crisis: is there a choice of alternatives?', in A. Evers, H. Nowotny and H. Wintersberger (eds), *The Changing Face of Welfare*, Aldershot: Gower.

Le Grand, J. (1991) *The Theory of Government Failure* (Studies in Decentralisation and Quasi-Markets 5), University of Bristol: School of Advanced Urban Studies, Bristol.

Le Grand, J. (1993) *Quasi-markets and Community Care* (Studies in Decentralisation and Quasi-Markets 17), University of Bristol: School of Advanced Urban Studies, Bristol.

Lorenz, W. (1994) *Social Work in a Changing Europe*, London, Routledge.

Ministry of Social Affairs (1992) *Pensioner in Denmark: Main features of Danish old age policy and care for the old*, Copenhagen: Ministry of Social Affairs.

Oliver, M. (1990) *The Politics of Disablement*, London: Macmillan.

Pijl, M.A. (1991) 'Netherlands', in A. Evers and I. Svetlik (eds), *New Welfare Mixes in Care for the Elderly*, vol. 2, Vienna: Euro Social.

Pinker, R. (1992) *Social Work in an Enterprise Society*, London: Routledge.

Thompson, G., J. Frances, R. Levacic and J. Mitchell (eds) (1991) *Markets, Hierarchies and Networks: The co-ordination of social life*, London: Sage.

Twigg, J. (1993) 'The interweaving of formal and informal care: policy models and problems', in A. Evers and G.H. van der Zanden (eds), *Better Care for Dependent People Living at Home: Meeting the new agenda in services for the elderly*, Bunnik: Netherlands Institute of Gerontology.

CHAPTER 5

Children and families

Nicola Madge and Karen Attridge

Recent years have witnessed dramatic changes in family structure and family life throughout Europe. There has at the same time been greater recognition of many family problems such as physical and sexual abuse, as well as ideological shifts regarding the positions of children and parents within families. All these changes have put enormous demands on services already faced with the effects of recession and often dwindling resources. This chapter looks at this changing context as well as policies for children and families from both pan-European and diverse national perspectives. It then examines a selection of services from different countries, presenting illustrations of provision rather than a comprehensive coverage of all that exists.

Changing families

The stereotypical family of two married parents and around two children, with a father at work and a mother at home much of the time, rarely exists anywhere in Europe. First, separation and divorce have markedly increased and recent statistics suggest that Britain now has the highest divorce rate in the European Union at 3 per 1,000 population (Eurostat 1994a). One consequence of this family breakdown is that more and more children face the likelihood of spending at least a period of time in a lone-parent household: at the end of the 1980s about 17 per cent of families in the United Kingdom, 15 per cent in Denmark and, at the other end of the scale, around 5 or 6 per cent in Greece, Italy and Spain, were headed by a lone parent (Roll 1992). Despite an increase in re-marriage over this period, there has also been a trend towards childbirth outside marriage: by 1990 over a quarter of live births in Denmark, France and the United Kingdom fell within this category.

The impact of these trends on family life can be illustrated by the case of Denmark, where, at the beginning of 1992, only 72.8 per cent of ten-year-old children were living with two natural parents. Instead, 9.1 per cent were living with their mother and a new partner, 14.1 per cent were with a lone mother, 1.2 per cent were with their father and his new partner, 1.9 per cent were with a lone father and 0.9 per cent were with neither natural parent (Qvist 1992).

Alongside these changes, fertility has decreased and families have become much smaller. Southern Europe, where large families were once the norm, has been particularly affected. World Health Organisation statistics show that the fertility rate (average number of children per woman of childbearing age) over the past five years was lower in Italy, followed in Europe by Spain, than anywhere else in the world, with rates of 1.3 and 1.4 respectively. Ireland led EU countries with a rate of 2.1 and was followed by Britain with a rate of 1.9.

Another noticeable trend is in the cultural and ethnic mix of national populations. All twelve EU countries except Portugal increased its population in 1991 as a result of migration from elsewhere. Luxembourg stands out for the proportion of residents from abroad, although other countries have higher proportions from non-EU countries. Germany, France and the United Kingdom have the greatest numbers of 'foreigners' from outside Europe (Eurostat 1991). These national population patterns have important implications for services provided for children and families. They have effects on the age structure of national populations: in the EU countries there are over-representations of people under forty years among 'foreigners' and almost twice as many infants in the total non-community population as among the EU population as a whole. Also, 'foreigners' are at particular risk of various forms of disadvantage, including discrimination. They may not share the culture and language of the national population, may be more isolated with fewer family resources and less family support.

Equal opportunities and the women's movement have also radi-
cally changed ideas about parental roles within the family and
hence the need for services. Far more women than in the past wish
to work and raise a family and, at the same time, the significance of
the father's role is increasingly appreciated. There are strong calls
for services which recognise the equal rights of women and men,
mothers and fathers, and which allow families flexibility to develop
their preferred individual lifestyles. These issues are addressed by
the European Commission Childcare Network (see below).

Last, but certainly not least, recent years have seen growing
awareness and public recognition of problems within families, and
in particular increased knowledge about child abuse and the forms
it may take. The acknowledgement of violence within the family is
fairly new throughout Europe, and indeed child protection registers were established only as late as 1974 in Britain. Public awareness of the problem has a similar history in Denmark and the
Netherlands, and is even newer in countries including Greece,
Italy, Portugal and Spain.

All these changes, which have taken place in a context of sharp
recession and rising unemployment, have strong implications for
provision. How, then, have policy-makers and services responded?

European policies for children and families

There are two senses in which European policies for children and
families can be considered. The first is in relation to measures with
a pan-European significance and the second is by cross-national
European comparison.

Pan-European perspectives

The most notable feature of pan-European perspectives is that there
is no unified European policy for children and families. The Treaty
of Rome, which describes the constitutional basis for the European
Union, as well as the Single European Act provide no mandate for
European competence in developing policies for them. The Treaty
on European Union (the Maastricht Treaty) expands European
competence within the social sphere, but still makes little

direct reference to children or families. It has, however, led to certain key proposals in the European Commission White Paper on European Social Policy (1994) which are relevant. These include following up the child care recommendation (see below) by considering the implementation of a regulation in this area, collecting further information on the provision of child care in the member states, and seeking ways of discouraging stereotyped sex roles in society. The European Commission will also introduce a recommendation urging member states to adapt their social protection systems to changing family structures. Although children and families have no explicit European focus, they do none the less receive attention from the various European institutions. Particularly important in this context is the European Commission Council Recommendation on child care of 31 March 1992, which urged EU member states to encourage certain initiatives to enable women and men to reconcile their occupational, family and upbringing responsibilities arising from the care of children and to report back on their actions in these areas within a three-year period. The four areas in which initiatives are encouraged (a recommendation is not legally binding) are as follows: the provision of child care services while parents are, or are seeking to become, employed or on a course of education; special leave for employed parents who have responsibility for bringing up children; more flexible employment conditions to suit employees with children; and greater equality of child care responsibilities between women and men. It is interesting to note, however, that this recommendation arose from a concern with equal employment opportunities for men and women rather than from any prime concern with child welfare.

Among other measures affecting young people in their own right is recent legislation on young workers. Since June 1994 there have been new common EU standards to ensure better protection for young people with paid jobs. Those aged 13–15 years may now work for up to twelve hours a week, although night work is not allowed and school commitments must be taken into account. In addition, children are affected by a number of standards regarding health and safety, such as regulations on wearing car seat belts, toy labelling and playground standards. More generally, they are affected by all measures designed to protect workers and their families in the European Union – including the Social Charter and the social chapter.

Besides the introduction of legislation, the European Commission has been responsible for developing or supporting a number of programmes, networks and observatories focusing on the interests and concerns of children and families. These include, to give a few examples, the EU Childcare Network (which gave rise to the child care recommendation mentioned above), the European Observatory of National Family Policies, the EU Observatory on National Policies to Combat Social Exclusion, programmes such as HELIOS that promote social integration of the disabled, and initiatives relating to a range of other areas including mental health, HIV and AIDS, and education.

The European Parliament has also become involved in the discussion of children's issues. In July 1992 it drew up and discussed a draft European Charter on the Rights of the Child to put the UN Convention into a European context. The Charter covers most aspects of a child's life and aims to safeguard all children from all forms of deprivation and disadvantage. Additionally the Parliament hosts a variety of working groups and committees focusing on women's rights, social issues and youth, culture, education, training and sport. It has recently set up a new all-party working group on Children, Families and Partnerships in Solidarity. These groups discuss issues of concern and produce reports, recommendations and proposals for change in policy and practice.

The Council of Europe has also been active in child and family protection and has over recent years drawn up a number of relevant treaties for member countries to sign and ratify. The main areas covered are the European Convention on Human Rights, the European Social Charter, social security, migrant workers, children and family law, and the media. Questions like the following have been considered: respect for private and family life, anti-discrimination, protection from danger, right of economic protection, minimum levels of social security, adoption and children born to unmarried parents, and custody of children. As a recent example, the Council of Europe produced a series of guidelines relating to child abuse in 1992 and called for harmonisation of child protection systems to cover legislation, training, resources and services.

Less formally, there has been extensive international exchange, with an emphasis on young people and their families in Europe. There are numerous cross-national networks and organisations, a range of international conferences and meetings, and many examples of exchange visits and experiences. Much of this activity has been organised by non-governmental organisations, and much has been stimulated by the UN Convention on the Rights of the Child. The focus of international exchange is, generally speaking, on the sharing of experiences and the identification of good practice rather than on the harmonisation of policies as such.

National perspectives

An examination of services for children and families highlights the problems there would be in attempting to harmonise provision to any great extent. These services vary markedly between but also within countries. There are various reasons for these differences. Some administrations are very decentralised, which almost inevitably leads to considerable variation in provision. Some rely much more heavily on private and voluntary services than public, or vice versa – and these patterns again affect provision.

Some countries have fairly co-ordinated services for children and families (with ministries or departments for children and/or families) while others are relatively fragmented. Belgium, France, Germany and Luxembourg, for instance, have a department or ministry of this kind. Denmark, the Netherlands and Spain have an interministerial committee or commission for children's issues which, although not responsible for legislation and administration, discuss children's issues from a coherent and integrated approach. It has been claimed that countries like Greece and the United Kingdom without such a department or ministry may show fragmentation and a serious lack of co-ordination and co-operation between services for children and families.

National populations also vary considerably in size and geographical characteristics, which in countries like Greece can impede the effective delivery of services. For these and many other reasons services emerge in many forms across Europe. Spain, Portugal, Ireland and Italy might be cited as countries displaying particularly uneven national services.

Attitudes to intervention within the family differ internationally. Some countries take on a major care-taking responsibility while others tend to leave it up to families to look after themselves.

France, for example, has a strong family policy and all political parties agree that supporting children and families is a sound investment for the future. Generous financial and other support is, as a consequence, provided. Denmark also aims to assist families in general and state intervention is taken for granted, as in the provision of care for young children. The former East Germany was also what might be termed a 'nanny state'. In the United Kingdom, social work has long been regarded as part of the welfare state.

By contrast Germany, Greece, Ireland and Italy in particular have traditionally relied heavily on self-help and resented 'interference' in family life. The principle of subsidiarity is particularly strong in former West Germany, where the state may provide family services only if an alternative private or voluntary agency cannot be found. As a result approximately two-thirds of child care services are provided in the private not-for-profit sector. There is none the less a strong tradition of German state intervention if the law is broken – parents would be 'punished' if their children did not go to school – although this is increasingly resisted in favour of a less punitive approach.

The focus of help and assistance also varies. Inevitably, the more widespread the services, the more generally they impinge on families. This can be illustrated by comparing the situation in Denmark, where much provision is for typical families – the dual-earning, reasonably well-off family – and Greece, where it is mainly targeted at those in difficulty. The impact of this is shown most clearly by the provision of day care for preschool children.

Finally, to what extent do national policies address the issue of equal opportunities? The UN Convention on the Rights of the Child was adopted in 1989 to protect children throughout the world from exploitation, abuse and neglect. It includes articles relating to children from ethnic, religious or linguistic minorities, children with disabilities and learning difficulties, and children separated from their families. All EU countries have signed or ratified this Convention since the beginning of 1990 and its articles have accordingly had an enormous impact on legislation and service development since then. It is therefore within the spirit of this legislation to ensure that a policy of equal opportunities towards children is pursued in all member states. How far practice matches this policy is harder to say and largely beyond the scope of this chapter.

In considering services for children and families it is worth noting that the priority currently accorded to children's rights in many countries may be in opposition to the interests, rights and responsibilities of parents. Although, as in Denmark, for example, it may be laid down by national law that assistance should respect the integrity of the family, it can sometimes be difficult to avoid a conflict of interests. It has been claimed that a considerable emphasis is placed on parental rights in Ireland, and also that social workers in France sometimes feel that 'the balance of rights and powers leans too far towards parents, sometimes at the expense of children's welfare' (Kent County Council Social Services 1993, p. 7).

Physical punishment of children raises interesting questions in this area. Five European countries – Sweden, Denmark, Norway, Finland and Austria – have now outlawed any form of smacking, and other countries have considered such a move. Children's rights have in a sense taken precedence over parental decisions on how to bring up their children. The increasing voice given to children in many countries may also sometimes mean that a child's wishes or views may be given higher priority than a parent's. Furthermore, preschool provision may be more for the convenience of parents than for the necessary welfare of children. Decisions have to be made in all these areas and the main question seems to be how services can best reconcile differing needs. The interests of children, their parents and their families as a whole are not necessarily the same.

Social work with children and families

Service needs, tasks and obligations

There is no single simple model of the social work role in Europe, either across countries or over time. Moreover, as noted, there are first differing levels of need and differing conceptions of appropriate intervention. These needs are uneven even within countries, as illustrated by Grazia (1994), who describes an Italian social worker's experience of two rather different neighbourhoods within her area. Although the two communities are of similar size and politics, one but not the other is socially cohesive and co-operative with well-run public services. The social work task is accordingly very different in the two locations.

Social work in its broad sense covers an enormous range of different jobs and orientations. Although social work trends in most European countries are increasingly generic, there are still many specialists to be found. There are, for example, school social workers, child care social workers, residential social workers and youth workers. Most countries also have some social workers who work mainly with children and families from abroad, while France has 'animateurs' who work specifically in leisure settings and on social action projects.

One of the more interesting distinctions for child and family services is between the social worker and the social pedagogue or educator. This is particularly evident in residential and other child care services. Social pedagogues or educators are dominant in child care in all countries except Ireland and the United Kingdom, where social work predominates, and Greece and Portugal, where there is no special profession. Social pedagogues are trained to work in a variety of settings, and pedagogy embraces:

> family, neighbours, friends . . . [and] the numerous organisations
> which offer nurturing, informal educational, leisure time and
> therapeutic support in, for example, nurseries, day care centres, youth
> clubs and children's homes. In the varied life of these interests the
> social pedagogues will work directly with people, seeking to facilitate
> their individual and social development. (Jones 1994, p. 2)

Child care is thus not necessarily more than one aspect of this role. It has been suggested that the social worker in the United Kingdom has a more restrictive role, with greater emphasis on pathology and problem-solving. This is particularly the case with the residential social worker.

As all European countries have social workers and as eight of the twelve also have pedagogues or educators, social work and social pedagogy can have quite distinct roles. Where both professions exist, the pedagogue is mainly concerned with the child's upbringing in a broad sense, while the social worker maintains links between the child and the family and community and does not generally act as 'therapist'. Very often the social worker role is largely administrative and office-based, and in countries such as France, Denmark, Germany and the Netherlands includes the administration of family benefits. Some confusion of roles can nevertheless arise. In Spain, for example, problems in delimiting areas of work do occur in practice, although the differences are becoming clearer as the professions develop their own associations.

Even within social work there can be contrasting perspectives and ways of working with children and families. An exchange between child care social workers in social services departments in Kent and in the Nord/Pas de Calais in France (Kent County Council Social Services 1993) identified several points of comparison: it was rare for social workers in France to specialise in child care; those in France spent much of their time providing financial aid; English social workers seemed to have more sense of meeting the psychological needs of clients; the French, unlike the English, operated on a strict generic patch-based system; the French had closer links with other agencies in the community – except for the police; the French statutory social workers had less power than the English and were not required to give evidence in court; the French had less autonomy than the English and referred to their superiors more often; and overall the job in France seemed less stressful and led to less conflict between social workers and families.

The tasks of social work are strongly related to statutory obligations which vary considerably across Europe in relation to children and families work. Lorenz (1991) has illustrated this by noting how Ireland is at one extreme of the continuum while Germany is at the other. Few statutory obligations exist in Ireland, where social workers work with families largely by tradition and not because they are required to do so by law, although there have been some changes since the Childcare Act 1991. By contrast, there is an increasing amount of legislation in Germany governing social work tasks and duties. While this means that families know their entitlements, it also leads to an inflexible system dominated by rules and regulations.

It may be that less statutory involvement is necessary in countries where traditionally the family is stronger. Smith (1994) contrasts the United Kingdom and Italy and notes that the statutory requirements of social workers in the former has no direct parallel in the latter. He suggests that the relative strength of the family is indeed contributory.

In many ways, and in line with the Resolution on Community Development proposed by the Standing Conference of Local and Regional Authorities of Europe and endorsed by the Council of Europe in 1989, the role of social work is demonstrating a shift towards community development, with growing emphasis in many countries on encouraging partnerships between citizens, local agencies and organisations to provide local services. As Cannan *et. al.* (1992, p. 46) note:

> The principles of solidarity and subsidiarity give social work a broader, preventive and community development mandate: not to separate individuals from society, but to promote healthy relations between and within groups, and to see that as a process of encouraging participation of the marginalised from below, aided by resources from above.

Cannan (1992) describes the social work role in France as being about strengthening communities by first setting up services for all and then encouraging those most at risk to use them.

This approach has clear implications for services available to children and families. Heaton and Sayer (1992) point out how community development has a preventative role in child abuse and other forms of family stress. Involvement in local activities can also help to counter isolation and encourage confidence. This role has been strongly recognised in Denmark, where government funding for the SUM project has since 1988 led to almost 2,000 experiments and programmes in the community. Over one-quarter of resources have been put into projects to support disadvantaged children and families through revitalising local communities by establishing or reviving activity centres, encouraging parenting skills while giving support to the whole family, or emphasising links with the family.

In recent times social work has had to cope with limited resources as well as increased family difficulties due to the economic situation and unemployment, family breakdown, weakening of the extended family, and greater numbers of families from abroad with language, cultural and support problems. Cannan (1992) suggests that as a result social workers have to prioritise their work more than in the past, and that increasingly they respond to crisis rather than carrying out preventative work. There has also been a changing balance between individual casework and empowering communities, as well as the increasing diversity in provision that comes with decentralisation and responses to local initiatives. Moreover, social work has more and more become an administrative job, especially in countries like Germany that impose a large number of obligations on social workers.

Another aspect of the social work role is the extent to which it involves links with other services and agencies. Jones and Bilton (1994) lament the failure of education, health and social services to work together in providing a comprehensive network of services in England. Although it is not possible in this chapter to examine European patterns of collaboration, it is worth noting that there are many examples of child and family services working together effectively across Europe as a whole.

In the Netherlands there are multidisciplinary youth assistance advice teams, staffed by paediatricians or other doctors, child or adolescent psychiatrists, psychologists and social workers. They collaborate in outlining local priorities and problems, in giving advice on the best assistance for particular children and in keeping records. In Italy, interdisciplinary community teams include social workers alongside doctors and psychologists, while in Greece all the major professions work together in the regional social welfare centres. Spanish social workers co-operate with doctors, teachers and other staff in primary care networks.

Another interesting example of co-operation is found in local teams in Denmark which include representatives from schools, social services and health departments, together with psychologists and psychiatrists. These new local and still often experimental teams are available to any professional seeking advice on how to deal with a particular problem, child or family. Finally, the strong links between social, health, educational and other services in Ireland should be mentioned. Many social workers are employed by health boards and work daily with a range of other professions in providing services for children and their families.

Patterns of services

In most countries there are first-stop services open to everybody including children and families. These include the public social welfare centres in every commune in Belgium, the *centres communaux d'action sociale* in France, the *consultorio familiare* in Italy, the regional social security centres in Portugal and the social services area offices in England. This type of provision is generally funded by the state and may be supplemented by other services provided by voluntary bodies or in some countries by employers.

The extent and accessibility of these services are quite variable both between and within countries. Whereas countries such as Belgium, Denmark, England, France and Germany have fairly widespread and uniform provision, others – particularly those in southern Europe – do not. An Italian social worker has claimed that social services in her country 'are not something you hear about. You can go through life without knowing of their existence' (Smith 1994, p. 7). In Spain services are highly variable and often very limited in their provision for children and families with social problems. Greece has very variable services which are likely to be particularly scarce in unpopulated and inaccessible rural areas.

These first-stop services provide material, financial, social and emotional assistance and put families in contact with appropriate agencies for specific problems. In addition, throughout the European Union there is an enormous range of different kinds of services and provision for children and families, some available to all and others targeted at specific population groups. This chapter provides some illustrations of this diversity, concentrating on the following seven categories of service:

1. Preventative work with young families.
2. Responses to child abuse.
3. Supporting families in the community.
4. Removing children from home.
5. Offering financial assistance.
6. Daytime care and clubs.
7. Services for young people.

Preventative work with young families

Most countries have some form of special service for pregnant women and mothers with young children, although the nature and scope of these services vary considerably. Belgium provides an example of effective provision with the state-run Kind en Gezin (Children and Families) located in Flanders, which since 1987 has provided a comprehensive service for 'future parents and families up to three years of age', which includes the provision of centres for prenatal and postnatal care. The service includes day care, child abuse aid centres, adoption services and crisis residential care. The agency also employs 700 social nurses who visit almost all homes before babies are born and then until infants are three years old. These home visits are very important in identifying children at risk, providing assistance, liaising with other services and agencies and making referrals to child abuse aid centres. Kind en Gezin subsidises, regulates and controls other services in the private and voluntary sectors. A parallel service is run by ONE (Office de la Naissance et de l'Enfance) in Wallonia, the French-speaking community of Belgium.

France also has a comprehensive service for young mothers and their children. The PMI (Protection Maternelle et Infantile) works with families including children up to six years old, and employs *puéricultrices* alongside doctors, midwives, social workers and psychologists in a multidisciplinary team. Their task is to identify and work with children at risk of a range of health and social problems. The prevention of child abuse is only a small part of this role. The PMI works closely with L'Aide Sociale à l'Enfance and Action Sociale to provide a social and health service. There is also close liaison with school health authorities.

It is interesting to compare the role of the French *puéricultrice* with that of its British counterpart, the health visitor (Foster 1988–9). Both are nurses with additional post-nursing training and both work predominantly with young children, even though technically the health visitor's responsibilities extend 'from the cradle to the grave'. Moreover both are concerned with surveying total populations of babies and infants. But as Foster points out, the role of the *puéricultrice* is considerably narrower than that of the health visitor. Despite greater French acceptance of a watchful eye over all children and more compulsory examinations, French home visits are not as regular as in Britain and tend to be less intensive and intrusive. Families are more likely to be regarded as able to sort out their own difficulties or referred on to other agencies if problems are found. Unlike the health visitor who has a specific brief to detect children at risk, the *puéricultrice* does not usually regard this as a main area of her work. Health visitors in Britain carry considerable responsibility for uncovering potential and actual instances of child abuse, and their decline – real in recent years and apparent in the future – is currently causing considerable alarm within their professional organisation.

Early and often continued visits to all young families are also usual in other countries, such as Denmark and the Netherlands. In Denmark the visiting nurses see the mother and her baby shortly after returning from the maternity ward and will continue the periodic visits according to needs during the infant's first years. In the Netherlands the usual pattern is for a first visit when the baby is a few days old and a second and last visit the following week.

Such services are not available everywhere. In Portugal, for instance, there is no service truly equivalent to the British health visiting programme. Despite some developments and an acknowledged need for home visiting to enable mothers and infants to be monitored more effectively, a general lack of nurses and other resources results in a very limited provision, particularly in non-urban areas. Home visiting is also rare in Greece, largely due to a shortage of nurses and the rural location of many families. For rather different reasons there is no home visiting service in Germany, where mothers and their babies consult family or child doctors at their surgeries.

Responses to child abuse

There is no common international definition of child abuse, and the term 'child protection' is commonly applied to policy and practice against forms of physical, sexual and emotional violence towards children. Issues in this area include prevention, detection and notification, investigation and assessment, follow-up intervention, treatment and review, training and research (Council of Europe 1992).

The services dealing with child abuse vary across Europe, ranging from the fairly comprehensive guidelines available in the United Kingdom (Home Office, Department of Health, Department of Education and Science and Welsh Office 1991) to relatively undeveloped services in much of southern Europe. The previous discussion on early preventative services for young families is relevant to policy and practice in this field. The remainder of this section is a brief examination of European practice regarding the reporting and registering of abuse as well as some approaches to service provision.

A first point of difference between European countries is in the reporting of child abuse. The Council of Europe has urged all countries to encourage the reporting of abuse, but there remains a contrast between countries who do and those who do not have a mandatory reporting system. Denmark, France (with the exception of doctors and midwives), Italy, Luxembourg and Portugal fall within the first group. Belgium, Germany, Greece, the Republic of Ireland, the Netherlands, Spain and the United Kingdom fall within the second group and rely on professionals and members of the public to report instances of suspected abuse.

There appear to be advantages and disadvantages of both mandatory and voluntary reporting procedures. It has been claimed that mandatory systems can encourage both under- and over-reporting of abuse and that they discourage families from approaching professionals for help with difficulties. On the other hand there is concern that voluntary systems can result in families in difficulty slipping through the net and remaining undetected. It is hard to evaluate these counterclaims, although it can be noted that although a voluntary system in the Netherlands was accompanied by a lower than expected level of abuse in years up to 1983 (Pieterse and van Urk 1989), recent statistics indicate that the rate of young people notified to authorities has more than quadrupled since then.

Another difference between countries is whether or not cases of child abuse are included on a central register (National Committee for Prevention of Child Abuse 1992). England (since 1974) and Northern Ireland (since 1977) do have central registers; Belgium and the Netherlands keep records of children reported to the confidential doctor centres (see below); and Denmark carries out regular national prevalence research studies. But there are no comparable registers in France, Germany, Greece, the Republic of Ireland, Italy or Spain. The lack of a central register may be due to a lack of resources or it may reflect national culture and ideology. Germany, for example, is a country where traditionally family matters have been seen as private and personal.

At one time child abuse was thought of as a straightforward criminal offence for which recourse to the law was necessary. More recently such views have been modified with the recognition that families may need help rather than punishment.

The introduction of a 'confidential doctor' system in the Netherlands some twenty years ago was probably the first formal step taken in this direction. This recognised that locking up parents rarely benefits anyone; it appreciated that unequivocal evidence of child abuse is hard to obtain; and it sought to shift the emphasis from the law to welfare. There are now eleven confidential doctor centres in the country. They are headed by general practitioners or paediatricians working in pairs, each on a part-time basis – one or other is on duty twenty-four hours per day – to co-ordinate provision for voluntarily reported cases of child abuse. They are usually assisted by a secretary and a social worker, their role being to provide advice to doctors and others as well as to organise appropriate assistance. They do not provide treatment themselves. They may collect information from health and educational records but deal with everything in confidence. They may approach the public prosecutor only if families refuse to co-operate and with their knowledge.

Child abuse aid centres, organised by Kind en Gezin in Flanders, operate on a similar model. These multidisciplinary 24-hour centres are required by the state to put social workers faced with cases of child abuse in contact with appropriate expert help, to co-ordinate the help given to families and to promote general awareness of child abuse.

Most countries, including Germany, Greece, Italy, Portugal, Spain and the United Kingdom, still place greater reliance on the legal system in cases of child abuse. In Britain, for example, local authorities are obliged by law to assist each other in safeguarding and promoting the welfare of children. They are required to work closely with all other professionals and agencies involved with children in order to do this, which entails co-operation between social services departments, doctors, midwives, health visitors, schools, voluntary agencies and the police. Although the police may also be involved in child protection in France, they have a much more restricted role and become involved only if ordered to do so by a judge. Children's judges play a very important role in this way and, as evidence of harm is not necessary for their involvement, they often review cases at an early stage (Cooper *et al.* 1992).

Supporting families in the community

Supporting families in the community is given a major emphasis everywhere, with an almost infinite variety of approaches. Quite apart from effective casework and community development which can make a considerable difference to the numbers of children and young people removed from home, interventions can range from the provision of financial assistance offered in many countries, through day care centres open to all young children and their parents, to a range of special centres and home-visiting programmes offering child and/or family therapy and support. This section describes a few examples of schemes to illustrate the wide diversity of approach across Europe as a whole. It looks first at an example of family centres open to all before turning to consider several special approaches targeted at children and families in difficulty.

Family centres of various kinds are found in many places. Those provided by the Caisse d'Allocations Familiales (CAF), a semi-public body working in accordance with state objectives and the main source of family and child services in France, provide an illustration (see Cannan 1992). These *centres sociaux* which complement the *centres communaux d'action sociale* and other forms of provision, employ family social workers, *animateurs* and some advisers. Others provide both family benefits and social action in the form of holidays, after-school care and casework. Provision is not uniform across the country as centres are run at departmental level, but aims to respond to local need. Centres, which are often found in large housing estates and may have nurseries attached to them, aim to be attractive to local inhabitants, promote good community relations and undertake preventative work. They are not set up specifically for families in difficulty, although specialists of various kinds are available to deal with specific family problems that may arise.

Besides services for all, there are many forms of community intervention developed for particular groups. An interesting and long-established response to child behaviour problems in the Netherlands has, since early this century, been to place children in special centres after school. There are now around a hundred of these centres across the country, with children attending at least three days a week over a period of around two years. The centres are staffed mainly by social workers, who also make contact with parents at least every two weeks. The strategy is to offer group therapy to the children while at the same time working with the families. Many of the children who attend the centres have social problems of some kind, and a majority come from minority ethnic backgrounds. Children are screened every six months to monitor their progress and usually leave the centre when both the child and the family seem able to cope on their own. There is apparently little stigma attached to attending these centres, attendance is generally good and demand for places outstrips supply.

A variation on this theme is the Danish Knude project – literally the 'knot' project – regarded as particularly successful in recent years. Using a family therapy model, this approach is to work intensively with the child as well as to a lesser extent with the whole family. Children aged between six and twelve years attend day care instead of school for a period of one or two years and are accompanied by other family members once a week for family therapy. Day care is provided in a special centre – usually an ordinary house in the neighbourhood – for groups of five or six children with a variety of problems who might otherwise be placed away from home.

Other countries also resort to highly intensive forms of social work intervention to resolve family problems. An interesting example with no direct parallel in other countries is Socialpedagogic Family Help (SF), which has been offered since 1969 and is available in some form or another in well over half of Germany. This long-term intensive treatment is aimed at families living under seriously deprived conditions who cannot be helped by more conventional means. Professionals (social workers, educators, family nurses) work with families for between 10 and 20 hours per week over one to three years, and may provide practical solutions to problems, counselling and therapy to improve parenting skills as well as family communications and relationships, or help to integrate families within the neighbourhood. They may work with the children, with the parents or with the whole family. Although the approach appears successful in about two-thirds of cases, it does have some drawbacks. In particular, social workers may become overinvolved and families overdependent (Textor 1990).

Video home training – very popular among social workers in the Netherlands in recent years – is another example of intensive intervention in the home. This is a shorter-term approach which seeks to reduce interpersonal difficulties by identifying and reinforcing successful aspects of family communication. The procedure is to film normal family activities and then view and discuss the recording with parents and older children some days later. The social worker uses the film to demonstrate effective forms of communication and behaviour that should be encouraged. The conclusion is that video home training can help families with child rearing or relationship problems as well as children with a range of behavioural difficulties. The technique has also proved valuable in helping a child to adapt or re-adapt to his or her family or a residential situation.

Mobile youth workers in Germany illustrate the kind of help that may be offered to young people who cannot be supported in traditional ways. These social workers seek out delinquents, drug users, gamblers and others showing aggressive and troublesome behaviour on the streets or in pubs, parks, stations and discos. They befriend them, gain their confidence and may then offer help to set up clubs or activities such as football matches or theatre groups. After this the social workers try to encourage the young people to make contact with schools, job centres, legal advisers and others as appropriate. This form of youth work is particularly important in big cities and neighbourhoods where young people are socially isolated from their communities. Mobile youth workers are employed by both statutory and voluntary agencies and, although not numerous, are growing in number. Similar workers are found in other countries.

There is an almost endless range of other forms of support for children and families within the community. The interested reader is referred to Munday (1993) for some further examples.

Removing children from home

Recent years have witnessed similar trends across Europe in the policies and practices adopted for children and families in difficulty. In line with articles of the UN Convention on the Rights of the Child, there has been a distinct move away from removing children from their families unless absolutely necessary, and towards more foster care, adoption and support within the community. Simultaneously there has been movement away from compulsory towards voluntary placements which marks a shift in emphasis from coercion to co-operation. Current thinking almost everywhere is that children are usually best with families, preferably with their own but alternatively with others, although it is recognised that residential care remains important. The primary aim of any arrangement away from home is to return the child wherever possible to his or her natural family as quickly as possible. Most countries have now written these requirements into their child and family legislation.

Residential care

The growing emphasis on keeping children at home has meant a decline almost everywhere in residential care as well as a reduction in the time a child is likely to stay in a residential placement. The young people in children's homes have also changed, the typical child now being more difficult and troublesome than previously, unable to remain at home or be found a suitable foster placement. These young people are also older on average than in the past.

Despite similar general trends, individual countries have shown enormous variation in the extent and speed of change. Although comparisons are difficult, it is clear that there are significant national differences in the relative use of residential care and foster care for children and young people placed away from home. Portugal and Spain, for example, place a high emphasis on residential relative to foster care, while at the other end of the spectrum the United Kingdom and Ireland rely heavily on foster care and much less on residential placements (see Madge 1994).

There have also been dramatic changes in the nature and meaning of residential care. Few large institutions remain in any country, and most children's homes are now much smaller than in the past. Small family homes in Belgium, for instance, house only six to ten children, while in Germany there are homes which accommodate only two or three children with substitute parents. This type of provision might also be called professional fostering.

There are many other kinds of provision, including observation or assessment centres, temporary homes where children stay while intensive work is carried out with their families, residential 'schools' for young people past the age of compulsory schooling, therapeutic units and communities, and children's villages. One particularly interesting development has been the growth in independent living opportunities in recent years. These were pioneered in Germany, although they are now found in Denmark, Belgium, Greece, Luxembourg and elsewhere, and provide flexible living arrangements for older teenagers. There is no single form of provision and varying levels of supervision are offered. Indeed the intention in Germany is that this type of facility should be created for the individual rather than the other way around. 'Human beings instead of walls' is the guiding philosophy.

Another interesting variation on the residential care theme is travelling projects which have been tried with some success in Denmark and Germany. The *Fulton*, an old Baltic schooner, provides an interesting example (Josephson 1994). For over twenty years this ship has included six to eight 13–18-year-old boys with severe familial, social or criminal problems among its crew. These boys offer instruction to other young people of their own age but with less experience of sailing, and co-operate with each other to ensure the smooth running of the ship. Boys coming to the *Fulton* are told that they are starting afresh, that their past histories are not of interest, but that heavy demands will be made of them. Life aboard the ship has, since 1980 and in recognition of the poor attainments of most of the boys, been supplemented by a voluntary educational programme offered at the land base. More recently it has been further supplemented by an after-care programme to help the young people find somewhere to live, manage their finances, and generally become independent and self-reliant.

A current concern about residential child care in Britain is the training and qualifications of staff. Quite apart from the issue of the most appropriate profession – the distinction between social work and social pedagogy has already been mentioned – there is considerable disquiet about the low levels of appropriately qualified staff in residential child care in comparison with proportions in comparable establishments in many other places. Germany and Luxembourg, followed by Denmark, stand out in having much higher proportions of qualified residential child care workers than England (Madge 1994).

Finally in this brief examination of residential child care, it is worth asking about the extent of abuse of children living away from home across Europe. While this has been a problem in the United Kingdom, it is less clear how far it has been elsewhere. Similar patterns seem to be found in France, Germany, Greece, Ireland and Italy, but countries such as Denmark, Luxembourg and Spain report that child abuse in children's homes is extremely rare.

Foster care

Foster care has a variable history across Europe but has in recent years become more popular almost everywhere. While it is likely to increase further in countries like Spain, where service development is rapid, it has probably reached a plateau in many other places, including Britain. A number of countries are currently experiencing problems in recruiting further foster carers, particularly those with professional experience.

Fostering arrangements, like residential placements, take a variety of forms. Children may be placed with relatives, with 'ordinary' families or with trained professional carers who offer treatment or therapeutic care. Placements may be 24-hour or daytime, weekday or holiday only. Generally speaking, foster parents have become foster carers to reflect the principle that fostered children are returned home as soon as possible. None the less stays may be short-term or long-term, and as with residential care a placement may be on a voluntary or compulsory basis.

The financial rewards for foster carers also vary. Trained pedagogues in Denmark and elsewhere can earn a salary, whereas others without specialised training may receive little more than necessary expenses. Foster care is increasingly used for children with disabilities or severe problem behaviour. It is evident that foster placements today do not much resemble those ten, twenty or thirty years ago.

Adoption

About one in every hundred children born in EU countries will become adopted before reaching adulthood, with the conditions under which this is likely to occur showing some differences between countries. Full adoption, involving the care givers completely taking over parental rights and responsibilities from the natural parents, can take place in all countries. Simple adoption, which leaves some rights and responsibilities with the birth parents, is possible in some countries.

Most countries place some age restrictions on adoption. All countries have an upper limit at which a young person can be adopted and this ranges from 14 to 18 years. Many also impose a lower limit: six weeks in Ireland, eight weeks in Germany and three months in Luxembourg and France. The ages of putative adoptive parents may also be important, as may be the age difference between the adults and the young person. Single persons can adopt in all countries apart from Italy. Nowhere, however, may an unmarried couple become adoptive parents.

Traditionally, the churches and other charitable bodies have been largely responsible for looking after abandoned children and placing them with alternative families. Often the role of the voluntary organisations has been retained, although in many places there are now restrictions on who can become involved. In the Netherlands and Denmark, for example, only authorised agencies are allowed to deal with adoption, and in Flanders Kind en Gezin has recently been given overall control of these matters. Before 1990 almost anybody could in principle organise adoption but now there are only eleven recognised adoption services, seven for children born in Flanders and four for children born abroad.

Offering financial assistance

Income support is an important family service because of the links that poverty commonly shows with a range of other problems and difficulties. Gartner (1991) was able to show from World Health Organisation data for seventeen countries how family characteristics – such as illegitimacy, teenage pregnancy and divorce – were accompanied by higher rates of infant and child homicide where welfare spending was lowest.

There is considerable variation between countries in the level of public expenditure for children and families. The EU average expenditure on social protection in 1992 was 292 ecus per head of the population. Whereas Belgium, Ireland, the Netherlands and the United Kingdom were fairly close to this average, Greece, Spain, Portugal and Italy – less so – were well below. Denmark, Luxembourg, Germany and France were above average, with expenditure in Denmark being six times greater than in Greece. The proportion of total benefits allocated to maternity and family relative to other categories has, in the European Union as a whole, dropped from 10.5 per cent in 1980 to 7.8 per cent in 1992. Individual countries differ in the extent to which this proportion has changed.

There are enormous differences in both statutory and discretionary payments made to families with children in different countries. Family benefits are available in one form or another in all countries. Everywhere except Italy, where the size of household is the critical factor, the amount given depends on the number and ages of children. Benefits are universal (although Germany offers an extra payment to those on low incomes) in nine of the twelve countries but dependent on income in Greece, Italy and Spain. They are tax-free except in Greece. Rates are higher for older children in Belgium, France, Luxembourg and the United Kingdom, and higher for younger children in Denmark. In about half the countries the total amount paid depends on family size. Benefits are paid for everyone up to 18 years in seven countries, but until 17 in the Netherlands, 16 in Germany, Ireland and the United Kingdom and 14 in Portugal. Additional payments may be made where young people enter vocational training or higher education or if they have a disability. Although it is difficult to compare rates paid, it appears that Belgium and Luxembourg are among the more generous countries while the United Kingdom and Portugal are among the least.

In times of severe family breakdown the arrangements made for the support or maintenance of children of former unions become very significant. In eight of the twelve current European Union countries there is a system of advanced payment of child support or maintenance payments with the state recovering money from the debtor. In Italy and Portugal employers can be required to advance payment, whereas in Greece and Spain no provision is made for advance payments.

Despite similar systems in principle, some countries are more successful than others in collecting child support or maintenance. Vedel-Petersen (1991) indicates that authorities in Denmark manage to collect 87 per cent of maintenance payments, and in Germany too most absent fathers who can be traced through their identity card pay child support costs. In the United Kingdom there has been less success in tracing absent fathers and enforcing maintenance payments despite the recent controversial introduction of the Child Support Agency. Besides maintenance or child support payments from absent partners, lone-parent families may expect to receive benefits from the state. Rather different levels of social protection in this area are found across Europe. Thus whereas Denmark and the Netherlands provide a benefit of more than 60 per cent of the average national income to unemployed lone parents, the figure is nearer one-third in Britain and Greece, one-sixth in Italy and nothing at all in Portugal or Spain.

This brief discussion of financial benefits available to families with children has not covered a variety of other grants and allowances found either universally or selectively in European countries. Funding for vocational training or higher education, birth allowances, new school year allowances, maternity leave and allowances are among those also relevant in this context.

Daytime care and clubs

This section looks mainly at preschool day care but also briefly considers provision for out-of-school hours.

Preschool day care

The availability of preschool day care is central to patterns of family life and employment (Eurobarometer 1991). It is important first because more mothers wish to go out to work, and because more are lone parents; and secondly because development during the early years is crucial for both current and later well-being. As already mentioned, early child care has, due to the activities of the European Commission Childcare Network, been one of the areas of family concern in which there has been greatest pan-European interest.

Public provision of day care for preschool children is highly variable across the European Union. The European Commission Childcare Network (1990) indicated that at the end of the 1980s Denmark, followed by Belgium and France (who still provided for only around one in five children), made the best *public* provision for children under three years, with the United Kingdom and Portugal being the worst providers. Despite some changes over the past few years, the picture remains similar. Types of care vary and detailed accounts are provided elsewhere (David 1993). In brief, many countries have both group care, such as day nurseries, nursery classes and playgroups, and family care, such as child-minders in the United Kingdom. In Denmark children under three years and in public care are usually in approved family day care where 'child-minders' look after three to five children although some take up limited places in the more popular but more expensive day nurseries.

Once children are aged three, opportunities for day care improve universally. Most 3–6-year-olds in Denmark and Germany attend kindergarten; most preschoolers attend pre-primary schooling from three years in Belgium, France, Italy and Luxembourg; and most from four years have places in Spain. Less formal provision is found elsewhere. The main options prior to compulsory schooling in the Netherlands are playgroups, which operate for a few hours only, or early attendance at school. Much the same, together with scarce nursery school places, is available in the United Kingdom, where compulsory schooling begins earlier than in most other European countries and where there is a growing trend for young children to be placed in primary school reception classes any time after the child's fourth birthday.

An interesting question is the orientation of day care: how far is it for 'care' and how far for 'education'? Many countries regard the preschool experience as primarily educational, this being the case in Belgium, France, Germany, Italy and Spain as well as in nursery and primary schools in the United Kingdom. In Denmark, however, there are local differences dependent on the views of the board of parents and staff who jointly decide on the children's activities. This board is in itself an innovatory practice as until recently child care workers were autonomous in these matters.

Policies for children with special needs are also not completely uniform although there is a marked trend away from segregation in preschool care. In Italy there is a total integration policy whereas most other countries recognise the value of integration but make some limited special provision. Children from minority ethnic backgrounds are similarly found in most forms of preschool provision even if they may sometimes be over- or underrepresented.

To what extent is the provision of day care adequate? There is a shortage of places everywhere for children under three years, even in countries like Denmark, Belgium and France, and a shortage almost everywhere else for older children. There have been enormous recent developments in Spain which have created day care places for almost all four- and five-year-olds although not yet for all three-year-olds. Change has been in the opposite direction in former East Germany, where unification has resulted in the closure of many creches and kindergartens that once provided for almost all children above one year of age.

The availability of day care places depends on national patterns and priorities. In Denmark the high level of day care reflects the fact that at least three-quarters of young mothers have educational qualifications and that two working parents are the norm. Even parents without employment often want day care places for their children, who would otherwise be isolated in residential areas that tend to contain few infants during the day. Traditionally, the situation has been rather different in former West Germany, where families have generally expected to bring up their own children without interference from the state. Recently, however, things have changed and the need for kindergarten places has become an important political issue as the proportion of working mothers and only children has increased. In Spain the reasons for infant care and education are different again and are intended to reduce disadvantage and inequalities. In France, widespread provision is part of a family policy aimed at encouraging increased fertility to reverse the falling birthrate.

The European Commission Childcare Network lists the following characteristics of effective child care services: high quality, equal access for all children, services available locally, no segregation of different groups of children, diversity should be supported but there should be coherence across services on certain subjects, care and education – broadly defined – are inseparable. They also note that the pay, conditions, status and training of workers in child care services are of fundamental importance.

Denmark, with its day care system distinguished both by wide coverage and the way in which it is organised and subsidised by public authorities, provides the best model of provision at the present time. The system allows parents to work and maintain a good standard of living, and it reduces reliance on state benefits. Moreover it is available to all children on an equal basis – there is not the two-tier system apparent in Britain, where services for low-income families are largely distinct from those for the more affluent – and it can offer good stimulation for children and encourage their development, well-being and independence. There is, none the less, still a shortage of places in some areas, particularly for the youngest children, and the service recognises that there are improvements yet to be made.

Out-of-school care

Besides preschool care, there is also a great need by many families for care out of school hours. As with preschool care, there are considerable differences in what is on offer across Europe. In general, most countries offer fragmented and piecemeal provision with a mixture of forms of care provided by a variety of agencies. Provision is frequently low, with very little at all provided in Greece, Ireland and Spain. Denmark provides the most, with the remaining countries offering a place to fewer than one in ten children (Children in Scotland/COFACE forthcoming, 1995).

Denmark again leads the field in out-of-school care and in principle provides leisure facilities for all school-age children. Local authorities must provide day care from ten years, which is usually in after-school clubs for 10–14-year-olds and in youth clubs for 14–18-year-olds. They also provide after-school centres for 6–10-year-olds, while others in this younger age group may attend school recreation schemes organised according to the Primary Education Act. Overall, most younger children attend one or other provision. The facilities operate in the afternoon following school and some are also open in the morning. No young person is denied a place in leisure-time or club facilities for financial reasons, and help is given if the subsidised cost of attendance cannot be met.

Leisure-time facilities and clubs are currently a high priority of the Danish government and emphasis is placed on the value of facilities for preventative and supportive work with children and young people. A recent proposal from the Ministry of Social Affairs suggests that, for the first time, the aims of these clubs in developing independence and encouraging solidarity should be formally written into the legislation. It is also recommended that young people should by law be given the right to influence how clubs are organised and run.

Services for young people

The UN Convention on the Rights of the Child, as well as recent national children's legislation in many individual countries, recognises the necessity to listen to children's views, to provide them with relevant information and advice, and to give them opportunities to voice their complaints. This section examines some ways in which 'good practice' is being implemented in some EU countries.

All countries provide telephone helplines that children can ring, generally free of charge. These include Børnetelefonen in

Denmark, BAG (Bundesarbeitsgemeinschaft Kinder- und Jugendtelefon) in Germany, ISPCC Childline in Ireland, Telefono Azurro in Italy, the number 12345 set up by the privately run Caritas in Luxembourg, Kindertelefoon in the Netherlands, SOS Criana in Portugal, Nuestro Teléfonon in Spain and ChildLine in Britain. These helplines play a particularly important role in dealing with child abuse, both because they offer young people somebody independent to talk to and because they can work with other agencies in the more serious cases. They can also inform the general public about the incidence of family problems. An informal analysis of calls to Telefono Azurro in Italy suggested that almost two-thirds of callers were aged eleven years or more, and over two-thirds were girls. One in three calls concerned difficulties with parents and 12 and 2 per cent respectively mentioned physical and sexual abuse. Similar analysis suggests that ChildLine in Britain also receives many more calls from girls than from boys – four times as many. More abuse is, however, reported, as 15 and 14 per cent respectively of the sample in question mentioned sexual and physical abuse, with only 11 per cent mentioning family problems.

Apart from somewhere to telephone, young people may like somewhere to visit. Opportunities for this are provided in the Netherlands through the JAB (Jongeren adviesburo). These advice centres were originally set up by local social services departments almost thirty years ago, providing young people between twelve and twenty-five years with information in areas such as education, health care, housing and employment, and counsel them on how to approach the institutions in these fields or on their own personal lifestyles and problems. Young people can approach the centres on their own or with a parent or friend, and in practice few under about twelve or thirteen years come unaccompanied. Most telephone for an appointment, although they can just drop in and wait until a social worker is free if they prefer. There is a high demand for this service but no waiting lists, as the aim is to solve problems as quickly as possible, although some young people do have longer-term contact with the centres.

Besides providing information, advice and counselling, the work of the JAB includes visiting families (although only with the permission of the young person), accompanying young people to appointments and interviews and group behaviour therapy. The advice centres are widely advertised and leaflets are distributed to all schools and other centres frequented by young people.

Views of children and young people on local rather than personal matters are given voice through municipal councils in France. Set up in agreement with municipalities, these councils comprise between fifteen and sixty members elected according to where they live, their age or their academic school level. Councillors, who are aged from nine to eighteen years, hold meetings to discuss issues and problems of general interest (e.g. the environment, culture and leisure, health, education, the third world and transport) and to map out projects and put them into practice using their own budget. Meetings for debate and decision-making take place in the town hall or educational establishments, and plenary sessions two to four times a year are attended by the mayor and local representatives.

The first of these municipal councils were set up in 1979 and now number about 750. In 1991 a national association was set up for support and advice, and an attitude survey of parents and young people at about the same time indicated that the vast majority of respondents were very much in favour of the councils and felt they promoted active citizenship. Councils can none the less run into difficulties. In particular it has been recognised that it can be difficult for the *animateur* – essential to keep councils going – to achieve a good balance between control and freedom during meetings. Furthermore, it can take a long time to develop projects and see them through, and there can also be problems of co-operation between councils and local authorities.

Germany, Italy and Portugal have looked at the French model, and Belgium has established approximately thirty councils along similar lines since 1987. The first of these achieved several objectives in its first six months, including relocating bus stops outside schools, installing new public benches and rubbish bins. Britain now seems to be following this model too. Chesham, for example, established a youth council with its own budget in 1994. Among its objectives it hopes to make the town more interesting for young people with places to go in the evenings and at weekends.

There has been much discussion in many countries about how best to represent the interests of children and young people at a national official, if not governmental, level. No country currently in the European Union has a children's ombudsman along the lines of the person in post in both Norway and Sweden. However,

Denmark has established a Børnerådet (Children's Council) to fulfil some of the same functions. This council is headed by a radio journalist well known to children and will include a four-person secretariat as well as a committee of elected members. It will be independent in status and will aim to take the point of view of children and young people through holding conferences, raising issues and other activities.

Conclusion

This chapter has reviewed a selection of policies and services for families, children and young people within the European Union. These policies and services have pan-European, national or local significance. Some are available to all, while others are targeted at special sub-groups in the population. Most have been influenced by changing trends and needs as well as by shifting approaches to social work. There is no useful sense in which a summary of the full spectrum of provision can be made.

Several themes can, however, be discerned from even this cursory look. First, there is a growing recognition of the importance of human rights. A respect for parental rights is witnessed, for example, in the current reluctance to remove parental responsibilities – as in the trend in England and Wales towards 'looking after' children rather than taking them into care. The UN Convention on the Rights of the Child has both reflected and encouraged this viewpoint so far as young people are concerned. Children's rights have been enhanced by the very many services developed specifically for them which allow their own points of view to be put forward and listened to.

The issue of rights is extended to the family as a whole and in many senses it seems that responsibility is being passed back to families to look after themselves, with the state relegated to a more subservient role. This is illustrated in the move towards supporting families in the community rather than removing children as a form of 'treatment', as well as in the current growing emphasis on help rather than punishment in cases of child abuse. The general orientation is more and more that co-operation is better than coercion. Moves towards community development and empowering local neighbourhoods to take charge reinforce this point. The state is of less significance – underlined by decentralisation in most countries and the emergence of services designed to meet the needs of communities rather than countries as a whole.

Prevention remains another theme even though a shortage of resources can mean that in reality it is not always a priority. It is generally recognised that it is cheaper in the long term to avoid problems than to have to deal with them once they have arisen. Adequate levels of family benefits, good child care and generally accessible services help to prevent difficulties, as do specific strategies such as the early detection of problems in young families, and working in the community in a preventative role. Prevention can also mean involving all relevant family members so that old problems do not resurface when the preventative service comes to an end. Good, widespread communication often seems to be the key to effective provision in this area.

Broad, although not universal, agreement is apparent that good communication should also occur between professions and services. Multidisciplinary teams are becoming the norm in many countries and many useful and effective models are found in countries such as Denmark and the Netherlands. Most national legislation urges inter-agency collaboration even if the mechanisms to carry this out require further development.

Despite national priorities, policies are established for a range of reasons and it is interesting to note that Jones and Bilton (1994) claim, for the United Kingdom at least, that the impact of service reorganisations on children is frequently an unintended consequence of other objectives. There is a continuing need to revise and develop child and family policies as needs and circumstances change and it is encouraging to note that discussion on this increasingly takes place at a pan-European level.

Until fairly recently there had been little interest or concern about comparability or harmonisation of services in different countries. The principle of subsidiarity has been dominant, with the European Union lacking competence in the family area. The situation is changing so that it is now appropriate to engage in greater European dialogue. The Single European Act has led to increased movement of families and children within the European Union, resulting in many new concerns. What happens, for instance, if a young person on a child protection register moves from one country to another? Is there, or should there be, any liaison between services internationally? Are there any procedures for monitoring the movement of adults known to have abused children? Can a family hope to receive a comparable service wherever they decide to live? These and other considerations need to be addressed in a frontier-free Europe.

Not only families but also child care professionals are now more likely to move around Europe during their working life. In this connection there have been various calls to consider the pedagogue model more seriously in the United Kingdom. There are good reasons for much greater harmonisation of professionalism in this and in other matters to do with children and families.

In summary, it is clear that children and families need to be on the European agenda not to draw up common European policies – the course of family life is very dependent on culture, history and ideology – but to ensure that all countries meet minimally acceptable standards of living for families wherever they live. Another goal is to facilitate the movement of professionals, children and families, a development which is particularly important as recent surveys of young people's attitudes have demonstrated their clear wish for closer ties with Europe.

References

Barbier, J.C. (1991) 'Comparing family policies in Europe: some methodological problems', in G. Kiely and V. Richardson (eds), *Family Policy: European Perspectives*, Dublin: Family Studies Centre, University College.

Cannan, C. (1992) *Changing Families Changing Welfare*, Hemel Hempstead: Harvester Wheatsheaf.

Cannan, C., L. Berry and K. Lyons (1992) *Social Work and Europe*, Basingstoke: Macmillan.

Children in Scotland/COFACE (forthcoming, 1995) *Out of School in the European Union: The contribution of schools, services and families to the care culture and recreation of primary school children out of school hours*, Dublin: Family Studies Centre, University College.

Cooper, A., V. Freund, A. Grevot, R. Hetherington and J. Pitts (1992) *The Social Work Role in Child Protection: An Anglo-French comparison. The report of a pilot study*, London: Centre for Comparative Social Work Studies, West London Institute and Association Jeunesse Culture Loisirs Technique.

Council of Europe (1990) *Proceedings of the Colloquy on Violence within the Family: Measures in the social field*, Strasbourg: Council of Europe.

Council of Europe (1992) *Recommendation No. R (92) Concerning the Medico-Social Aspects of Child Abuse and Explanatory Memorandum, European Health Committee, 32nd meeting, Strasbourg, 24–26 November*, Strasburg: Council of Europe.

David, T. (ed.) (1993) *Educational Provision for our Youngest Children: European perspectives*, London: Paul Chapman.

Eurobarometer (1991) *Lifestyles in the European Community*, Brussels: Commission of the European Communities.

European Commission (1994) *European Social Policy – A Way Forward for the Union*, Com (94) 33, 27.7.94, Brussels: Commission of the European Communities.

European Commission Childcare Network (1990) *Childcare in the European Community 1985–90: Women in Europe supplement No. 31*, Brussels: Commission of the European Communities.

European Observatory of National Family Policies (1992) *National Family Policies in EC-Countries*, Brussels: Commission of the European Communities.

Eurostat (1991) *A Social Portrait of Europe*, Brussels: Statistical Office of the European Communities.

Eurostat (1994a) *Demographic Statistics*, Brussels: Statistical Office of the European Communities.

Eurostat (1994b) *Social Protection in the European Union: Rapid report on population and social conditions*, Brussels: Statistical Office of the European Communities.

Foster, M.-C. (1988–9) 'The French puéricultrice', *Children and Society* 4, pp. 319–34.

Gartner, R. (1991) 'Family structure, welfare spending, and child homicide in developed democracies', *Journal of Marriage and the Family* 53, pp. 231–40.

Grazia, E. (1994) 'A tale of two villages', *Social Work in Europe* 1, 1, pp. 5–6.

Heaton, K. and J. Sayer (1992) *Community Development and Child Welfare: Community Development Briefing Paper, 4*, London: Children's Society/Community Development Foundation.

Hill, M. (ed.) (1991) *Social Work and the European Community: Research highlights in social work 23*, London: Jessica Kingsley.

Home Office, Department of Health, Department of Education and Science and Welsh Office (1991) *Working Together under the Children Act 1989: A guide to arrangements for inter-agency co-operation for the protection of children from abuse*, London: HMSO.

Jones, A. and K. Bilton (1994) *The Future Shape of Children's Services*, London: National Children's Bureau.

Jones, H.D. (1994) *Social Workers, or Social Educators? The international context for developing social care, paper no. 2*, London: National Institute of Social Work International Centre.

Josephson, J. (1994) 'Fulton: a pedagogical experiment', in M. Gottesman (ed.), *Recent Changes and New Trends in Extrafamilial Childcare: An international perspective*, Zurich: FICE.

Kent County Council Social Services (1993) 'Exchanges of childcare social workers with Pas de Calais', in *Information on Kent County Council's*

European Work with Nord/Pas de Calais, Maidstone: Kent County Council.

Lorenz, W. (1991) 'Social work practice in Europe: continuity in diversity', in M. Hill (ed.) *Social Work and the European Community: Research highlights in social work 23*, London: Jessica Kingsley.

Madge, N. (1994) *Children and Residential Care in Europe*, London: National Children's Bureau.

Munday, B. (ed.) (1993) *European Social Services*, Canterbury: European Institute of Social Services.

National Committee for Prevention of Child Abuse (1992) *World Perspectives on Child Abuse: An international resource book, prepared for the International Society for Prevention of Child Abuse and Neglect, with support from UNICEF*, Chicago: National Center on Child Abuse Prevention Research.

Pieterse, J.J. and H. van Urk (1989) 'Maltreatment of children in the Netherlands: an update after ten years', *Child Abuse and Neglect* 13, pp. 263–69.

Qvist, A. (1992) 'Husstands- og familiestatistik 1. januar 1992 (Household and family statistics on 1 January 1992)', *Befolkning og valg* 8, pp. 1–10.

Roll, J. (1992) *Lone Parents in the European Community*, London: European Family and Social Policy Unit, Family Policy Studies Centre.

Sale, A. and M. Davies (1990) *Child Protection Policies and Practice in Europe*, London: National Society for the Prevention of Cruelty to Children.

Smith, P. (1994) 'Culture, family and welfare: Italian perspectives', *Social Work in Europe* 1, 1, pp. 6–8.

Textor, M.R. (1990) 'Helping multi-problem families in West Germany: a new approach to social work', *Practice* 4, 1, pp. 56–62.

Vedel-Petersen, J. (1991) 'Families with young children: the situation in Denmark', in M. Hill (ed.), *Social Work and the European Community: Research highlights in social work 23*, London: Jessica Kingsley.

CHAPTER 6

People with disabilities

Vanessa Wilson

Introduction and context

According to published European Community research (1991) there are around 30 million individuals in the European Union with some form of physical or learning disability. All researchers and experts estimate a range of between 10 and 14 per cent amongst the adult population. Disabled people, whichever statistics are used, are therefore a very significant minority of the population of the countries of the European Union.

Moreover there is increasing concern amongst professionals about disability amongst older people. On no criteria do current estimates of the proportion of disabled people who are over sixty years of age fall below 70 per cent (Daunt 1991). This figure will continue to rise both because of the general rise in the proportion of the general population who are elderly people (and especially older elderly people) who may incur disability in association with ageing, and because of the increasing longevity of people with long-standing disabilities which are not age-related. The substantial increase in the disabled population because of a larger elderly population is unlikely to be compensated for by a reduction in disability amongst children. This is because medical advances in prevention and cure and treatment will be countered partly by the extent to which people who would have died in the past survive, but with a long-term disability. Thus for the policy-maker, the large and increasing number of people who are disabled is of particular importance for the provision of personal care services.

The term 'disabled' will be used in this chapter to refer to those people who have physical or intellectual impairments or long-term mental illness. The term is not universally used throughout Europe: some countries refer to impairment; others use the term 'disability' only where physical impairment is concerned and speak of 'handicapped' when referring to intellectual impairments. Some countries in Europe have no word which translates the English word 'disabled', for example France, using only the word *handicapé*. The selection of the term is used for two reasons: first, the terminology is based on the International Classification of Impairments, Disabilities and Handicaps (ICDH) of the World Health Organisation (WHO); and secondly, it is generally acceptable to disabled people themselves. It is acceptable because 'disability' is a relatively objective term, indicating loss of function resulting from an impairment of some kind, whereas handicap is the disadvantageous consequence of the interaction between the disability and an environment which has failed to respond or adapt to it. Since it is the aim of disability policies to reduce or, if possible, eliminate handicaps, being handicapped is merely a contingent state and it is incorrect to describe the long-term condition of someone experiencing the consequences of an impairment as that of being handicapped rather than disabled (Daunt 1991, p. 18).

It is now generally accepted that it is largely the society and environment in which people live which disable, not the particular impairment a disabled person has. Disabled people therefore reject the medical model of disability which concentrates on the impairment rather than environment. The emphasis should be on the steps, not the wheelchair.

Two further points need to be developed before launching into a discussion of services in Europe. First, the services provided for disabled people, under what we are here describing as social care, tend to cover a much wider spectrum of the life of the disabled person than services for other client groups. In this chapter issues ranging from employment and housing through to cash benefits will therefore be discussed in addition to the more ubiquitous services provided by social services agencies. In relation to disabled people, social services organisations have an inter-relationship with other departments which is more significant than in other aspects of their work.

The second point is that of the often controversial issues which surround the idea of services *for* people with disabilities. The very notion of 'services for' is rejected by many as perpetuating the passivity, dependency tradition in relation to disability. The relationship between social care organisations and people with disabilities has traditionally been one of service providers and service users. This is still the predominant relationship; however, changes are under way recognising the right of people with disabilities to have a voice in determining the content and method of delivery of services and in the assumptions that underpin the relationship. Many organisations of people with disabilities stress that emphasis should be placed on 'normalisation' not rehabilitation, competitive not sheltered employment, a social rather than medical model, all contributing to the goal of independent living. The philosophies of normalisation, competitive work and the social model emanate from different sources, and can be read about in more detail elsewhere (see Brown and Smith 1992; Finkelstein 1990; Grover and Gladstone 1981; Oliver 1990; Shakespeare 1992), but broadly speaking these state that disabled people have a right to live in an environment as close as possible to normal, exercising independence, having privacy and access to work and leisure pursuits in normal community settings, that is, independent living.

Confusion and disagreement about these philosophies and resulting services are paramount amongst professionals and disabled people themselves, but there is some common ground, including the value placed on independence rather than dependency, on individual-centred rather than service-led provision of support and care, and on maximising flexibility and choice. In terms of evaluating good practice, this common ground, as an absolute minimum, can be used as a guideline whilst taking into account the ultimate goal of independent living.

This chapter explains policies and practices of social services organisations throughout Europe in providing a wide variety of services for disabled people. The subject matter is placed in an historical context, followed by an examination of the major types of services provided across Europe. The chapter then considers the role of the European Union in this field, concluding with an evaluation and outline of future trends.

Historical context

The spread of industrialisation in the eighteenth and nineteenth centuries, followed by the continuous drive to more efficient production systems, seems to have operated progressively on disabled people by making them, as a social group, unemployable. Disabled people, therefore, suffered the more serious endless problem of unemployability rather than simple unemployment. Disability itself came to mean 'unable to work' and, as non-earners, disabled people were fundamentally identified as incapable as home-makers.

During the nineteenth and earlier part of the twentieth century the main lines of progress in responding to disability consisted of improvements in medical treatment and the creation of specialised institutions of education and residential care. A person with a serious disability of any kind was perceived as a patient. The task of the professional was to reduce the consequences of a tragic infliction as far as possible.

The large number of young disabled soldiers returning from the First World War led to a new sense of responsibility in Europe to find means for reconciling disablement with the chance of an active and productive life; hence the creation of special workshops, reserved occupations and reserved places on public transport. The situation after the Second World War was somewhat different, but the effects on the perception of disability and the services needed to respond to it were even more striking. There were relatively fewer disabled veterans, but the economic situation, so far from being one of imminent depression, promised a prolonged boom with a consequent severe shortage of labour.

This market-driven impulse to find a means of employing disabled people previously supposed to be unemployable was reinforced by two other factors: the notion of a welfare state and the growth of independent organisations working with people with learning disabilities. In the 1940s, 1950s and 1960s there was dramatic legislative development in Europe aimed at promoting the training and employment of disabled people:

1944: UK – Disabled Persons (Employment) Act.
1947: Netherlands – placement of less able-bodied workers.
1957: France – vocational and social rehabilitation.

1959:   Luxembourg – retraining and placement.
1963:   Belgium – social resettlement.
1968:   Italy – obligatory employment of disabled persons.

The notion that there should be positive action for the employment of disabled people was firmly established almost throughout western Europe by the late 1960s, mainly because of the economic boom. This initiative did not, however, go far enough to meet the demands for equal opportunities in society. This would require a recognition of the right of disabled people, however severe their functional loss, to the same life chances as everyone else.

Movements *of* disabled people, rather than *for* disabled people, began to spring up across the world, first in America but rapidly replicated in Europe. The principle aim of this movement was independent living, as opposed to rehabilitation with all its paternalistic associations. Instead of being an irremediable misfortune calling for charity, handicap had to be seen as an intolerable injustice which could be eliminated. The founders of the independent living movement based their political demands on the provision of effective services, and gained considerable support coming, serendipitously, with a growing drive from professionals to close down long-stay institutions.

Founded in 1964, the GIHP (Groupment pour l'Insertion des Personnes Handicappées Physiques) in Nancy, France, developed into one of the most dynamic organisations run by and for disabled people in Europe, its political demands based on effective service provision. In Italy in the 1960s, inspired by the idea of Professor Basaglia in Trieste, a nationwide movement took place to close the psychiatric hospitals and integrate their former patients, people with learning disabilities and those with mental health problems, as fully recognised citizens in the open community. This initiative was paralleled by innovation in schools aiming at the integration of children with disabilities into the normal education system.

The education initiatives were mirrored in Scandinavia. In 1969 the Danish parliament recommended educational mainstreaming. There was also a trend to enable children with moderate or severe learning disabilities to participate in the education system. The United Kingdom in 1970 followed this trend with the publishing of the Warnock report, which also recommended educational integration of those with physical and learning disabilities.

In the 1970s the European Community's first initiatives for disabled people were established. The European Social Fund, the Community's largest programme for combating unemployment, was divided in such a way that for a number of years 10 per cent of funds were devoted to the vocational rehabilitation of disabled people. In 1975 the European Commission launched a scheme to support housing projects for disabled people and presented a report on architectural barriers to mobility. The European Community also funded research activities relating to technical aids and medical research.

Although there was no European Community legislation, the principle was established that the Community could be active in a field such as housing as well as in the more strictly vocational areas. Major interventions of the European Social Fund were having a dramatic impact, particularly in Italy and Ireland. Any ambiguity about concern for those with learning as well as physical disability had been eliminated.

The year 1981 was the United Nations' International Year of Disabled People and, although many were critical of its organisation and effectiveness, it had a big impact on attitudes to disabled people and was an inspiration to disabled people themselves, leading to an awareness of each other. The European Community's first action programme for disabled people, HELIOS (Handicapped People in the European Community Living Independently in an Open Society), 1982–7, was now about integration not rehabilitation.

Policies and services in Europe today

The most striking conclusion to be drawn from research into the policies and practices of social services for disabled people throughout Europe is the degree of commonality which exists. Whilst in many respects individual European countries differ from each other in the details and emphases of their disability policies and provision, when set against non-European countries uniformity is more apparent than diversity.

The current trends are also very similar: deinstitutionalisation leading to increased emphasis on living in the community; decentralisation of administration of services; a mixed economy of

care; debate about the need for the provision of integrated services; and the debate about the rights of disabled people and their
control over the services provided for them. These trends are pre-
valent virtually throughout Europe.

There are of course differences, in the legislative base for action
and in the nature of some of the services, and there are many
examples of good practice in individual areas which could be more
widely adopted. This section of the chapter will look at the similarities and differences and highlight some of the 'good practice'.
For the purposes of this chapter good practice refers to that which
is innovatory or different and for which there is some evidence of
success in meeting the needs of disabled people, that is, moving
towards the goal of independent living.

The most distinctive feature of social service provision for disabled people is the wide range of services provided and this range
varies from country to country. Some have a wider remit than
others but in general any or all of the following may be directly
provided by social services, or have a direct bearing on the responsibility borne by social services: day care and residential services,
employment and vocational training, transport, education, housing
and financial benefits.

This section of the chapter first gives a selective overview of the
legislative, policy and organisational background which determines the provision of services for disabled people on a country-
by-country basis, and then looks at the specific services provided.
It does not attempt to be comprehensive but aims to pick out the
most interesting or peculiar features.

Legislative and policy background

Belgium (French community)

There are some social services in the public sector but most provision, with state funding, is private or voluntary. The range of services provided includes boarding schools, centres of observation
and guidance, family placement agencies (fostering) and day centres. Early help operated without a legal framework for several
years but has now been formalised by a decree in 1990. From birth
to age six social and psychological support is provided for parents,

and educational help for children; a multidisciplinary team takes responsibility for assessment.

Belgium (Flemish community)

A minimum income is guaranteed for disabled people. In 1990 legislation was passed establishing a fund for the social integration of disabled people. It established for the first time an integrated package of assistance which can include both funding for organisations involved with the integration of disabled people and financial benefits to individuals for the purchase of assistance.

Denmark

The main aim of current Danish social policy is to ensure a satisfactory standard of living for disabled people. Counties and municipalities are obliged to provide the necessary support to physically disabled people in the form of guidance, education, training, stays in institutions and so on, and if necessary economic support. Disabled children are educated mainly in mainstream schools. There is a national institution for basic vocational training. Means-tested financial assistance is offered to the families of disabled children and to disabled adults living at home.

France

Disabled people and their families are exempted from the responsibility of paying for all services. Services are provided free to children, and adults make a contribution according to their means. For adults, entitlement to allowances and services is through assessment of the degree of disability by a multidisciplinary team.

Many feared that the division of funding and responsibility between state and *département* following decentralisation would hinder the development of a co-ordinated service and perpetuate investment in outdated segregative provisions. These possibilities have been tempered by the general contracting out of provision to not-for-profit associations. For example, the association La Vie Active, centred in Arras, has 100 employees of the state and the *département* seconded to it, and manages establishments for children, including specialised *clubs de prevention* to provide day relief to parents. For adults it has sheltered workshops, a training centre, a service for placing people in work, guardianship, holidays and residential facilities. It has a membership of 3,700 organised into seventeen clubs, and more than 750 employees. Its field of activity spans the health, educational, social security, employment and social services sectors (Ely and Saunders 1993).

Greece

The Greek Red Cross and Orthodox Church are significant in the provision of services but it is the responsibility of the state to take special measures to protect individuals with special needs. Allowances are paid which aim to assist with independent living or life within the family, primarily to prevent the need for permanent stay in a residential institution. Assistance is not universally available to all disabled people but is dependent on official recognition of the disability, categories of individuals who are granted financial assistance are specified in precise detail in Article 21 of the constitution of 1975, with very rigid categories.

Germany

At the end of June 1994 the German constitution was changed to include disabled people as a sub-section in the equal protection clause. 'Nobody shall be discriminated against because of a disability' has been added to paragraph 3 of the constitution. Legislation to enact this new clause in the constitution must certainly follow. This makes Germany the only European country to have such anti-discrimination legislation, but it remains to be seen what effect this will have on provision of services.

The aim of assistance for disabled people is avoidance of marginalisation from society, to support rehabilitation and to expedite re-integration. Besides early diagnosis of disabilities, the primary goal is to enable people with disabilities to participate in community life. The measures employed for this purpose address vocational education, work, living conditions, leisure, and mobility. Only medical and vocational rehabilitation are explicitly regulated by law. Social assistance is the provider of 'last resort'. In law there is no difference between the causes of disability, only the effects.

Ireland

Current services include domiciliary care, principally home nursing and home helps. Care attendants – a new service – provide relief for relatives at times they identify as essential, and family support through short-term alternative family care, that is, respite care. Day care is underdeveloped, with few satisfactory services, and is not particularly widespread. Support services, including social work, are only available through voluntary organisations and are dependent upon geographical area and type of disability.

Because of concern about the paucity and inconsistency of services, the Irish government established a Commission in November 1993 on the status of people with disabilities. Its terms of reference are as follows:

1. To advise the government on practical measures necessary to ensure that people with a disability can exercise their rights to participate, to the fullest extent of their potential, in economic, social and cultural life.
2. To examine the current situation of disabled people and the organisation and adequacy of all types of existing services to meet those needs.
3. To make recommendations setting out necessary changes, in legislation, policies, organisation, practices and structures to ensure that the needs of people with disabilities are met in a cohesive, comprehensive and cost-effective way.
4. To establish the estimated costs of all recommendations made.
5. To report to the government within two years.

Italy

Public intervention for the care of people with disabilities, although structured and based on contemporary principles, is afflicted by unsystematic growth which has often occurred under the pressure of demands from the different categories of disabled people, creating a lack of uniformity and consequent shortcomings.

A minimum level of financial aid is guaranteed by the state. Action is aimed at providing support for the disabled person and their family to meet basic needs; however, there is also a significant undertaking to promote and achieve conditions which favour the social integration and wider participation of the disabled person in the life of their own community. Thus there has been a spread of initiatives for integration in schools and access to work as well as action to create special services or socio-recreational activities and to facilitate access to sports and cultural activities.

Social services are in principle available to everyone and not just those on low incomes. In practice, priority is given to the 0–18 age group especially for the use of social centres, rehabilitation services, home helps and some residential services, on the assumption that situations tackled early enough have a better chance of evolving in a positive direction.

A personal care attendance allowance is available, as is enhanced social assistance. A quota of state-subsidised public housing is reserved for disabled people. Educational integration has been achieved to a great extent, as has vocational integration, except for those with learning disabilities. There are a few sheltered workshops or placements. Training and rehabilitation vary according to region.

Luxembourg

The main services are provided by private and voluntary bodies, with local administrations playing very little part in service provision. Public financial support comes largely at state level. The position of disabled people was clarified in law in 1960 which created the National Solidarity Fund. Its main purpose is to ensure that the elderly and those deemed unable to work should have sufficient means to avoid them being in need. This is a very basic policy with no mention of integration at all.

Netherlands

Sociale Vernieuwing (restructuring) was launched with the change of government in 1989. This social restructuring aims at re-integration and reactivation of those disadvantaged because of disability or other circumstances. This social restructuring policy was introduced at the same time as lower levels of funding and government decentralisation. There are three planks to this policy: training and education, the environment and the accessibility of social provisions. Decentralisation has given municipalities the freedom to operate independently once their plans have been approved, with increasingly marked differences in the provision of services across the country.

The policy aims at the integration, emancipation and independence of disabled people. Part of the policy is to encourage organisations with a remit to provide services for the community as a whole to pay attention to special groups. In general no distinction is made between different forms of disability. Employment quotas vary from 3 to 7 per cent but are much lower in practice, there being little enforcement. Educational integration is well advanced. Vocational training and rehabilitation centres are mainly run by local authorities, emphasising new technology. Disabled people are entitled to a personal attendant allowance.

There is partial non-discrimination legislation. Far-reaching draft legislation on the empowerment and extension of disabled people's rights was formulated in the early 1980s and this continues to be a major focus of debate, although the government has not addressed the issue for some time.

Portugal

The policy aim is to provide services and professional advice to support disabled people and their families. The services provided include early technical support, home helps, socio-educational centres, occupational support centres and residential care.

Spain

Care for disabled people is shared by social services with health, education, labour protection, housing, social policy, town planning and transport. There is a complex system of finance, aids and services in health, education, labour and social services. The existence of a network of specialist first-stage services for disabled people is a key provision. The services include a range of diagnosis/evaluation and functional and vocational rehabilitation functions. Home help and advice on the management of financial benefits are also provided.

United Kingdom

The most recent legislation of 1986, which placed statutory duties on local authorities in respect of services, representation and consultation, has not been fully implemented, due to lack of funding. Services are still largely governed by 1948 and 1970 legislation and the 1990 NHS and Community Care Act.

Local authorities must provide advice on what services are available, on how to overcome some aspects of disability, on workshop provision, on work which can be done at home and on recreation facilities. They must also compile a register.

The 1970 Act requires local authorities to inform themselves of the number of disabled people in their area, to publish information on services available and to ensure disabled people are informed of relevant services. Section 2 requires local authorities to provide a number of services, for example, practical assistance in the home, television and radio, assistance with taking holidays, provision of a telephone and assistance in arranging any works or adaptations in the home such as a lift or bath rail. Implementation varies considerably.

Most local authorities provide day centres, transport to and from day centres, dial-a-ride or taxis, occupational therapists, grants to or, increasingly, contracts with voluntary organisations to provide services, long-term care purchased in voluntary or private sector residential care homes, home helps, skills assessment and vocational training.

Scotland has a different legislative base, contained in Section 12 of the Social Work (Scotland) Act 1968, which places a duty on social work departments to promote social welfare in the community through the provision of assistance in cash or in kind for persons in need. This places them in a unique position to provide flexible and imaginative support. Some local authorities provide home-makers who can support a person with learning disabilities living in their own home; they may help with budgeting, shopping and other aspects of home-making.

The civil rights bill, which was presented to the UK parliament in April 1994, aimed to give Britain's 6.5 million disabled people equal rights of access to work, transport, education and public buildings. The government rejected the bill on the grounds of potential cost to employers. In November 1994 the government did, however, announce its intention to introduce a bill to tackle discrimination against disabled people in employment and in access to goods and services, and to establish a National Disability Council.

Day care and residential services

Provision for people with physical and/or mental disabilities is most likely to be made through domiciliary, day care or residential services provided by agencies in the voluntary sector who are subsidised by the state. In the Netherlands current concern about the large number of disabled people dependent on state benefits is resulting in attempts to integrate more disabled people into paid employment in the public and private sectors. A recent trend towards putting increased resources into domiciliary care indicates a move away from a well-established tradition of residential care for disabled people. This provision has often been of a high standard, but on an immense scale (up to 1,000 residents and catering for a wide age range, from five to eighty years), although again recent policy changes suggest a reduction in scale, perhaps to homes for 200 people. It is also recognised that a move to care in the community will lead to an increase in demand for sheltered workshops, and may lead to less availability in specialist equipment and social work expertise.

In Denmark concerns over the loss of specialist resources and expertise which can be found in large-scale organisations occurred in 1988, when services for people with disabilities were devolved from fourteen regional authorities to 275 local authorities, who now sometimes subcontract responsibility for these provisions to the voluntary or private sectors.

In both Dutch and German provisions age and disability groups are mixed. In Germany such centres are run on a regional basis by the National Association for Disabled People for a potential population of 1.5 million. While this is not one of the Big Six voluntary organisations, it does receive some state funding as well as drawing on parental contributions and fund-raising. A typical centre is staffed on an interdisciplinary basis.

Virtually all countries in Europe regard the use of residential care as a last resort, at least in principle, when there is no family support and no possibility of some form of independence. In Italy a reorganisation of residential provision is under way which focuses on residence communities and family-type homes. In Belgium home guidance services provide help to families. When parents are no longer able to look after their child the service provides the required aid and advice to try to avoid a crisis admission. In France in 1989 a law was passed permitting funding for individuals who could provide accommodation for elderly or disabled people in their own homes. This does not apply to relatives and has a number of limitations, but it may allow disabled individuals to stay in their home towns rather than move to an institution in an unfamiliar area.

Employment and vocational training

Paid work is seen by disabled people and their campaigners as one of the chief components of equal opportunity. A 1993 EC survey (Eurostat 1993) shows that in 1988 only 13 per cent of German disabled people were unemployed, while there were 16 per cent in France, 25 per cent in Spain and a high 30 per cent in the United Kingdom. The British quota system was also shown by the research to be less successful than similar schemes in other EC countries.

Most European countries have some form of employment quota system. These vary not only in their effectiveness but also in their application, enforcement and take-up. Italy, the United Kingdom, the Netherlands and Belgium have quota systems which are not enforced, others, like France and Germany, have quota systems but offer employers the opportunity to pay contributions or fines in lieu of filling their quotas.

In Germany the 'equalisation' quota system is relatively successful. All employers with a workforce of fifteen or more are obliged to employ 6 per cent (the figure actually achieved is around 5 per cent) of severely disabled people on a penalty of approximately £50 per month for each place unfilled. The funds collected are spent exclusively on practical action to promote and support the employment of disabled people. The system has recently been reviewed and updated.

In France, once assessed by COTOREP (Commission Technique d'Orientation et de Reclassement Professionel), the disabled worker counts against a quota for employers established by a law of 1987 called the *loi Seguin*, which sets a target for 1992 of 6 per cent of disabled workers in each enterprise. Employers unable to fill this quota pay a levy to AGEFIPH (Association National de Gestion du Fonds pour l'Insertion Professionelle des Handicappés), which in turn funds its regional offices providing advice to disabled potential workers and acting as a catalyst motivating employers to think about how they could widen employment opportunities in their firms. For example, an agreement was signed between AGEFIPH and the *préfet* of the Ile-de-France region in 1990 with the aim of creating 2,000 jobs for disabled people in two years. Each *département* set up an employment team and made agreements with various state, departmental, not-for-profit and business organisations for training, employment and follow-up support. By the end of the first year, of 10,000 referrals, 6,000 received specific advice, 3,200 obtained places at pre-employment centres, 1,800 found employment and a further 1,000 were placed on training courses for a full skills assessment (Ely and Saunders 1993). AGIFIPH's own estimate is that since the *loi Seguin* came into operation, some 55,000–60,000 disabled people have directly benefited, over one quarter of those seeking employment (*ibid*).

Portugal and Denmark have no quotas. In Denmark in the context of employment policy there is no definition of 'disabled'. All who need help including the disadvantaged are considered together. There is an effective disability lobby which campaigns against quotas and instead calls for positive discrimination in terms of access to jobs.

In France, for those in employment there is a minimum wage irrespective of output. In Germany a recent measure enables disabled people to take up employment without economic risk, benefits are only proportionally decreased and reinstated immediately if the employment does not work out.

In many centres of vocational training the value and quality of training have been enhanced by its setting in a wider context of operations including education, medical and community services.

National networks also enhance quality. These exist in Spain, Italy and Germany. In Greece the development of special education and special vocational training is relatively recent and is 55 per cent subsidised by the European Social Fund. In Portugal, occupational support centres, which aim at creating the conditions to enable clients to carry out socially useful occupational activities, also operate in individual homes where mobility is a problem.

Sheltered workshops exist in all countries except Greece, Italy and Portugal. Commonly they operate as competitive enterprises but also receive government subsidy. In the United Kingdom and Ireland there are single organisations. In the Netherlands, sheltered workshops are open to disadvantaged as well as disabled people.

Innovatory structures also exist. In an EC study of 1988 (Seyfried and Lambert 1988) which studied semi-sheltered forms of employment and analysed landmark measures in the member states of the European Community, it was found that small groups of disabled people working together within normal enterprises – the enclave model of competitive employment – had some success but that there was a danger of perpetuating 'ghettoisation'. Sheltered posts for individuals were considered to be a better option, this being well developed in Denmark particularly.

In Italy the Co-operation movement, which involves the participation (including decision-making) of non-disabled and disabled people together in mixed co-operatives, is provided for by law. Co-operatives have also been established in the United Kingdom, Germany, the Netherlands and Ireland, although they do not all contain mixed ability communities. An example of a successful mixed enterprise outside Italy is the Goodwill project in Glasgow.

In France, Spain and Luxembourg there are specially designed enterprises operating on the open market mostly run by voluntary organisations, sometimes with vocational training playing a part. These are neither sheltered workshops nor co-operatives but include disabled and non-disabled people. This is called the 'work crew model of supported competitive employment'. A good example exists in Montpelier, France, where 60 per cent of the employees are disabled, the work consisting of office cleaning, the maintenance of buildings and the upkeep of parks and open spaces. The large Promi Centre in Spain and the Rehabilitation Centre at Capellen in Luxembourg include programmes for integrated housing in addition to employment.

There are other positive measures to promote employment and training for disabled people. In Belgium there is a remarkable strategy for financing employment and training for disabled people, with quite considerable funds accumulated by a small premium on motor insurance, paid by every Belgian driver. The fund gives direct support to individuals, employers and training and rehabilitation centres. In Spain, France and the United Kingdom there are incentives to employers in the form of grants for technical adaptations and training for disabled people.

Special mention should be made of ONCE, the national organisation of Spanish blind people. It is a voluntary association, but is statutorily empowered with public functions. It has a licence to operate the national lottery as its main financial resource. Selling tickets guarantees employment for many blind people and benefits from the lottery pay for social and other services for blind people.

Too much emphasis should not be placed on employment and training policies and projects because it is not clear that this is a realistic option for all disabled people. Those with the greatest difficulties could be even more downgraded and marginalised if there is too much concentration on this aspect.

Special transport services

In Denmark the only initiatives are in the public sector. The most developed services are in Copenhagen, with door-to-door services run by the city's transport company on behalf of the department of health and social welfare. In Belgium – in Brussels only – a similar very popular scheme is in operation but because of cost is constantly under threat of closure.

In the Netherlands there are many diverse services. An initiative of particular interest has been a research and development pilot programme launched by central government in the province of Groningen, aimed at extending a special service for disabled children to include all disabled people in all municipalities.

In Germany services are numerous, in both the public and the voluntary sectors, in many cases offered without charge. The most celebrated is the Telebus service of West Berlin, originally launched with substantial federal support and now the responsibility of the local social services department. The service, possibly the most highly developed in Europe, operates for twenty-four hours a day every day of the year. The research on which it has been established offers valuable evidence about the needs and wishes of disabled people. In the United Kingdom local authorities fund schemes such as dial-a-ride in London, but provision throughout the country is patchy.

Special transport services throughout Europe have proved their worth, but consumer-friendliness appears to vary considerably. Requirements to make arrangements twenty-four hours in advance and restrictions as to geographical limit, frequency or purpose of personal journeys are quite often encountered and naturally unpopular. Not all services operate at weekends or on public holidays, or during unsocial hours. Restriction of use to local members is also common and, though understandable, evidently not compatible with the longer-term mobility aspirations of disabled people. Standards of management in terms of cost-effectiveness are also somewhat variable.

Many European countries also offer assistance with privately owned vehicles, though there is considerable variation in the quality and range of provision. In Belgium, Germany, Ireland and Italy financial help is virtually restricted to those who need a vehicle for the purposes of work or training. In Denmark and Luxembourg this restriction does not apply. In both Denmark and the Netherlands provision of grant aid is made by local authorities and workers' welfare organisations respectively. In Greece certain categories of disabled people (those with particular physical needs) are entitled to import cars without paying taxes and some severely disabled people are also granted a monthly allowance for fuel. In the United Kingdom the existence of the mobility allowance puts disabled people who receive it in an exceptional position of choice.

Housing

Many of the most useful projects have concerned the provision of urban apartments fully adapted for people with severe physical disabilities. One of the first of these to be supported by the European Commission was a project to establish fifteen new and fifty-seven adapted dwellings in the new town of Evry on the outskirts of Paris. Of the Belgian projects, the most celebrated is perhaps the Cité de l'Amitié, where some 15 per cent of apartments in a large development were designed for physically disabled people. The Association Nationale pour le Logement des Handicappés (ANLH, national association for the housing of disabled people), responsible for the project, was one of the pioneers too of the principle of 'care without institutionalisation', by providing for assistance in the home.

The problem of the link between the provision of the domestic assistance needed on the one hand and the possibility of living independently in adapted housing on the other was studied in 1988 by a member of the HELIOS experts team, Mary Kyriasopoulou. She undertook an analysis of three approaches in different member states. The first was Crossroads Care, a British voluntary organisation which employs 1,300 staff and volunteers bringing care to some 11,000 people each year in 132 projects. The scheme is also being taken up in the Netherlands. One of its main merits is the flexibility with which it meets the needs of disabled people and their carers for regular, occasional or emergency care provision. Two other systems studied were Fokus in the Netherlands (originating in Sweden) and the 'individual assistance' method widespread in Denmark. The disadvantage for Fokus clients is that they have to be grouped together in designated accommodation, whereas those benefiting from the Danish scheme can live in any accessible accommodation they choose. The so-called '48.3' scheme in Denmark, initiated in Aarhus, offers an exceptionally well-funded and flexible system which enables disabled people committed to an active and independent life to employ their own assistants for as many hours as has been agreed with the local authority. Yet there is a very considerable difference of cost, estimates of 72 ecus in Fokus and 175 ecus in Denmark (Daunt 1991). The Danish Handicap Association tries to find appropriate habitation for seriously disabled people through the Disabled People's Building Society, working for the establishment of housing specially designed for motor handicapped people.

The needs of people with learning disabilities should not be forgotten in this context. The philosophy of 'democratic psychiatry' in Italy has led to centres such as Trieste and Rieti facing the consequences of deinstitutionalisation with the provision of housing projects and domestic support. In Ireland too important use has been made of a scheme providing small-scale supported housing for people with learning disabilities, and a scheme of adapted housing linked to new communal facilities has been launched.

Education

Educational integration is very much on the agenda in most European countries, with a variety of approaches to the issue. A radical approach in Italy and Denmark, a gradualist approach in France and the United Kingdom, a cautious approach in Germany and the Netherlands, and an innovatory approach in Spain.

In Italy there was no history of special-needs education so the move to integration, at the same time as deinstitutionalisation, was relatively easy with no system to dismantle. Italy also has small class sizes because teachers are in protected employment and school numbers are declining. Full integration was achieved in 1971. A new innovation is local support centres for disabled children. In Denmark in 1984, 88 per cent of disabled children were fully integrated in normal classes, 6.2 per cent in special classes and only 5.7 per cent in separate provision (Daunt 1991). They have good staffing levels and teachers who tend to be with the children throughout their education.

In France emphasis on the educational need of each child leads to the principle that flexibility of provision, including separate education for a lesser or greater period of the child's education, is paramount. This view is promoted by the health sector in France, which is very powerful in influencing policy as well as programmes for individual children. In the United Kingdom the Warnock report and subsequent legislation created a good base for integration but the subsequent implementation of a national curriculum and removal of autonomy from local authorities to schools themselves mean that development is patchy and not the subject of much educational focus. In Germany and the Netherlands elaborate special school systems have been developed and there is no national impetus to change this structure, although there are local examples of integration, particularly in former West Germany.

Spain has recently launched an eight-year programme to integrate disabled children into mainstream education. This programme aims to have 50 per cent of all schools providing integrated education in eight years. The choice of schools to become integrated will be arranged so that there will be at least one for each geographical area each year. The plan is accompanied by provision for early intervention, teacher training, the operation of multidisciplinary teams, the adaptation of the curriculum and information initiatives for parents and teachers.

Social protection

All European countries pay some kind of cash benefits to disabled people, although systems are diverse and frequently amended. Benefits are a contentious issue for governments and disabled people alike. In some of the wealthier European nations benefits are considered to be so generous as to militate against a disabled person seeking work. In Germany, particularly, this problem has recently been addressed (see below). The more vocal disabled groups claim that the goal of increased control over their own lives can be achieved if they are in receipt of sufficient financial benefits to purchase their own care and assistance. Passively receiving such help from social services does not contribute to independence. Governments have reacted in different ways to these issues. Germany has recently introduced legislation which allows a disabled person to keep their benefits in the early days of new employment, having them reduced only proportionately as the employment continues, with a right to full re-instatement if the employment fails. Countries such as Denmark, France, Germany and Scotland offer care allowances to disabled people in order that they may purchase their domestic assistance independently of social services, but there are also a full range of services on offer. In other European countries disabled people receive whatever assistance is available from social services without any element of choice.

Benefits are bestowed in a variety of ways throughout Europe. In Germany and Belgium benefits take the form of minimum income and are unrelated to the type of disability or its cause. In France benefits depend on whether the disabled person has formerly worked. If so, higher benefits are received; for the disabled person who has not worked benefit is roughly equal to the retirement pension. In Italy the cause of disability determines the level of benefit paid, legislation distinguishes between war-disabled, service-disabled, industrially disabled, the blind, the deaf and the civilian disabled.

Additional benefits and loans beyond the minimum are also payable in some countries. Greece provides loans to pay for housing or holidays. Countries including France and Greece offer income tax exemptions for the employed disabled person.

The European Union

European Community plans and programmes to help disabled people play a full and satisfying part in the European Community started in a small way in 1981 and have been strengthened in recent years by the increasing importance attached to the social conditions for all workers. The European Union currently spends in the region of £56 billion a year on programmes specifically designed for disabled people.

In 1988 the European Commission presented a report on the application of its recommendation on the employment of disabled people in the Community. Having considered the report, the Council stressed the importance of programmes, both at national and Community level, which promote the integration of people with disabilities into the labour market. The Council invited the Commission to develop measures which would highlight the difficulties facing disabled people in relation to employment and proposed employment measures to ensure better co-ordination and consistency between member states.

The European Community's 'Community Charter of the Fundamental Social Rights of Workers', adopted in December 1989, had this to say about disabled people:

> disabled people, whatever the origin and nature of their disablement, must be entitled to additional concrete measures aimed at improving their social and professional integration. . . . These measures must concern, in particular, according to the capacities of the beneficiaries, vocational training, ergonomics, accessibility, mobility, means of transport and housing. (1990, p. 19)

A further communication from the European Commission (1992) concerning the action programme designed to implement the Charter stated:

> The social and economic integration of disabled people is an important element of the social dimension of the single market. It is

not only a question of social justice. It is an economic issue in so far as their economic integration in a regular working environment may often represent an asset for the Community. (p. 53)

The Social Action Programme, which aimed to implement the Charter, in fact contained only one, minor, proposal for legislative action specifically aimed at disabled people. This is the 'Directive on the introduction of measures aimed at promoting an improvement in the travel conditions of workers with motor disabilities'. The draft directive was published in 1991. To date, there has been little progress towards agreement or implementation by the Community.

HELIOS is the oldest of European Community programmes addressing the concerns of the disabled. HELIOS was a new step towards integration and independent living for disabled people in the European Community. The first action programme, running from 1984 to 1987, had as its objective 'to provide a pragmatic response to the growing needs and new aspirations of disabled people with a view to the promotion of social and economic integration and independent living' (Social Europe Supplement 1986).

HELIOS I and now HELIOS II seek to promote integration broadly by the dissemination of good practice between the member states. HELIOS II involves 676 disability organisations across the twelve EU member states participating in this programme which runs until December 1996. The HELIOS II programme is divided into four sectors: social integration and independent living, functional rehabilitation and economic integration, vocational training and employment rehabilitation, and educational integration. Funding is intended to cover the selected projects' expenditure on conferences, study visits, group visits and training sessions that the participants arrange between themselves.

HANDYNET, which is part of the HELIOS programme, is a specialised, computerised information system which aims to make available tens of thousands of items of information to disabled people and rehabilitation professionals. This information relates to technical aids, the manufacturers and distributors of these products in Europe, and the national procedures and regulations which disabled people should follow to obtain these aids. The information is compiled in a data bank in nine languages and supplied on CD ROM, which is accessible in the centres designated by the twelve member states.

Organisations representing disabled people are less than impressed by the work of HELIOS: very small amounts of money are available; the team of 'experts' which run HELIOS does not contain any disabled people amongst its members; and HELIOS II has been called a 'tired version of HELIOS I' (Disabled Persons International 1994). HANDYNET has been a disappointment to those seeking to use it; the information is not particularly comprehensive or useful in the view of many; there seems to be no clear view of who the information is for and therefore presentation and content are rather muddled.

HORIZON was adopted in 1990, as part of the European Social Fund set up to help member states combat unemployment and regenerate areas of industrial and rural decline. The central aim of HORIZON was to transfer expertise between member states through transnational projects which seek to improve access to the labour market for people with disabilities and those who are disadvantaged. It has now finished and the Council of Ministers is currently considering its successor. HORIZON was a programme taken up by many social services organisations throughout Europe. It increased contact between member states' organisations and brought very useful additional income for innovative projects. The criticism most often made by those running such programmes is that the emphasis is always on innovation and that once a project has started, no matter how successful, when HORIZON money runs out there is no further EC or national/local money to be had to keep a project going.

Two further EC programmes relate to disabled people: TIDE, a new technology initiative for disabled and elderly people, and EUCREA, which aims to stimulate artistic and creative projects involving people with disabilities.

In 1993 the European Commission published its Green Paper on social policy. The paper highlights concerns about disabled people particularly in relation to high unemployment and consequent 'social exclusion'. The views of at least one organisation of disabled people, the Disabled Persons International (DPI), are, however, that the paper is disappointing, noting that there are few references to disabled people in the document when compared with the sections on women and the elderly, which are much longer and more specific. The DPI also takes exception to the language referring to disabled people, stating that much of it 'is offensive and reflects the general view held by able-bodied people that disabled people "suffer" from impairments when the reality is that they "suffer" from the discrimination of negative attitudes, segregating policies, and environmental barriers' (Disabled Persons International 1994).

The follow-up to the Green Paper, 'European Social Policy – a Way Forward for the Union – a White Paper', published in July 1994, recognises that 'as a group, people with disabilities undoubtedly face a wide range of obstacles which prevent them from achieving full economic and social integration. There is therefore a need to build the fundamental right to equal opportunities into Union policies' (Flynn 1994). Most importantly, the paper states that at the next opportunity to revise the treaties of the European Union 'serious consideration must be given to the introduction of a specific reference to combatting discrimination on the grounds of race, religion, age and disability' (Flynn 1994). It also presents a number of concrete proposals, including adoption of the UN Standard Rules on the Equalisation of Opportunities for People with Disabilities and disability equality training for Commission staff. Interestingly, a draft of the White Paper distributed to members of the European Parliament's Social Affairs Committee only a few days prior to publication had some much stronger proposals, including the statement that 'an explicit commitment to equal rights for disabled people should be included in the Treaty' and 'explicit powers should be introduced to combat discrimination' (Disabled Persons International 1994). Thus the final proposals are a somewhat weaker version, serious consideration rather than explicit commitments.

In December 1993 the first European Day of Disabled People was held, the initiative coming from the HELIOS forum. The aim was to draw the attention of the Community institutions, national authorities and general public to the work still needed to achieve the full integration of disabled people; it focused specifically on human rights. The European Parliament was taken over by a European disabled people's parliament for the day and a resolution was passed on disability as a human rights issue, including equal opportunities, discrimination and the right to consultation on issues affecting them.

The present European policy on rehabilitation and social integration is based on the individual or medical model of disability and does not provide a comprehensive framework for non-discriminatory practices. Disabled groups would like to see this replaced by a policy of human rights for disabled people. The special department that now runs HELIOS could have a far wider remit and act as a focal point for monitoring all EC policy and departments to ensure that disabled people's rights are included in everything that directly affects disabled people, and ensure that disabled people are employed within the Commission.

Conclusion

A number of trends and issues have surfaced repeatedly in this rather whirlwind description of social care for disabled people in Europe: the increasing disabled elderly population, care in the community, integration of services and control over services are clearly paramount.

The proportion of the population disabled in some way is likely to increase significantly with the growing elderly population. Estimates for increasing numbers are striking, but the implications are greatly aggravated by qualitative factors. The increasing longevity resulting from improvements in medical care, diet and housing has already created demands for care and support which cannot be adequately met either in institutions or in the open community; many of these demands are specific to disability. What is more, the problems are not only increasing in number – this is widely understood and accepted – but also in severity, owing to the accumulation and deterioration of disabling conditions.

Western culture since the war has tended to favour the manifestations of growth, success, youthfulness, activity and speed. It is often complacently assumed that the elderly and disabled people in general do not have the same range of needs as others and are therefore, or should be, content with restricted opportunities and facilities. The persistence of a traditional concentration on exclusively medical models can widen the gap between the theory and practice of independent living. The mere size of the problem, with its menace of increasing demand on resources, means that it is a convenient one to put aside in the hope that it might somehow go away. Ageing itself is a big enough problem without the aggravation of disability superimposed.

The effect of this trend of increasing numbers of disabled people in a context of determined policies in all European member states to reduce or close long-stay institutions has been to increase the extent to which authorities are looking to the 'informal carers' – that is, above all families – to save the situation. Yet this is only to shift responsibility from one scene of crisis to another. People with disabilities which in the past would have rarely have allowed them to outlive their parents now do this commonly; the increase in the number of broken homes reduces the availability of family support; caring spouses may break down under the triple burden of their own age and of the age and disability of their partner; a significant number of long-term disabled people do not have children; smaller families can offer less by way of sibling support. Demand for long-stay places continues, so the criteria for reception tend to become more severe and delays more grievous.

The integration of services for disabled people is an issue made all the more important by the increased emphasis on community care. Fragmentation and lack of co-ordination remain the norm, services are organised in relation to specific needs so that at the same time a disabled person has to relate to a number of professionals or agencies, none of which is capable of looking at his or her problems as a whole or is concerned to consider the impact of one intervention on other aspects of the person's life. There is little evidence that national governments are willing to think in terms of a national comprehensive plan to meet the needs of disabled people; response appears to be very *ad hoc*.

Moreover, the universal trend towards community care across Europe has mixed motives. The drive underlying the move would seem to be as much about cutting costs as aiming to offer the user a better way of life. In so far as cost-cutting figures significantly among the aims, there is the certainty of a direct conflict of objectives, since for some disabled people, particularly the elderly disabled, community living, so professionals are agreed, can only save money if standards of care are lowered (Daunt 1991).

In Europe most disabled people remain the passive recipients of services after their needs have been assessed by others. In an innovative project in the London Borough of Southwark, partly mirroring a successful initiative in Canada, a successful attempt has been made to change this situation for a small number of people with learning difficulties. The two key elements of this approach are handing over control of individualised funding to the people and their families, and using service brokers. The changes have not been welcomed by many social workers and other professionals who see them as a threat to their role. The pilot project in Southwark has been running since January 1993, funded jointly by Southwark Consortium and the South East London Health Authority, and employs two service brokers, each working with up to twenty people with learning difficulties. In Southwark, only a few people control their own funding, but individualised funding is to be extended this year. The evaluation of services in Southwark and the findings indicate service brokers have contributed to significant beneficial changes to individual lives. The initial evidence is that individualised funding and service brokerage piloted by people with learning difficulties costs no more than the existing system (Holman 1994).

Independent living as a concept and movement has continued to grow since the 1970s, although often one step forward has often been followed by two steps back due particularly to cuts in funding. The European Network on Independent Living (ENIL), which was formed in April 1989, organises conferences on diverse topics, including legislation and services in different European countries. Self-determined living, as it is called in Germany, is on the increase and has more than ten centres. There is a strong and expanding National Council of Centres for Independent Living in Helsinki, Vienna and Dublin, providing examples of the still slow but constant and permanent development throughout Europe.

The move to involve disabled people in decisions about their way of life and future is a slowly increasing trend, albeit in its infancy, especially where those with learning disabilities or mental health problems are concerned. Empowerment of mental health users was the subject of a workshop in a recent European Social Services conference (Warner and Munday 1994) which drew on the experience in Prato, Italy. This experience started with a 1989 conference on 'psychiatric self-help' and led to the establishment of user groups that insisted on being independent of the health authority and professionals. As the project developed, people could join self-help groups without going via a health agency or professionals. This has caused difficulties for professionals as they have become uncertain about their roles.

People with learning disabilities have also been seeking greater independence. By accessing state benefits to buy the services they need people with learning disabilities in Denmark have achieved considerable user empowerment. More generally, Danish people with all forms of disabilities seem to be in relatively greater control, as compared with the rest of Europe, of the major service providers, although there are isolated examples of this type of control in other countries. In Italy, Project South in Calabria is a voluntary project supported by public money which aims to involve people with learning and physical disabilities in the planning of services. In Ireland the Cheeverstown voluntary project is developing a range of community-based services for people with learning and physical disabilities involved in the planning of services.

Paternalism or overprotection can inhibit a disabled person from developing his or her individuality or active potential. The effect of this may be extremely serious if the accustomed protection is suddenly removed, for example on the death of parents or the closure of an establishment. Direct employment of their own care assistants by disabled people themselves using an allowance of money granted to them personally by the state for this purpose is a prominent part of some programmes and would address this problem for many.

Perceptively and increasingly (though not rapidly) disabled people themselves are responding actively to this complex of predicament and opportunity. In all community countries the association of parents and families of disabled people and of disabled people themselves are more or less influential and the trend is for this influence to grow.

We have seen, in the section on historical context and those following, that not only services for but attitudes towards and organisation of disabled people have undergone change during the course of the twentieth century. Recently, however, media reports have shown that violence against disabled people is on the increase in some regions of Europe and cases of discrimination and exclusion are still too numerous by far. For example, a court in Germany in 1993 awarded damages to a couple of tourists on the pretext that their holidays had been spoiled by the presence of disabled people in their hotel restaurant.

Disabled people are still two or three times as likely to be unemployed as any one else. The current trends, technological and economic progress together with changes in attitudes, offer no real grounds for either pessimism or optimism as regards the future for disabled people.

Positive factors include the fact that new technology has provided new learning possibilities for those with learning disabilities as well as physical disabilities. Educational mainstreaming has increased and is likely to continue to do so, albeit slowly. The contribution of technology has also enabled considerable practical achievement by disabled people resulting from and further encouraging changes of attitude.

There are also many negative factors. For administrators and providers of services the diversity of disabilities constitutes an intractable difficulty; they are perpetually either trying to find a narrow path between overspecialisation and overgeneralisation in their definition of the problems to be confronted, or they are having to make a series of discrete decisions to take comparatively narrow or broad approaches to specific situations or needs.

The highly competitive environment developed in western Europe over the past ten years will create difficulties for those who have to struggle for equality of opportunity. Where public budgets are perpetually under severe scrutiny, the service needs of minorities with special problems are always likely to be at risk.

Since the 1950s and 1960s there has been a development of legislation and facilitating measures, official agencies, improvements in the attitudes of professionals and the general public and increased self-determination amongst disabled people. Moreover in spite of economic constraint and emphasis on creation of wealth and competition progress in many fields continues.

It is, however, not an exaggeration to speak of an ongoing struggle. There have been cuts in benefits and services in many countries. There are many examples of progress being reversed.

The treaties governing the European Union need to be extended for it to pursue further work for disabled people. The current treaties only cover disabled workers, thus disabled elderly people, disabled home-makers and all those on full disability pensions are excluded from the impact of EU legislation and programmes. The organisation Disabled Persons International calls for action: to include disability in the European Convention for the Protection of Human Rights as well as the Maastricht Treaty; by the EU to issue directives in support of equality of opportunity and

provision of information; and by European member states to provide legislation on human rights and anti-discrimination (Disabled
Persons International 1994).

A new model is needed, interpreting disability as a result of
social and attitudinal barriers constructed by a world built for able-
bodied living, with associated integrated living support systems.
This would change and develop the main role of social workers as
one of advocates in support of and working with disabled people in
identifying and helping to remove social and physical barriers in
the local environment.

Canada, Australia and particularly the United States (with the
Disability Act 1990) are far ahead of Europe with legislation
aimed at the prevention and prohibition of discrimination and the
achievement of equal opportunities through the provision of rea-
sonable accommodation for disabled people.

References

Baine, S., J. Benington and J. Russell (1992) *Changing Europe: Challenges
    facing the voluntary and community sectors in the 1990s*, London:
    NCVO.
Booth, T. (ed.) (1990) *Better Lives: Changing services for people with
    learning difficulties* (Occasional Series monographs), Sheffield: Sheffield
    University.
Brown, H. and H. Smith (eds) (1992) *Normalisation: A reader for the
    nineties*, London: Tavistock/Routledge.
Connolly, N. (1990) *Raising Voices: Social services departments and people
    with disabilities*, London: Policy Studies Institute.
Commission of the European Community (1989–94), *HELIOS FLASH,
    Quarterly Magazine of the HELIOS Programme*.
Commission of the European Communities (1990) 'The Community Char-
    ter of Fundamental Social Rights of Workers', Commission of the Euro-
    pean Communities, Luxembourg.
Commission of the European Communities (1992) 'Communication from
    the Commission concerning the action programme on implementation
    of basic rights for workers', Com. 89 568, Commission of the European
    Communities, Luxembourg.
Daunt, P. (1990) *Age and Disability: A challenge for Europe*, London:
    Eurolink Age.
Daunt, P. (1991) *Meeting Disability: A European response*, London: Cas-
    sell Education.
Disabled Persons International (1994) *Newsletter of Disabled People's In-
    ternational European Region*, May and June.

Ely, P. and R. Saunders (1993) 'France', in B. Munday (ed.), *European Social Services*, University of Kent at Canterbury: European Institute of Social Services.

European Community (1991) *Single Market Fact Sheet 11*, Brussels: Commission of the European Union.

European Community (1994) *Disabled People in the European Union, Fact Sheet 13*, Brussels: Commission of the European Union.

Eurostat Survey (1993) *Disabled Persons: Statistical data*, Brussels: Commission of the European Union.

Finkelstein, V. (1990) 'Disability – an administrative challenge' in Oliver.

Flynn, P. (1993) *Green Paper. European Social Policy: Options for the Union*, Brussels: Directorate-General V, Commission of the European Union.

Flynn, P. (1994) *White Paper. European Social Policy: A way forward for the Union*, Brussels: Directorate-General V, Commission of the European Union.

George, M. (1991) *'Disability in Europe'*, *Community Care*, September.

Grover, R. and F. Gladstone (1981) *Disabled People: A right to work*, London: Bedford Square Press.

Holman, A. (1994) 'The Southwark Consortium evaluation: how services change to meet the needs and wishes of people who use them, values into action', *Community Care*, March.

Lunt, N. and P. Thornton (1993) *Employment Policies for Disabled People: A review of legislation and services in fifteen countries*, York: Social Policy Research Unit, University of York.

Mobility International (1994) *Mobility International News*, Spring.

Munday, B. (ed.) (1993) *European Social Services*, University of Kent at Canterbury: European Institute of Social Services.

Oliver, M. (1990) *The Politics of Disablement*, Basingstoke: Macmillan.

Oliver, M. (ed.) (1991) *Social Work: Disabled people and disabling environments*, London: Jessica Kingsley.

Samoy, E. (1992) *Sheltered Employment in the European Community*, Brussels: Commission of the European Union.

Seyfried, E. and T. Lambert (1988) *New Semi-Sheltered Forms of Employment for Disabled Persons: An analysis of landmark measures in the member states of the European Communities*, Berlin: CEDEFOP.

Shakespear, T. (1992) 'Reviewing the social model', *Coalition*, September.

Shearer, A. (1981) *Disability: Whose handicap?*, Oxford: Basil Blackwell.

Social Europe Supplement (1986) *The Social Integration of Disabled People*, Brussels: Commission of the European Union.

Waddington, P. (1986) *Local Services for Disabled People: A European Community guide*, Amsterdam: International Union of Local Authorities.

Waddington, P. (1989) *Local Services for Disabled People: Portugal and Spain*, Amsterdam: International Union of Local Authorities.

Warner, N. and B. Munday (eds) (1994) *Commissioning Community Alternatives in European Social and Health Care*, Canterbury: European Institute of Social Services.

CHAPTER 7

Social care for elderly people in Europe

The central problem of home care

John Baldock and Peter Ely

Introduction: a simple classification

Elderly people are the source of the largest category of people receiving social care in European countries. It is provided to them in hospitals (where social care may be subsidiary to some kind of medical treatment), nursing homes, residential homes, various forms of sheltered housing, a variety of day centres and, most importantly, in people's own homes. Each of these milieux is associated with particular problems and policy issues: for example, there is a large literature on ways of making the experience of institutional care as rich and positive as possible. It would not be feasible in one chapter to do more than touch on these issues. Therefore, we have chosen to concentrate mainly on the provision of social care to older people in their homes; on home care. This is in any case the aspect of social care which is receiving the most attention from policy-makers and service professionals as they seek ways to avoid the need for people to have to move into institutions of some kind when they come to need care.

The principal theme of this chapter is that what may be called 'home care services for elderly people in Europe' exhibit great variety and even unpredictability between countries and even within them. Home care systems are not amenable to easy generalisation. In other areas of social policy there are much greater similarities in the broad patterns of provision. In the core social

Table 7.1 Some basic data about elderly people in Europe, c. 1990

	Aged dependency ratio	85+ as % total population	Growth 80+ group 1990–9	65+ % living alone	65+ % in institutions	65+ % receiving home help
Austria	21.7	1.4	–1.0	36.0		1.0
Belgium	21.1	1.4	0.0	38.0	6.6	6.0
Denmark	22.6	1.4	10.0	53.0	5.3	20.0
Germany	22.3	1.0		41.0	5.9	4.0
France	20.9	1.5	3.0	28.0	4.5	8.0
Greece	18.2	1.0		14.0	0.6	1.0
Italy	20.1	1.1	33.0	31.0	2.3	1.0
Ireland	18.5	0.7		20.0	5.0	3.0
Netherlands	18.4	1.1	21.0	31.0	9.7	12.0
Portugal	17.9	0.8	18.0	18.0	2.0	1.0
Spain	19.4	0.9	21.0	19.0	2.0	1.0
Sweden	27.3	1.6	22.0	41.0	10.0	16.0
UK	23.0	1.5	14.0	36.0	5.0	9.0

Sources: OECD (1988); OECD (1994, Table 11); Glendinning and McLaughlin (1993, Table 1.6); Hennessy (1994, Table 2.8); Walker *et al.* (1993a, Table 4.4).

spending areas such as social security, the provision of medical care and the education and training of young people, while the generosity of provision may vary between countries, the nature of the benefits and services are broadly similar in design and intention. For example, all EU countries run hospitals and have a system of primary medical treatment from local doctors. All have schools to educate their children. In the case of the care of dependent elderly people, in contrast, there are wide differences not only in the amounts that are spent by the state but in the very nature of the services. Furthermore, this diversity makes any form of classification of countries rather arbitrary.

However, it is possible to begin with a limited degree of focus. Amongst the group of thirteen EU nations listed in Table 7.1 there are certain broad core features to their home care services. In all the countries the state is directly or indirectly responsible for the provision of some home help services, some personal care services and some home nursing services. In most cases these services will not have developed solely to serve the elderly; indeed home help services and community nursing usually emerged first to help families with children and younger disabled people. With the ageing of European populations so the retired population, and more particularly the very old and frail, have come to dominate these areas of provision.

'Domiciliary care may be said to be an approach rather than a specific service' (Hugman 1994, p. 100). Its essential characteristic is that it is delivered within the person's own home. Within this constraint there is great variety in the nature and intensity of the services and the degree to which, at one end of the spectrum, they allow an old person to remain at home despite great frailty or, at the other, to which they merely make life marginally more comfortable for people who are largely self-sufficient anyway. The most common forms are help with domestic work, shopping, laundry and cleaning, the delivery of meals or the cooking of them in the home. Increasingly, as in most countries the target groups have become more frail and disabled, so home care services have shifted from largely domestic work to help with personal care such as bathing and dressing, eating, communicating and getting about. To these may be added speech and physiotherapy, counselling for both users and their carers, and carer substitute services that offer periods of relief to the existing, usually informal, carer. The degree to which home care includes medical and nursing services can also vary a great deal. In some countries bathing, overseeing the taking of drugs, changing bandages or administering injections may be seen as specifically medical interventions requiring a qualified nurse; in other countries such services can be provided as part of a more general personal care service. There are also considerable and crucial differences in when the services are provided: they may be limited to working hours during weekdays and require advance booking and planning or they may be available at any time of the day or night on an emergency call-out basis. In its most developed forms home care can sustain a chair- or bed-bound old person in their own home with a level and range of support comparable to that available in a hospital ward.

This very broad and basic outline is, however, the limit to which generalisation may go. The dominating characteristic of home care services across Europe, and even within countries, is their variety. As Table 7.1 shows, using a broad definition of home helps as an indicator, the proportion of elderly people provided with services is very varied. Only in the Scandinavian countries such as Sweden and Denmark, together with the exceptional addition of the Netherlands, are home care services available in sufficient quantity to be regarded as a standard or routine form of support for frail elderly people. In the Netherlands, for example, the home help services reach at any one time 30 per cent of those over eighty who are living at home and the home nursing service visits some 20 per cent of the over-65 population (Huijsman 1993). Even more generous and dispersed levels of provision can be found in Sweden and Denmark and amount to near universal provision for those who are likely to need the services.

Elsewhere in Europe the proportion of the elderly population reached by home help services is very small. This is not because services are carefully targeted on the most dependent elderly people but more a function of the general economic stage of the country: the countries with the most limited domiciliary services are also those with proportionately smaller institutional provision for the elderly in residential homes, nursing homes and the hospital sector.

Home care services also vary considerably in the way in which they are financed and provided, and these factors can have implications for their quality. A mix of sources of finance is usually the rule, leading to considerable problems of co-ordination. In all of the countries there are three principal types of public funding: the social insurance system, the health insurance system and the local, often municipal, public welfare or social services. Thus, some provision will be funded through the public assistance system which is only available on the basis of a means test and to those on very low incomes. This is the basis upon which home help and home care services are often financed in Germany and France, for example, and reflects their origins in forms of outdoor relief for the poor. The health care system usually forms a significant source of home nursing funding. In some countries this may be quite generous, such as in the Netherlands, where a special general medical expenses insurance fund (Algemene Wet Bijzondere Ziektekosten or AWBZ), paid for through an income tax levy, is largely responsible for financing nursing homes and community nursing services. However, the most general rule in European countries where health care is funded through an insurance system is that the schemes specifically exclude the funding of long-term domiciliary social care. As a result problems of collaboration and co-operation between health services and community social services are a central theme in accounts of home care almost everywhere. The third major source of funding is the local community or municipal welfare system. Depending usually on when these systems were first developed their contribution may be universal or highly selective. In Britain, France and Germany, for example, local welfare provisions can usually be traced back to the late nineteenth or early twentieth centuries and consequently provide services that are limited and hedged about with restrictions. They tend to be relatively less used by the middle classes. In most Scandinavian countries, in contrast, local municipal services are the product of the more recent post-war development of comprehensive, citizenship-based welfare and are generously funded and universally used by all classes.

Just as the funding of home care is mixed, so too the organisations which provide it are of great variety and differ significantly from country to country. In Germany and the Netherlands the actual delivery of both home help and home nursing has long been contracted out to large national voluntary organisations which originally grew out of the charitable work of the Catholic and Protestant churches (Dieck and Garms-Homolová 1991; Pijl 1993). The result has tended to be relatively bureaucratic, inflexible and high-cost services which are careful to demarcate the limits of their responsibilities but seek to maximise the demand for their services. In contrast, in Britain and the Scandinavian countries the dominance of local authority social services in the delivery of services has meant that provision has been characterised by a civil service culture of response; that is to say provision that has been relatively unaccountable and insensitive to user and carer demands, or even changes in the distribution of need, and co-operation between local welfare services and the often separately (regionally) organised health services has been poor. In Italy and Greece and the other southern Mediterranean countries public provision is very limited and the church-based organisations and the religious orders have been significant providers of services (Facchini 1993; Ziomas and Bousas 1993) but largely in the context of a value system that places the primary obligation on the family and sees all other sources as a last resort.

Given the varied character and organisation of their home care services, it is not really justifiable to classify European systems according to precise criteria – as is more often done in the case of social security or health care systems. This chapter will simply follow the fairly common practice (e.g. Walker 1993a) of distinguishing three broad bands of countries in terms of the generosity of their home care services: first, southern countries and

Ireland, where public provision is minimal but developing; secondly, those core European nations, such as Germany, where home care is more developed but is still a residual category marginal to the insurance-based health care system; thirdly, those countries, usually Scandinavian but including Britain in principle, where home care is part of the core institutional welfare state and available as a basic entitlement alongside health care and income maintenance. These three groups can be distinguished in table 7.1 largely by the level at which home help support (used as an indicator of home care more generally) is available: group 1 below 4 per cent; group 2 from 5 to 8 per cent; group 3 from 9 per cent (the United Kingdom) but closer to 15–20 per cent in Scandinavia.

The 'problem' of home care

At one level the provision of care to elderly people who need help to live their lives is a mundane and even simple matter; in one way or another all societies manage to provide it and always have done. At first sight it should not constitute a major social policy problem. At another level it has become one of the most complex and intractable areas of social policy development, subject to quite abrupt shifts and turnabouts in policy as governments seek to deal with unexpected or unsatisfactory outcomes. Anne-Marie Guillemard has warned of the dangers of not getting it right: 'A certitude has taken shape: if we do not soon adopt new ways of handling the risk of dependence in old age, the progress achieved during the twentieth century in lengthening the life-span will turn out to be a tragedy' (Guillemard and Frossard 1993, p. 253).

Why and how has fulfilling such a basic function as providing care for old people developed this potential for disaster? Most discussions of the issue begin by setting out in detail, often in as dramatic a way as possible, demographic predictions about the size of the various categories of older people in future years. This is not always a helpful perspective: to see a class of people as a problem tends to imply they are in some way less eligible citizens or even that they are blameworthy to a degree. It is a perspective that has rightly been called 'ageism' and it is a form of prejudice (Bytheway 1995). We would be most unlikely to speak of the need for care amongst the young as a problem in the same negative way. Yet we often fail to recognise that the dependencies of age are as natural as those of youth and, to a greater or lesser degree, will beset all of us at one time or another.

One of the ways in which the 'burden' of elderly people is emphasised is the tendency to predict the growth in their numbers over very long periods. Thus, for example, it has been pointed out that over the period to 2025 the Netherlands, Germany, Denmark and the United Kingdom will face the highest increases in the proportion of people over sixty-five in Europe (Glendinning and McLaughlin 1993). This way of presenting a social policy 'problem' might be thought curious if it were not so common. Looking thirty years ahead tends to obscure the more immediate issues and it suggests a mode of social policy development that is unrealistic. It is surely rare for governments to look at the policy implications of such a distant era. How relevant would one expect plans to meet the care needs of elderly people that were made in 1965 to be to today's problems? It seems particularly ill-focused and even cruel that today's population of frail elderly, who even in the most populous of European countries amount to no more than a few hundred thousand, should have their needs exaggerated and obscured by potential 'burdens' in thirty years' time.

If more immediate, and policy-relevant, demographics are focused upon, the 'problems' look rather different. As table 7.1 indicates, what distinguishes some of the richest European nations such as Belgium and France is that they currently face rather low or even negative growth in the number of 'very old' in their populations. Even where growth is fast, it rarely exceeds 1 per cent a year, though there are some spectacular exceptions which highlight the fact that the immediate problem can vary greatly from one European country to another. Indeed, the more immediate demographic dimension to the issue of care provision is that the relevant population group may vary quite abruptly in size from year to year. This is a factor well understood by those responsible for providing services for the young, particularly education. In all industrial countries year upon year birthrates can vary quite abruptly due to a variety of social and economic factors (Coleman and Salt 1992, ch. 4). This means that the school entry population can be sharply different from year to year, affecting the size of classes and demand for teachers. Because the frailties of old age are slightly less age-specific than the start of education, the demand for the services of social workers and other care resources will vary less abruptly. None the less the short-term fluctuations remain quite significant. For example (see table 7.1), in the current decade from 1990 to 2000 the number of people over eighty actually falls in Austria and remains roughly constant in Belgium, Germany and France. This is due to low birthrates and sometimes infant survival rates in those countries in the years 1905–1920. In contrast Britain, Sweden, Spain and Italy are experiencing a decade in which the size of the care-needing elderly population will grow between 14 per cent and 33 per cent because those country's birthrates were less or not at all affected by the ravages of recession, war and disease in the early years of the century.

So, given that the need for domiciliary care in old age is a relatively small and unpredictable demand on welfare states, why is it so often seen as a difficult social policy issue requiring new and innovative social policy responses?

The actual tasks that need to be carried out are quite straightforward: when age brings frailties and incapacities people may need help with washing, toileting, dressing, cooking, cleaning, eating, mobility and communication. They need help to do the things that have hitherto constituted their adult autonomy. As a result, in any particular instance, any other able adult will see quite easily and clearly what help is needed, what needs to be done. The helping tasks that are required may be onerous, they may be tedious and time consuming, they may be regarded as very menial, but they are not complex or difficult. Why then are they seen as so difficult to organise and provide in reliable, cost-effective and acceptable ways? Why should so many people dread the frailties of old age and fear that they will not be helped in a manner they will find acceptable? Why is it that social policy systems that are capable of financing and delivering social security benefits to millions and of building sophisticated acute medical care provision should find it so difficult to ensure adequate personal care in old age?

The 'paradox of complex mundaneity'

It is suggested here that the answer lies in the fact that the apparent simplicity of social care is deceptive and that its provision is in practice inherently complex. We call this the 'paradox of complex mundaneity' or what in French can be called *la complexité quoti-dienne*, the complexity of everyday life. This complexity takes various forms. The most obvious can be classified as cultural, or-ganisational and economic forms of complexity.

Social care policies raise a whole range of *cultural difficulties*. They are an excellent example of the point at which the public, in the form of social policies, collides with the private, in the form of those activities of daily life which are essentially the province of personal and family routine (Ungerson 1987). The classic way of dealing with this difficulty is to remove the activities from the household and have them conducted by 'professionals' in some different, usually institutional, environment; a nursing home, a hospital or a clinic. However, the defining characteristic of home care is that it takes place in people's private homes. With the advent of frailty in old age, the state or its agents may quite liter-ally step into the private home and start to play a part in carrying out the routine personal activities that previously defined a per-son's essential adulthood and individuality. Home care is culturally and emotionally loaded, and accepting it requires important ad-justments in self-image and identity (Baldock and Ungerson 1994). For this reason the help that individuals will feel they need and the forms in which they will find it acceptable vary in ways which are not necessarily closely linked to the objective disabilities which they have. Not all people who cannot clean their homes, or dress, or bathe, will find the same sorts of solutions acceptable or desir-able. People with similar disabilities will not be similarly satisfied with the same solutions.

Home care has been found by providers and researchers who study it to present exceptional *organisational problems*. These or-ganisational problems arise directly because the distribution of care needs amongst older people is unpredictable and unstable. While the nature and volume of need in a particular elderly popu-lation may be quite small and predictable in a global sense, quite which old people will need what combinations of help, and for how long, is always very uncertain. This is particularly so in the case of those who are very frail and have high levels of need: their cir-cumstances and requirements can change very abruptly – as a result of a fall or an infection, for example – requiring a complete review and re-arrangement of the services they are receiving. In practice this immense uncertainty at the individual level is a great disincentive to those whose job it is to arrange care. They are often reluctant to invest the time and energy required to set up an appropriate package of care services if it seems likely that these arrangements are suddenly to be rendered inappropriate, possibly within days of being set up. This can even be a major problem for researchers into innovative schemes of care. Their research reports frequently point to the difficulties of recruiting a sample of appropriately needy people a high proportion of whom then fall out of whatever scheme of care is being provided because their needs change abruptly (Challis *et al.* 1990; Askham and Thomson 1990). This central problem of the instability and unpredictability of need at the individual level is what distinguishes the frail elderly from other groups needing social care such as children, younger physically disabled people and those with learning difficulties. Within these groups the pattern of need tends to be stable or at least predictable in the case of individuals. Only in the case of mentally ill people does a similar problem of uncertainty arise and, even then, it is often reduced through the use of drugs which stabilise, if not heal, the afflicted.

Much public and user criticism is based upon what are seen to be the crude, inflexible, overstandardised and unco-ordinated ways in which social care services are provided to people at home. Much of the emphasis in innovation and reform is on finding ways to tailor services to the needs and wishes of users and their carers (Baldock and Evers 1992). There is a growing realisation that a core reason for the failure of services to deliver acceptable outcomes derives from insufficient attention to managerial issues (Davies and Challis 1986). Sophisticated systems of care management are required to cope with the great variety of needs, the numerous sources from which they can be met and the speed and unpredictability of changes in service need at the individual level.

The *economic and financial complexities* of home care are also a consequence of its position at the boundaries of the public and private. The routine home care of an old person is likely to involve a wide mix of sectors in terms of both financing and provision. Much research has examined the complex ways in which home care is likely to be financed out of a combination of private income and assets, public subsidy, reciprocal relations established with friends and neighbours and outright gifts of time or money (from family, friends and charities). In no other area is the mix of finance so complex and so different from case to case. In comparison the financing of medical care, or education or even housing are relatively simple. Just as costs are often hard to define and allocate so too are the benefits of home care. Whose judgements should be used to value the outcomes of the home care of a frail old person? Only those of the cared for individual? There is much evidence that their judgements will be seen as unreliable and perverse by those around them (Qureshi *et al.* 1988). Researchers have found that old people often prefer ways of organising their time and the things around them in ways that seem quite illogical and even dangerous to others. How are acceptable trade-offs to be established between the benefits as perceived by users, carers, the wider community and the state?

These complexities of home care have not gone unnoticed. They have given rise to an equally complex and varied research and normative literature that explores all the cultural, organisational and economic problems that can only be alluded to here. Home care of the elderly is a spectacularly multidisciplinary area of study, attracting the attention of philosophers, anthropologists and sociologists, psychologists and medical researchers as well as economists and management scientists. This variety of the literature is surely a testament to what we have called the 'paradox of mundaneity'. Unfortunately, this has one important negative consequence; that is that policy-makers and practitioners tend to ignore much academic and research-based writing on home care. They see it as too esoteric and therefore tend to follow common sense and conventional wisdom in the construction and implementation of policies (Coolen 1993a). As a result, home care as a policy area within European welfare systems still exhibits a range of basic and important policy dilemmas.

The main policy dilemmas

1. The provision of formal home care services may have relatively little to do with the volume of home care actually provided in a country. As Table 7.1 shows, the probability of receiving publicly provided or funded home care services varies considerably from country to country. It also often varies even more between different localities within a country. However, it is not clear that the

presence or absence of these services has much effect on the general level of home care, defined more widely, in a society. Since in all countries this is provided overwhelmingly by families and informal carers, without any state help, we cannot conclude that because, for example, Greece and Italy have low levels of home help services that therefore home care is lacking in amount or quality in those societies.

With the exception of Denmark – and possibly Sweden – where services previously aspired to replace family care, services have nowhere aspired to do more than complement and prolong informal care and stand in its place when there was no family available to undertake care. Services also have a role when the dependency level is too high for the family to cope.

2. There is little correlation between the degree of functional dependence (i.e. inability to perform tasks of daily living) of the *individual*, and what services they receive. In the different countries discussed in this chapter, research into who actually receives home care services shows that there is a wide variety of recipients from across the spectrum of need and that the amount of service they receive bears little relationship to the degree of their dependency (Boffi and Facchini 1991; Davies *et al.* 1990; Huijsman and de Klerk 1993). The chief independent variable is, of course, the presence or absence of informal help from spouses, children, friends and neighbours. Others are differences in the facilities of the home and its environment and the determination of the old person to remain at home; or conversely, their state of anxiety which leads them to seek residential care.

It is not possible to tie assessment of need for services to wholly 'hard', objective criteria, which leaves scope for subjective bias. There are also commonly obstacles to a needs-based distribution of services within the structures of service provision: cash limits, budgetary instability, eligibility based on insurance entitlement or means-testing, or the service providers' current desire either to husband scarce resources or to utilise all that is available in the face of fluctuating and unpredictable demand, the users' and carers' own preferences and willingness to offer support. Certainly, unless there is some need-based logic to the distribution of home care services, it is difficult for policy-makers to justify any particular level or type of provision. It would also explain the wide variety of types and volumes of provision across Europe, which seems unrelated to factors other than history and tradition.

3. One of the most common justifications for the expansion of public home care services is that it will allow a reduction in the use of institutional care in residential homes, nursing homes and hospitals. Thus it is those countries with the highest levels of institutional care that tend to be most vigorous in the pursuit of alternative community-based care. This is true of Britain, France, Sweden and the Netherlands for example. However, it has been found that the provision of better home care services tends not just to draw people away from the use of institutional care but to attract to the use of public services people who hitherto were not being helped by the state at all (Coolen 1993b; Monk 1993; Thorslund 1993). Two principal responses to this problem have been tried. One is to limit or reduce the availability of institutional care at the same time as home care services are increased. This policy has been followed in Britain and Sweden, for example. The other is to develop more effective screening or targeting methods that will ensure that those who receive the expanded home care services are indeed those who would otherwise have gone into some form of residential care. To do this comprehensive systems are required to assess and screen potential users of services and to ensure that only those who are eligible are helped. Assessments and targeting lie at the heart of the recent reforms to the community care process in Britain following the NHS and Community Care Act 1990 (Audit Commission 1994). In practice, assessments are both difficult to do and the strict formal criteria tend to be undermined by more subtle, and perhaps inefficient, social judgements (Davies 1992, 1994; Ellis 1993). In short, intensive home care does not appear to operate entirely or mainly as a substitute for institutional care even when that is the primary policy intention but rather draws into the formal care system people who would otherwise have gone without services.

For the remainder of this chapter the complexities of home care that have been outlined are further illustrated by describing the patterns of domiciliary provision in five countries (France and Germany, Greece and Italy, Sweden) chosen from across the three groups distinguished earlier.

Domiciliary provision in five countries

France

France can be placed in the middle group of our classification. Services are available, but not universally so; the French arrangements for domiciliary care are extremely complex. There are multiple sources of funding: pension funds (both statutory and complementary), public assistance and health insurance. Old people who employ their own home helps do not have to pay national insurance contributions. Service provision is almost everywhere through voluntary associations set up for this purpose, usually by pension funds and local governments. These associations are able to draw on and co-ordinate the various funding sources on behalf of the users, and offer examples of integrated services which could act as models for other countries.

Pension funds topslice their contribution income to provide themselves with finance for *action sociale*, the largest part of which is spent on domiciliary care. Funds typically provide finance for a fixed number of home help hours per month (typically fifteen or thirty hours) to those of their pensioners who are assessed in need of the service, though this entitlement is means-tested. The assessment is carried out by the service-providing association which arranges for and receives the finance. Associations can also register themselves as an *association mandataire*, in which case they can act as agencies for old people wishing to employ help on their own account and take advantage of favourable tax allowances for doing so. Associations can advise as to what fiscal advantages are available and apply on behalf of the old person if necessary. They supply their own trained personnel for self-employment. The advantages to all sides are obvious.

The same association may also supply a range of domiciliary help under the direction of qualified nursing staff. Home care assistants are trained to carry out personal care tasks and have a wider range of functions than home helps. They too are frequently employed by the old person themselves, often with the assistance of a cash benefit (*Allocation compensatrice pour tierce personne*) intended to compensate disabled people for the services of a third person. Again, the same association using sickness insurance funding can purchase professional nursing inputs from freelance qualified nurses on a fee-for-service basis.

French arrangements for domiciliary care have benefited from the gradual extension of provisions originally intended for younger disabled people, and also from measures to increase employment such as the concessions over employers' insurance contributions. While the complexity of administration is considerable, at their best provisions integrate health and social care and encourage the users to manage their helpers. The French arrangements for service provision are characterised by a high level of training and a correspondingly low investment in monitoring. The disadvantage of the French arrangements is the degree to which complexities in eligibility and funding may obstruct the tailoring of services to needs.

As in many other European countries, French research into the distribution of social provision finds little correlation with the pattern of need. Of people with high needs (confined to a bed or wheelchair) 75 per cent are to be found in the community, largely cared for by informal, family carers, 47 per cent of whom have no public support (Colvez 1990).

In a number of studies, Frossard and his collaborators (Frossard *et al.* 1990) set out to test the common assumption that because of the economies of scale achieved by large institutions, home care costs less below, and institutionalisation less above, a certain threshold of dependence. The researchers calculated the care costs of institutions on the basis of the hours staff spent attending to each resident, as a proportion of their salaries. In domiciliary care, the costs of professional help were calculated similarly, but to these were added the opportunity costs of unpaid carers in terms of actual or potential earnings forgone.

On this basis, the real costs of living at home were either the same as or greater than those of institutional care, whether in a residential or a medical facility. But Guillemard and Frossard (1993) consider that the economies of scale in care costs achieved by large institutions are probably offset by their greater capital costs and overheads. Less is spent at home on housing and food. In addition, large institutions seldom succeed in establishing a friendly atmosphere or a good quality of life for residents.

The research draws attention to the way in which the exercise of elderly people's choice of a setting suitable for their needs is distorted by considerations of who would bear the financial cost. This difficulty is probably found in all European countries. In the French context, though the opportunity costs to informal carers can be heavy, it is in the family's financial interest to keep the old person at home, as the high cost of residential care would otherwise fall on them and the resident. As a result, most admissions to care take place as emergencies. Statutory pension schemes bear the main costs of home help provision, so that schemes have an interest in placing their pensioners in residential institutions; in fact they construct and own institutions for this purpose. Finally, the costs of acute medical and psychiatric care are almost entirely covered by statutory sickness insurance, and Guillemard and Frossard (1993) report that there is no medical reason for the presence of some 40 per cent of the elderly people found on these wards.

Germany

Germany, like France, can be placed in the middle category of countries. Indeed, Germany presents a good example of the difficulties in classifying and passing easy judgements on a country's home care system. It has often been portrayed as having a comparatively harsh and minimal system. This image had several sources.

First, it was due to the unfavourable position of those who needed long-term care due to the disabilities of old age rather than needing medical intervention to deal with illness. Germany's compulsory national medical insurance system is particularly generous; at 9 per cent of GDP, expenditure on health care is one of the highest in the world (Commission of the European Communities 1993). Under the national health insurance scheme, 'rehabilitative' domiciliary care is available for a strictly limited period following an acute medical episode – typically on discharge from hospital. In contrast, until recently, state payment for long-term care was mainly only available under the means-tested system of national assistance (Evers and Olk 1991). It was stigmatising, dependent on bureaucratic income assessments, and required one and one's family to spend their savings before becoming eligible. Even then, it was often easier to get for institutional care than for assistance in one's home – a paradox common across Europe and, before the 1990 reforms, true of the United Kingdom. It was particularly true in former East Germany where residential homes were the main form of care in society where housing was crowded and women's employment high.

Secondly, all welfare provision in Germany is governed by the Bismarckian principle of subsidiarity, which is deeply embedded in national values (Jamieson 1991). This defines a hierarchy of obligation to care, both financially and in kind, starting with close kin (spouses followed by children) and extending only when they are not available to local voluntary organisations, the local municipality, the provincial government (*Länder*) and only lastly the federal state. Thus both practice and ideology meant an entitlement to social care by the state was not an integral part of German citizenship in that there was no formal right or entitlement for the individual (Baldock and Evers 1991).

However, this explicit approach to welfare entitlements and family obligations has in recent years led to remarkably widespread public debate about the 'care crisis', the *Pflegenotstand*, typified by articles in the popular press such as *Der Speigel* and *Stern* magazine (Evers and Olk 1991). This debate has led to a series of major reforms to the health insurance scheme (the *Gesundheitsreformgesetz*), culminating in 1993 in the introduction of a new category of risk to be covered under the system of health insurance – the risk of becoming in need of long-term domiciliary care (Dieck 1994). The new system remains typically bureaucratic but provides a clear basis for the expansion of a system of home care. People in need of long-term domiciliary care are assessed and allocated to a hierarchy of need categories. These entitle them to choose between payments for care (varying between DM400 and DM1,200 a month in 1994, depending on their need assessment) or services in kind, of between twenty-five and seventy-five hours a month, bought on their behalf by the insurance funds. This choice between cash or kind can be varied on a monthly basis. The monetary value of the hours of help is greater than the alternative cash payment so as to discourage misuse of funds. What is perhaps most remarkable, from a British point of view, about the *Gezundheitsreform* is that the political debate and compromises that preceded it centred explicitly round the additional costs to the economy and how they should be met. It is expected that additional social insurance payments equivalent to between 1 and 2 per cent of payrolls will be required and, as part of the overall settlement, the major unions and employers reached specific agreements about the length of the working week (Dieck 1994).

The recent reforms in Germany have given elderly people and their families the option of receiving cash rather than care services. This is an example of what may be an important general trend in Europe, the development of what has been called 'payment for care' as an alternative to public home care provision. We therefore digress briefly at this point to outline these developments.

Payment for care

Payments for care may include payments in various forms to carers and/or payments to users to enable them to purchase their own packages of services. In Britain the payment of money to relatives to care for their frail elderly has been the fastest growing sector of the social security budget (Leat and Ungerson 1993). In Austria the payment of money to people to arrange their own care has been made the central idea in a revolutionary new care policy for elderly people in which cash will largely replace the, until recently, limited provision of public home care (Evers, Leichsenring and Pruckner 1994). It is expected that much of this money will be paid to relatives. In Sweden there is a well-established practice for local authorities to pay family members for care they undertake (Glendinning and McLaughlin 1993). In Finland there have been experiments involving the payment of what are effectively salaries to family members to care for their elderly (Sipilä and Anttonen 1994).

What is effectively happening is that governments are seeking, or are been drawn into, supporting family care arrangements that are sometimes close to paid, contractual relationships between old person and carer, or between the state and the family carer. There is much debate about whether this is a positive or negative development (Evers, Pijl and Ungerson 1994; Ungerson 1995). On one hand it amounts to an overdue recognition of the existing reality; that is, that in almost all European countries the vast bulk of caring for dependent older people has always been carried out by the family. There has been a tendency on the part of welfare systems to depend on this reality but not to give it formal recognition (Kraan *et al.* 1991). Family carers have had to bear the bulk of the burden of caring but have received little recognition or co-operation from the public health and social services. Rather, the carers have often had to devote considerable energy to fitting in with the bureaucratic ways of working of the public system. Now we are seeing explicit attempts by the public providers to work with the family carers, to adapt services to suit their timetables and to support and sustain the work they do. Payment for care pushes this approach to its limit, making service provision directly dependent upon what users are prepared to pay for.

On the other hand, it has been argued that payment for care policies may present considerable dangers for the informal sector and that women in particular are at risk of systematic exploitation by what may appear to be progressive social policies (Baldock and Ungerson 1991). Payments for care are often well below market rates and, although there is evidence that they are popular, they do take advantage of women's disadvantaged labour market position and of their socialisation into the caring role. Payment for care seeks to tie women into the care plan for a dependent old person and so could be seen as a subtle form of entrapment; on the other hand cash payments are popular. Under the new system in Germany more people are choosing to receive the monthly payments than are accepting the higher-value hours of care in kind.

Italy

Italy falls into the category of those countries with low levels of home care provision. It presents perhaps the most acute example of a society whose modes of care for the elderly are difficult to classify and to fit into the categories and classifications derived from more northern European states. Similar difficulties, but by no means identical ones, arise in the case of Spain and Portugal. The crude conventional wisdom that these are societies in which tradition and extended family networks are an important source of care tends to be wrong. It also is possible to find examples of innovative forms of provision such as payment for care.

Perhaps the chief distinguishing characteristic of care provision for the elderly in these countries is even greater variety than can be found in the more developed welfare states. There is, for example, much greater variation in the age structure of the population. In 1991 in Italy the proportion of the population over sixty varied between 15 per cent in the south and 22 per cent in more northern regions such as Tuscany and Trieste (Glendinning and McLaughlin 1993). Similarly, levels of employment amongst women vary between over 60 per cent in northern cities and less than 25 per cent in parts of the south – so to a degree affecting the availability of informal care. The provision of financial subsidy to meet home care needs varies from commune to commune. In some regions, for example in Emilia-Romagna, Bolzano and Trentino, there are levels of home help provision available, largely financed by the municipalities (communes), at levels that compare well with the United Kingdom (Bianchi 1991; Glendinning and McLaughlin 1993). At the same time half of the communes in Italy provide no home help service at all.

It is also true that these societies have relatively low levels of institutionalisation (Table 7.1), but this is less because residential care is unnecessary or undesired and is rather a consequence of a lack of state provision and insufficient private demand. In Italy, as in Greece, in those parts of the country where there are people who can afford them, private residential and nursing homes are much more common than in the poorer, usually more rural parts of the country. In the relatively affluent north, for example in Turin, private demand for institutional care is as high or even higher than in northern Europe, where the alternative of domiciliary support is more likely (Mengani and Gagliardi 1991). In the south of Italy, as in the rural parts of Greece, where residential facilities are almost non-existent, the image of high-quality family support, while clearly not unknown, must be set against reports of high levels of loneliness amongst older people (Mengani and Gagliardi 1991; Walker 1993b) and growing evidence that family care can be of a low quality and even cruel and exploitative (Bianchi 1991).

In Italy, as has already been discussed for Europe generally, the fastest growing form of support for the care needs of the elderly, and other disability groups, has been a form of payment for care, the *indennita di accompagnamento*, or 'companion payment'. Like the British attendance allowance, this is paid directly to the disabled person but is intended, in principle, to pay for informal, family support. The value of the *indennita di accompagnamento* varies according to a percentage measure of disability assessed by a doctor. Where disability is assessed at 100 per cent the payment is generous by European standards, equivalent to £300 a month or nearly £4,000 a year in 1991. These payments are index-linked. The proportion of people over sixty-five receiving them varies considerably across the country, varying between 1 to 9 per cent in 1988 (Ministero dell'Interno 1989, reported in Glendinning and McLaughlin 1993). These differences cannot reflect the real incidence of disability but rather reflect the differential application of the criteria in what has been called variously a 'clientalistic' or 'particularistic–meritocratic' state (Ascoli forthcoming). However, it may be unwise to attribute the growth in care payments only to what is effectively a euphemism for nepotism and corruption. The experience of the phenomenal growth in the payment of disability benefits elsewhere in Europe, such as in the United Kingdom, Germany and Greece, tends to indicate, as we have already pointed out, that a substantial proportion of users and carers of community care prefer cash to kind.

Greece

Purely because levels of publicly supported home care are so low (see Table 7.1) Greece too falls into the first group in our classification; those countries with undeveloped and minimal state-provided home care. However, Greece also usefully illustrates the difficulties in attempting to place countries and their patterns of home care in neat categories. In some important ways it is a society which has many characteristics associated with northern Europe. Life expectancy is one of the highest in Europe, fertility rates amongst the lowest and the proportion of over-65 age group in the population is near the European average (Eurostat 1991). Yet on the other hand these characteristics have to be understood within the context of a country which simultaneously presents aspects of a more traditional, rural society. While Greece is a highly urbanised country (a large proportion of the population live in and around Athens), it is also one in which many families still retain strong links to the land and to relatively isolated members, often elderly, who live in rural villages, often cut off even from easy telephone contact. On some of the islands more than 30 per cent of the population may be over sixty-five (Triantafillou and Mestheneos 1990, reported in Hugman 1994). At the same time the proportion of elderly living on their own is lower than in most northern European countries, older people sharing the family home is more common, and contact with family members is more frequent and intense (Age Concern 1992; Jylhä and Jokela 1990). Greece has one of most relatively generous old age pension systems in Europe: the average pension/wage replacement rate is close to 100 per cent compared with 60 per cent in the United Kingdom (Eurostat 1991). At the same time because many older Greeks have not experienced lives of continuous employment (and therefore not accumulated a pension entitlement), the level of poverty amongst older people is high (Eurostat 1990).

What these gross figures therefore hide is a wider variety in the experience of old age than is to be found in the more northern countries: there is a greater range of what constitutes 'typicality' (Hugman 1994, p. 37). These patterns should also be understood in the context of expectations of old age engendered by a culture which old people are traditionally held in high esteem, are likely to be holders of 'family' property and in which the role and values of the Greek Orthodox Church remain important (Hugman 1994, pp. 31–43). One consequence of this particular national combination of social patterns and values is that while there is evidence that the Greek elderly, on average, have high levels of contact with their families they are also much more likely to declare themselves lonely and isolated (Jylhä and Jokela 1990; Walker 1993b).

As Table 7.1 shows formal services for the care of elderly people are relatively undeveloped in Greece. On the other hand the more traditional sources of support from family (divorce is a good deal less common than in northern Europe) and particularly the church play a larger role (Hugman 1994, p. 32). Health care is insurance-based and covered by the same complex system that provides pensions through a large number of separate occupational funds (Dontas 1987). Again a consequence is a great variety of access to services: the better-off in the cities relying on private provision; those on lower incomes having to use often crowded public hospital facilities and those in the rural areas depending on the local GP. During the late 1970s and much of the 1980s the Greek economy prospered and governments moved towards developing a more formalised set of services for elderly people, much of it within the traditional mould of the state-financed and -provided welfare state. A special Division for the Protection of the Aged was created within the Ministry of Health, Welfare and Social Security. However, before an infrastructure of planned health and community services could be built, the recession of the early 1990s brought developments to a halt and at the same time increasingly influential right-wing politicians began to express doubts about the wisdom of attempting to develop a northern-style welfare state (Hugman 1994, p. 40). The national government's commitment to building a system of state-supported home care services was reiterated in legislation passed in 1992 (Ziomas and Bouzas 1993), but it is not clear how rapidly this will lead to real changes in provision.

The aspect of Greek support for elderly people that has received most international attention are the Open Care Centres for the Elderly (OCCs or 'KAPI'). These grew out of community centres established in Athens in the 1960s by the Orthodox Church. In 1981 the idea was taken up by central government and funds provided for municipalities to encourage the spread of KAPI, of which there were 234 by 1991 (Ziomas and Bouzas 1993). These centres, which use available buildings in suburbs and small towns and villages, are a combination of social club and day centre which seems particularly suited to the Greek pattern of social life. In the cases of the best examples, they are staffed by social workers, a nurse, a physiotherapist, an occupational therapist, a home help and a part-time doctor. They may operate as a base from which services are provided to those not mobile enough to reach the centre (Hugman 1994, p. 163). However, their social functions do appear to be more important than the care role and there is evidence that the relatively fit and male elderly are over-represented amongst those using the centres (*ibid.*, p. 164). None the less the 'open access' characteristic, which allows people to use the services without waiting for a referral or an assessment, has been taken up in some more established welfare systems; in Aaborg in Denmark, for example, and in Sweden (Daatland 1992). At best it offers the possibility of a demand-led, flexible and potentially preventative service. What it is unlikely to do is reach those elderly people whose needs are such that they have already become isolated from the wider community.

Sweden

Sweden presents the classic example of a society in which support for older people, both financially and in kind, is deeply embedded in national institutions and the political culture. Despite severe economic pressures in recent years (leading to very high interest rates, steep falls in the value of the currency and growing unemployment; Olsson and McMurphy 1993), Sweden has maintained levels of provision which often exceed provision in the United Kingdom by factors of 3 or 4 (Kraan *et al.* 1991). For example there are municipalities in Sweden where over 80 per cent of people over eighty receive public home help services (Johansson and Sundström 1994). The average national figure may be as high as 16 per cent for people aged sixty-five and over (Swedish Institute 1992). The scope of home help is also likely to be more generous than in many other European countries, often including, when necessary, elements of personal care. Most municipalities now provide some home help and nursing cover out of hours and at weekends. Residential and nursing home care provision is also generous by most European standards. Again specific comparisons are made difficult by the fact that many of the residential homes of the 1960s and 1970s have now been converted to or replaced by serviced flats in which the residents have a greater degree of autonomy and privacy. However, support in these 'institutions' is usually considerably greater than that which is associated with sheltered housing in Britain – communal activities, communal eating facilities and full cleaning services are common. If one includes these serviced flats in the definition of institutional care, then the level of provision rises to over 12 per cent of the over-65 age group (Swedish Institute 1992) and over 65 per cent of the care budget for elderly people still goes on institutional care (Johansson, Thorslund and Smedby 1993). One reason for these high levels of residential provision may be that demand remains high, and that in turn may be due to the high quality of the provision and the degree to which many of the 'homes' are integrated into the life of the local community, particularly in the small towns and villages.

These high levels of provision are the more remarkable when one observes that Sweden, compared with other European countries, is currently going through a period of high growth of the key need group, the over-eighties. Because of higher birthrates 80–95 years ago, during the 1980s Sweden saw the size of this age cohort grow by 44 per cent, and during the 1990s the growth will be 22 per cent (Swedish Institute 1992).

This optimistic picture of the position in their country would very likely be queried by Swedish service providers and policy researchers (authors' contacts). This is not because they would deny the facts and figures but because they are interpreted in Sweden in the context of a different set of assumptions about the normal entitlements of older people than would be found in the United Kingdom or many other European nations. From a Swedish perspective the last decade has seen the provision of services under demographic and budgetary pressure and as even in decline. Neither institutional nor domiciliary services have been able to match the growth of the key need group (generally the over-eighties). The numbers actually receiving domiciliary care have not risen in the last twenty years, though there is evidence that hours of provision per person have risen (Johannson 1991). In consequence bed blocking in hospitals (because nursing homes were already full or because the expected level of domiciliary support could not be arranged) became an important issue. At the same time home help and personal care support from the municipality became less of an automatic right as providers sought to ration higher levels of support for those in the most need (Swedish Institute 1992). The result has been a lengthy and public debate about the future direction of policy and a series of official and parliamentary reports culminating in the Care of the Elderly Act passed by parliament at the end of 1990 and which came into effect in January 1992 (Johansson and Thorslund 1993). This bears interesting comparison with the United Kingdom's contemporaneous NHS and Community Care Act 1991. Unlike all British legislation since the 1948 National Assistance Act (Part 111), the Swedish law does not merely permit the local authorities (municipalities) to provide services, it requires them to do so. The legislation includes clear statements of rights and entitlements to support from the local state (Baldock and Evers 1991). The main organisational consequence of the new legislation has been to transfer the responsibility for the primary health care of elderly people from the county councils to the municipalities (who were already responsible for the provision of housing and social care). Secondary hospital services remain with the counties but a financial penalty has been imposed on municipalities who cause hospital bed-blocking through failing to arrange community care quickly or adequately (Swedish Institute 1992).

One consequence of the high levels of provision in Sweden, and of the general level of expectations that they have induced over the years, is that some of the ideas which are regarded as innovatory solutions elsewhere have little appeal. Payment for care in Sweden is in decline rather than seen as a solution to the inadequacies of domiciliary services. In the 1960s and 1970s full-employment Sweden faced severe pressures on the availability of staff to provide local services and in consequence arrangements emerged whereby municipalities paid relatives either by the hour or by the task for care they gave or took them onto the payroll as council employees. These arrangements prospered in an *ad hoc* sort of way and peaked in the late 1970s or early 1980s. The most recent figures for direct cash payments for family carers are from 1984, when some 21,000 people received hourly payments (Glendinning and McLaughlin 1993). It is believed that the numbers have fallen considerably since then. Similarly the numbers of family carers taken onto the public payroll have fallen: from 18,500 in 1970, to 10,500 in 1980 and 6,500 in 1991 (Johansson and Sundström 1994). Little is known of the reasons for the decline in these systems of payment to carers. It may be that as the labour market has become less tight local authorities have felt less need to recruit labour in this way. It is argued that both the public and the municipalities regard this system as a second-best; both expect and prefer the state to provide services in kind where possible. There is clear evidence that the Swedish public prefer care services in kind to cash payments (Glendinning and McLaughlin 1993). There is a concern on the part of municipalities that standards of care, driven by money in this way, might not always be satisfactory and that the costs of monitoring quality would be high.

Conclusion

Social care provision for elderly people is sometimes portrayed as being in crisis. This negative portrayal is also often made more dramatic by pointing to the substantial growth all European nations will see in the numbers of very old, and potentially frail people, over the next thirty years. The reality, it has been argued here, is more complicated and more positive. While, sadly, it will probably always be possible to find some cases in all countries of old people who are getting very poor or even no support despite great frailty, most old people are well supported and integrated into their families and the community. The ways in which they are helped are almost impossible to generalise about; not only is each case always somewhat unique, but the care of elderly people constitutes the most complex example of the 'mixed economy of care' it is possible to find.

References

Age Concern (1992) *The Coming of Age in Europe: Older people in the European Community*, London: Ace Books (Age Concern).

Anderson, R. (1992) 'Health and community care', in Age Concern, *The Coming of Age in Europe: Older people in the European Community*, London: Ace Books (Age Concern).

Ascoli, U. (forthcoming) 'The growth of the social welfare system in the post-war period', in L. Balbo and H. Nowotny (eds), *Time to Care in Tomorrow's Welfare Systems*, Vienna: Euro Social, European Centre.

Askham, J. and C. Thompson (1990) *Dementia and Home Care: A research report on a home support scheme*, Mitcham: Age Concern.

Audit Commission (1994) *Taking Stock: Progress with community care* (Community Care Bulletin no. 2), London: HMSO.

Baldock, J. and A. Evers (1991) 'Citizenship and frail old people: changing patterns of provision in Europe', in N. Manning (ed.), *Social Policy Review 1990–91*, London: Longman.

Baldock, J. and A. Evers (1992) 'Innovations and care of the elderly: the cutting edge of change for social welfare systems', *Ageing and Society* 12, pp. 289–312.

Baldock, J. and C. Ungerson (1991) 'Whatd'ya want if you don' want money? A feminist critique of paid volunteering', in M. Maclean and D. Groves (eds), *Women's Issues in Social Policy*, London: Routledge.

Baldock, J. and C. Ungerson (1994) *Becoming Consumers of Community Care: Households within the mixed economy of welfare* (Community Care into Practice series), York: Joseph Rowntree Foundation.

Bianchi, M. (1991) 'Policy for the elderly: innovation or modernisation?', in *New Welfare Mixes in Care for the Elderly* (EuroSocial Report, vol. 40, no. 3), Vienna: European Centre for Social Welfare Policy and Research.

Boffi, M. and C. Facchini (1991) *Condizioni di vita e utilizzo dei servizi nella popolazione anziana*, Milan: CUESP.

Bytheway, B. (1995) *Ageism*, Buckingham: Open University Press.

Challis, D., R. Chessum, J. Chesterman, R. Luckett and K. Traske (1990) *Case Management in Social and Health Care: The Gateshead Community Health Scheme*, University of Kent, Canterbury: Personal Social Services Research Unit.

Coleman, D. and J. Salt (1992) *The British Population: Patterns, trends and processes*, Oxford: Oxford University Press.

Colvez, A. (1990) 'Panorama de la dépendance en France', *Revue Française des Affaires Sociales* 2, pp. 15–21.

Commission of the European Communities (1993) *Social Protection in Europe*, Luxembourg: Directorate-General Employment, Industrial Relations and Social Affairs.

Coolen, J.A.I. (1993a) 'Discussion and conclusion', in J. Coolen (ed.) *Changing Care for the Elderly in the Netherlands: Experiences and research findings from policy experiments*, Assen/Maastricht: Van Gorcum.

Coolen, J.A.I. (1993b) 'Towards a coordinated pluralism of care providers: experiences and research findings from the Netherlands', in A. Evers and G.H. van der Zanden (eds), *Better Care for Dependent People Living at Home: Meeting the new agenda in services for the elderly*, Bunnik: Netherlands Institute of Gerontology.

Daatland, S.O. (1992) 'Ideals cost? Current trends in Scandinavian welfare policy on ageing', *Journal of European Social Policy* 2, 1, pp. 33–47.

Davies, B. (1992) *Care Management, Equity and Efficiency: The international experience*, University of Kent, Canterbury: Personal Social Services Research Unit.

Davies, B. (1994) 'Improving the case management process', in P. Hennessy (ed.), *Caring for Frail Elderly People: New directions in care*, (Social Policy Studies no. 16), Paris: OECD.

Davies, B.P., A. Bebbington, H. Charnley and B. Baines (1990) *Resources, Needs and Outcomes in Community-based Care: A comparative study of the production of welfare for the elderly*, Aldershot: Avebury.

Davies, B.P. and D. Challis (1986) *Matching Resources to Needs in Community Care: An evaluated demonstration of a longterm care model*, Aldershot: Gower.

Dieck, M. (1994) 'Reforming against the grain: longterm care in Germany', in R. Page and J. Baldock (eds), *Social Policy Review 6*, London: Social Policy Association.

Dieck, M. and V. Garms-Homolová (1991) 'Home-care services in the Federal Republic of Germany', in A. Jamieson (ed.), *Home Care for Older People in Europe: A comparison of policies and practices*, Oxford: Oxford University Press.

Dontas, A.S. (1987) 'Primary health and social services for the elderly in Greece', in S. di Gregorio (ed.), *Social Gerontology: New directions*, London: Croom Helm.

Ellis, K. (1993) *Squaring the Circle: User and carer participation*, York: Joseph Rowntree Foundation.

Eurostat (1990) *Inequality and Poverty in Europe*, Luxembourg: Office for Official Publications of the European Committees.

Eurostat (1991) *Income Replacement Ratio at the Date of Retirement*, Luxembourg: Office for Official Publications of the European Committees.

Evers, A., K. Leichsenring and B. Pruckner (1994) 'Payments for care: the case of Austria', in A. Evers, M. Pijl and C. Ungerson (eds), *Payments for Care: A comparative overview*, Aldershot: Avebury.

Evers, A. and T. Olk (1991) 'The mix of care provision for the frail elderly in the Federal Republic of Germany', in A. Evers and I. Svetlik (eds), *New Welfare Mixes in Care for the Elderly*, vol. 3, Vienna: European Centre for Social Welfare Policy and Research.

Evers, A., M. Pijl and C. Ungerson (eds) (1994) *Payments for Care: A comparative overview*, Aldershot: Avebury.

Facchini, C. (1993) 'Risks and achievements in strengthening home care for the elderly: the Italian situation', in A. Evers and G.H. van der Zanden (eds), *Better Care for Dependent People Living at Home: Meeting the new agenda in services for the elderly*, Bunnik: Netherlands Institute of Gerontology.

Frossard, M., D. Bouget, R. Tartarin and P. Tripier (eds) (1990) *Le Prix de la dépendance*, Paris: Documentation Française.

Glendinning, C. and E. McLaughlin (1993) *Paying for Care: Lesson from Europe* (Social Security Advisory Committee, Research Paper 5), London: HMSO.

Guillemard, A-M. and M. Frossard (1993) 'Risks and achievements in strengthening home care: the case of France', in A. Evers and G.H. van der Zanden (eds), *Better Care for Dependent People Living at Home: Meeting the new agenda in services for the elderly*, Bunnik: Netherlands Institute of Gerontology.

Hennessy, P. (ed.) (1994) *Caring for Frail Elderly People: New directions in care* (Social Policy Studies no. 14), Paris: OECD.

Hugman, R. (1994) *Ageing and the Care of Older People in Europe*, Basingstoke: Macmillan.

Huijsman, R. (1993) 'Care provisions for the elderly: a review', in J.A.I. Coolen (ed.), *Changing Care for the Elderly in the Netherlands: Experiences and research findings from policy experiments*, Assen/Maastricht: Van Gorcum.

Huijsman, R. and M. de Klerk (1993) 'The elderly in the Netherlands: a review', in J.A.I. Coolen (ed.), *Changing Care for the Elderly in the Netherlands: Experiences and research findings from policy experiments*, Assen/Maastricht: Van Gorcum.

Hunter, D. (1986) *Care Delivery Systems for the Elderly*, Bath: Age Concern/University of Bath.

Jamieson, A. (1991) 'Community care for older people', in G. Room (ed.), *Towards a European Welfare State*, Bristol: School of Advanced Urban Studies.

Johansson, L. (1991) 'Informal care of dependent elderly at home: some Swedish experiences', *Ageing and Society* 1, 1, pp. 41–58.

Johansson, L. and G. Sundström (1994) 'Sweden', in A. Evers, M. Pijl and C. Ungerson (eds), *Payments for Care: A comparative overview*, Aldershot: Avebury.

Johansson, L. and M. Thorslund (1993) 'Care for the elderly in Sweden: formal and informal support', in F. Lesemann and C. Martin (eds), *Home-Based Care, the Elderly, the Family and the Welfare State: An international comparison*, Ottawa: University of Ottawa Press.

Johansson, L., M. Thorslund and B. Smedby (1993) 'Formal and informal support in a rural setting in Sweden', *Journal of Gerontological Social Work* 20, 1/2, pp. 79–94.

Jylhä, M. and J. Jokela (1990) 'Individual experiences as cultural: a cross-cultural study on loneliness among the elderly', *Ageing and Society* 10, pp. 295–315.

Kraan, R., J. Baldock, B. Davies, A. Evers, L. Johansson, M. Knapen, M. Thorslund and C. Tunissen (1991) *Care for the Elderly: Significant innovations in three European countries*, Frankfurt: Campus; Boulder, Co: Westview.

Leat, D. and C. Ungerson (1993) *Creating Care at the Boundaries*, York: Joseph Rowntree Foundation.

Little, V. (1979) 'For the elderly: an overview of services in industrially developed and developing countries', in M.I. Teicher, D. Thursz and J. L. Vigilante (eds), *Researching the Aged: Social services in forty four countries*, Beverley Hills: Sage.

Mengani, M. and C. Gagliardi (1991) *Family Assistance Programmes for the Very Elderly Population*, Ancona: Centro Studi, Economica-Sociali.

Ministero dell'Interno (1989) *Provvidenze Legislative a favore dei mutilati ed invalidi civili, ciechi civili e sordomuti: tutel economica. Compendio informativo-statistico 1988*, Rome: Ministero dell'Interno.

Monk, A. (1993) 'Innovations in home care: trends and problems in service implementation in several European countries', in A. Evers and G. H. van der Zanden (eds), *Better Care for Dependent People Living at Home: Meeting the new agenda in services for the elderly*, Bunnik: Netherlands Institute of Gerontology.

OECD (1988) *Ageing Populations: The social policy implications*, Paris: OECD.

OECD (1994) *New Orientations for Social Policy* (OECD Social Policy Studies no. 12), Paris: OECD.

Olsson, S. and S. McMurphy (1993) 'Social policy in Sweden: the Swedish model in transition', in R. Page and J. Baldock (eds), *Social Policy Review 5*, London: Social Policy Association.

Pijl, M. (1993) 'The Dutch welfare state: a product of religious and political pluralism', in R. Page and J. Baldock (eds), *Social Policy Review 5*, London: Social Policy Association.

Pitaud, P., R. Vercauteren and B. Dherbey (1991) 'France', in A. Evers and I. Svetlik (eds), *New Welfare Mixes in Care for the Elderly*, vol. 3, Vienna: European Centre for Social Welfare Policy and Research.

Qureshi, H., D. Challis and B.P. Davies (1988) *Helpers in Case-Managed Community Care*, Aldershot: Gower.

Sipilä, J. and A. Anttonen (1994) 'Payments for care: the case of Finland', in A. Evers, M. Pijl and C. Ungerson (eds) *Payments for Care: A comparative overview*, Aldershot: Avebury.

Swedish Institute (1992) *Fact Sheet on Care of the Elderly*, Stockholm.

Thorslund, M. (1993) 'Home care in Sweden: past and future trends', in A. Evers and G.H. van der Zanden (eds), *Better Care for Dependent People Living at Home: Meeting the new agenda in services for the elderly*, Bunnik: Netherlands Institute of Gerontology.

Triantafillou, J.H. and E. Mestheneos (1990) *Pathways to Care: A study of Greek elderly people and their use of hospital emergency department services*, Athens: Centre for Studies of Age-related Changes in Man.

Ungerson, C. (1987) *Policy is Personal: Sex, gender and informal care*, London: Tavistock Publications.

Ungerson, C. (1995) 'Gender, cash and informal care: European perpectives and dilemmas', in *Journal of Social Policy* 24, 1, pp. 31–52.

Walker, A. (1993a) 'Living standards and way of life', in A. Walker, A.-M. Guillemard and J. Alber (eds), *Older People in Europe: Social and ecomomic policies. The 1993 Report of the European Community Observatory*, Brussels: Directorate-General V, Commission of the European Communities.

Walker, A. (1993b) *Age and Attitudes: Main results from a Eurobarometer Survey*, Brussels: Directorate-General V, Commission of the European Communities.

Walker, A. (1993c) 'Towards a European agenda in home care for older people: convergences and controversies', in A. Evers and G.H. van der Zanden (eds), *Better Care for Dependent People Living at Home: Meeting the new agenda in services for the elderly*, Bunnik: Netherlands Institute of Gerontology.

Ziomas, D. and N. Bouzas (1993) 'Social integration of older people in Greece', in A. Walker (ed.), *Older People in Europe: Social integration*, Brussels: Directorate-General V, Commission of the European Communities.

CHAPTER 8

Conclusion

The future for social care in Europe

Brian Munday

Chapter 2's panoramic review of social care in the twelve member states of the European Union concluded with a reference to dominant themes and issues emerging from the study. The intention in this short final chapter is not to engage in a wide-ranging conclusion touching on all subjects but instead to concentrate on two major topics of special relevance to the future for social care in Europe.

The dominance of the mixed economy of social care in Europe

This ever-increasing characteristic of European social care has been discussed extensively in this book, particularly in chapter 4. All the evidence points to the establishment of this all-pervasive policy throughout Europe, varying in its precise form from country to country. It is well established that *convergence* rather than *harmonisation* is the agreed approach to social policy by the European Union. Certainly, there is a very clear convergence across Europe towards the development of social care systems that place less emphasis on state agencies as *providers* of social care, with increasing attention on provision by the informal sector of family, friends and neighbours, the independent not-for-profit sector, and, to a lesser degree, the commercial care organisations.

Countries in the European Union arrive at a mixed economy of social care from many starting points. Some, such as Germany, the

Netherlands and Luxembourg, have been there some time for historical, political and cultural reasons. The majority are adopting this policy primarily out of economic necessity. The timing of this book did not allow discussion of social care in the three new member states. Two – Sweden and Finland – are of special interest in relation to the policy of mixed economies in social care. Both are Scandinavian countries within the tradition of dominant and well-resourced state social care provision, with small independent care sectors. Adverse economic and fiscal factors have been largely responsible for both countries changing direction in social care as part of a broader review of the future for their welfare states. They are now drawing selectively on experience elsewhere in Europe to enable them to develop their relatively underdeveloped independent social care sectors.

Within a wider definition of Europe converging trends in social care are also seen in countries that previously lacked other than rather rudimentary services. This applies particularly to countries emerging from the dominance of totalitarian regimes, whether of right or left ideologies. For example, chapter 2 referred to the emergence of formal social care services in Spain in the early 1980s following the end of the Franco era. Initial hopes for extensive state-provided services had to be tempered by economic realities and the subsequent emphasis on support for the growth of the independent sector. Economic realities also figure strongly in the approach to building up social care services in the former communist countries of eastern and central Europe. In Hungary and the Czech republic, for example, EU and other outside assistance concentrates on support for the development of independent social care organisations rather than on an extensive, well-resourced new state sector.

Opposition to policies of mixed economies of social care is mostly muted. Gone – mostly – are the Marxist arguments of the 1970s which portrayed the state as by definition the best and necessarily near monopolistic provider of social care, the socialist task being to expand its role and the quantity of its provision. The independent/voluntary sector was to play a strictly minor role in the state-dominated system, while for-profit social care was to be resisted at all costs. Centrist 'socialist' parties such as in Britain seem very unlikely to reverse the introduction in recent years of quasi-markets in social and health care by right-wing governments,

arguing that when in power they will make the market more accountable. Across the now somewhat narrower political spectrum
in most European countries it is argued that markets give choice to
the service users and make providers more responsive to users'
preferences. This perceived advantage of 'the market' is much less
obvious in the case of social care, where the user is often not
paying for services, is poor and is frequently disadvantaged in
other ways.

What is the future for social care in Europe under mixed economy systems? A major concern is that, as governments progressively withdraw from provider roles, both the quantity and the
quality of social care services will deteriorate. Families – women in
particular – will again be expected to assume greater responsibility
for dependent members; while changes in the financing for social
care will lead to an American-style two-tier system, with state
agencies as the providers of last resort, leaving better-off users
able to buy superior-quality services from the independent agencies. American experience in social care is worrying in this respect,
even if as yet there is no serious sign of extreme right-wing Newt
Gingrich style anti-welfare policies emerging in Europe.

Lower-level, but nevertheless important, changes are already
under way as mixed economies of social care gain hold. In chapter
4 and elsewhere reference has been made to significant shifts in the
role and style of operation of both state and independent social
care agencies in the world of contracts and competition. Employment opportunities for social workers and other social care staff
are shifting from state to the independent sectors, causing serious
unease for some and welcome opportunities for others. Professional training for social workers has to keep pace with these rapid
changes in employment, requiring the introduction of training in
care management skills to replace to some degree the traditional
emphasis on the more direct service counselling skills. Debates
continue as to whether this 'new world' of the mixed economy in
social care constitutes the greatest threat to the professional status
of social work this century.

The writer hesitates to make predictions as to the extent to
which users of social care will be better served in this future of
mixed economies. Again, to some extent it will depend on the
starting point of particular countries. Given the relatively low level
of provision in some countries for either/and political or economic

reasons, then there are grounds for optimism in some countries within both the European Union and the new Europe. In countries such as Sweden, Finland, Denmark and Britain the concern is that policies of a mixed economy of social care are designed essentially to reduce costs and keep taxation at a politically acceptable level. Recent changes in community care in Britain suggest that publicly financed social care may be progressively reduced under finance-driven policies.

The future role of the European Union in social care

Chapter 3 included a detailed discussion of the role and types of involvement of the European Union in social care. Since then the European Commission has published (1995) its *Medium Term Social Action Programme 1995–1997*, outlining its intentions following the publication of the White Paper (1994) on the future of social policy. The terminology – some would say rhetoric – is familiar: a 'balance between competition, cooperation and solidarity'; 'harmonisation of social policies is not an objective'; 'preserving diversity because of subsidiarity'; 'economic and social dimensions are inter-dependent, no social progress without competitiveness and growth'; 'the Commission to play a greater role as a catalyst for transnational exchange of experience and action to deal with common problems.'

As the recent document states and as is illustrated in chapter 3 above, the approach of the European Union in social policy to date has been

> to take the form of targeted measures for specific groups with specific needs, such as those excluded from the labour market, disabled people and older people. What is needed in the future is a more broadly based approach which is still sensitive to the specific problems of certain groups but which seeks to help Member States in their efforts to address the larger policy issues such as the functioning and the financing of social protection systems and the overall quality of life. (p. 21)

The Commission intends to launch a *framework initiative on the future of social protection*, the purpose of this being to enable member states 'to develop and adjust their national systems on the basis of optimum understanding of what is happening in other

Member States' (p. 22). The reference is only to social protection (cash benefit) systems, with no mention of social care systems throughout the document. However, there is now the possibility that the Commission may be persuaded to include social care within this initiative on the future of social protection in the European Union. As shown at points in this book (e.g. chapter 1) 'cash and care' are integrated in some EU countries, while the Commission document goes on to refer specifically to the future of care for an increasing number of elderly people in Europe, a group of citizens for whom cash and care are ever more closely connected.

An optimist therefore sees a new opportunity for social care to become more centre stage in EU social policy, being considered alongside hitherto higher priority subjects such as social protection and public health. A reduced marginalisation of social care in EU policies and programmes would in turn have a similar effect in at least some member states, with an eventual beneficial impact on services for many of the most disadvantaged citizens in what Delors referred to as a 'citizens' Europe'.

References

Commission of the European Communities (1995) *Medium Term Social Action Programme 1995–1997*, Communication from the Commission to the Council, the European Parliament and the Committee of the Regions, Brussels.

European Commission: Directorate-General for Employment, Industrial Relations and Social Affairs (1994) *European Social Policy: A way forward for the Union*, Luxembourg: Office for Official Publications of the European Communities.

Index